The Weight of the World

Book II
in the
My Brave Little Man Series

Written by
T.A. DEGNER

A BANDI BOOK

Printed in the United States of America

Library of Congress Control Number: 2018905014
ISBN: 978-0-9836636-1-4

Terry A. Degner 1945 -
www.tadegner.com

The Bandi Media Group LLC
8567 Powers Place, Chanhassen, MN 55317

This book is dedicated to my adopted father and mother, Walter and Winifred Degner, and to Grandpa Walter Ash. May the gift of love you blessed me with be with you eternally.

Author's Introduction

This is a true story. Some of the names have been changes and in one instance, I changed both the names and the location. I did not change the name and location of one individual due to his position in the community. Had what took place turned out to be a one-time affair I would have skipped it altogether, but his personality entered my life on a number of occasions, so I felt compelled to write about what took place. In his, and in all cases, I did my best to focus on facts and the impact an incident had on me; not on the motives of others.

I share my memories with you, the reader, not to boast about my life, but because things happened to me that today would be beneficial to many young boys growing up in divided homes and in the inner cities of America. To understand where I'm coming from, it would be beneficial for you to read my first book, titled, *My Brave Little Man*. In the book, I cover the first eight years of my life during which I spent three plus yeas in an orphanage.

In this book, I cover the years I spent with my adoptive parents on a farm in western Minnesota. As you will see, my father and mother had a real challenge on their hands for I not only came with an established identity, but as an adult/child accustomed to making decisions on my own. This is a story about a troubled young boy moving into a world of truth, beauty, and goodness and how this impacted his life.

The hunger of the soul cannot be satisfied with physical pleasures; the love of home and children is not augmented by the unwise pursuit of pleasure. Though you exhaust the resources of art, color, sound, rhythm, music, and adornment of person, you cannot hope thereby to elevate the soul or to nourish the spirit. Vanity and fashion cannot minister to home building and child culture; pride and rivalry are powerless to enhance the survival qualities of succeeding generations. ~ The Urantia Book, (84:8.4)

PROLOGUE

May 1964

"Mom, where are you!" I shouted, as I stepped into the kitchen. I knew she was home because her car was parked in front of the garage.

"I'm upstairs," I heard a far-away voice say.

What the heck was she doing upstairs? I thought, as I walked through the kitchen toward the living room and the door that led to the staircase.

It was 5:30, the school bus had just dropped me off, and I had things I wanted to show her. Tomorrow was Career Day and I couldn't wait to tell her my plans. Where my sister Jean was, I had no idea. We were seniors in high school and we seldom talked. She had been dating a classmate for some years and it wasn't unusual for him to swing by later in the evening to drop her off.

"I'm going to be a Marine," I yelled excitedly as I scurried up the stairs, holding up an ad I had picked up at school. "It's either them or the Green Berets."

Just as I reached the top of the staircase, I saw her exit my bedroom and step into the hall.

"What are you doing up here?" I asked in surprise.

"You got some letters in the mail today and I was just about ready to put them on your desk when I heard you come in," she replied, holding up the envelopes.

"Really? Someone sent me a letter? I wonder what that's all about?" I couldn't remember the last time anyone had sent me a letter.

"Well, they seem to be from colleges. Did you apply?" "No. Let me see," I said, holding out my hand.

She handed them over and I looked at the return address on the top one: University of Oklahoma.

I ripped open the envelope. To my astonishment, it was a scholarship offer. "What does this mean?"

She took it out of my hands and scanned it. "Well, it looks like they're offering you a wrestling scholarship. I wonder if that's what the other ones are about. Here, look at them," she said, handing me three more letters—one from the University of Wisconsin, one from North Dakota State, and the other from Iowa State. Each contained scholarship offers in wrestling. I would have never, and I mean never, considered applying for a scholarship in wrestling, let alone to the top four programs in the country.

"Well, that's something," Mom said. "How did they get your name?"

"I have no idea." And with that, I walked past her into the bedroom and tossed them into the waste basket next to my desk.

"So, you're just going to ignore them?"

"Yes!" I replied, holding up the glossy ad for the Marines.

I knew I'd go to college, but I wasn't ready to jump right from high school back into a classroom, so the Marines seemed to be a good fit. They wanted only the best, and I'd been the best wrestler in high school.

Mom looked at the ad in my hands and in her gentle, soft voice, said, "Well, if you're not going to college, you might want to consider going into the military for an education instead."

"Education," I said, shaking my head. "What kind of education can you get in the military?"

"Well, I'm not sure, but I would think the Navy has more to offer in the way of education than the Marines, but you do what you think is best." And with that she walked downstairs.

CHAPTER 1

The Adoption

On July 1, 1953, Miss Marion Lee, a Child Welfare Worker in Duluth, Minnesota, sent a letter to a Walter and Winifred Degner of Wendell, Minnesota. The letter read:

Dear Mr. and Mrs. Degner:
You have been referred to us as a family interested in taking one or two children into your home on an adoptive basis. We have in our county a brother and sister who would fit into your home very nicely and we would be interested in talking with you further about this.

Terry was born in August 1945, and his sister, Jean, was born in October 1946. Both children are alert and attractive and they are most anxious to have a new "mother and daddy." Terry has clear blue eyes and medium blond hair, and Jeanie has much the same coloring. Jeanie is an outgoing, well-adjusted child who has made good progress in school. Terry is of good average intelligence too, but he is socially somewhat immature. We feel that with warm under-standing parents, Terry will soon catch up. He does need, however, stable parents, and from your home study, we know that you have the ability to offer this to him.

You do live some distance from Duluth but if you are interested in considering these two children, I would like to have you come and talk with us directly. At that time, I can give you complete information on the children and answer your questions regarding their background and present adjustment. If you are interested in the children, I will set a tentative ap-pointment for July 8th at 10:00 A.M. My office is in the Court House in Duluth, Room 306. If, after our interview you are interested in meeting the children, this can be arranged. It might be well for you to plan to stay in Duluth for a day or so because it does take a little time to get to know the children.

Will you kindly let me know immediately if you are interested in keeping the appointment to discuss Ter-ry and Jeanie?

Mr. and Mrs. Degner rescheduled the appointment for Friday, July 10, 1953 and the entire process took four days. Ironically, July 10 was also the day I ran away from the Chil-dren's Home to find my biological mother. Had the meeting taken place at the orphanage instead of the social services office downtown, there's a good chance our perspective parents would have learned about my flight, but for reasons known only to the staff at the orphanage, they were never told.

On the morning of July 11, Mrs. Hemphill, the superinten-dent, approached me at the breakfast table. "Terry, after you're done eating, please go to your room and wait until I call for you. I've already told Jean to do the same thing, so you don't need to tell her."

"How come?" I asked.

"Well, as I told you before, this is the day you're going to meet your new parents. I think you're going to like them. I know your sister is very excited."

I had expected her to scold me for running away, so I didn't bother to answer. I just kept looking at her, a blank expression on my face.

"OK! You come when I call for you." And with that she walked out of the dining hall and into her office.

Mrs. Hemphill had told me about the adoption on Fri-day. That's why I'd run away, but I was still in denial because I didn't know what to expect. Unlike Jean, I had not given adoption any thought. The matrons at the orphanage had been discussing the positive virtues of getting a new mom and dad with Jean for some time and she was excited about the idea, but no one had taken the time to enlighten me. In hindsight, I'm not sure if I would've listened anyway.

"Are you OK?" a voice asked. Looking up I saw Jean walk-ing toward me.

"Yes. Why?"

"I was just wondering. Did you see Mom yesterday?"

"Yes."

"Well, what was it like? Was she glad to see you?"

"I guess. I don't think I was supposed to see her, but the sisters at the school were really nice."

"That's why we need to have a new mom and dad," she said. "Maybe they'll be nice to us."

"How do you know that?"

"I don't, but I think it will be better than staying here," she said emphatically. "We can't stay here forever and our mom isn't coming to get us."

I knew Jean was right. She wasn't our mom anymore and we had to go on with our lives. I just wasn't sure what "going on" meant.

"My friends are excited for me and I'm going, so there. You can do what you want!" And with that, my sister got up and walked out of the dining room.

I returned to my bedroom and curled up on the bed. *What's going to happen to us?* I thought. *Where are we going, and will I ever see my mom again?* Finally, I drifted off into a state of total confusion.

At about mid-morning, Mr. Kolander, the supervisor of the third floor, walked into my room without knocking.

"Terry, get up," he shouted. "Mrs. Hemphill wants you in her office. If you need to go to the bathroom, now is the time."

I got up, walked to the bathroom to relieve myself, and then descended the steps to the first floor.

Jean was waiting for me in the hallway and together we walked into the secretary's office.

"Go right in, they're waiting for you," the secretary said, pointing at the superintendent's office.

There were three people sitting on chairs in front of Mrs. Hemphill's desk. When we entered, they all stood and faced us.

"Hi Terry and Jean, come on in. This is Miss Lee," Mrs. Hemphill said, pointing at a prudish woman in a black dress with a white collar that came up to her chin. "And these two people are Mr. and Mrs. Degner. They've been waiting to meet you. Walter and Winifred, this is Terry and his sister, Jean."

The woman was shorter than both Miss Lee and Mrs. Hemphill. She had pure-white hair, every strand neatly brushed back from a face that registered something akin to concern, or maybe it was just kindness. The man wasn't much taller, maybe an inch or two. He had thinning gray-brown hair and a face that seemed frozen in time. It wasn't a smile or a frown, it was more like bewilderment or confusion; as if he didn't know what he was doing here. Unlike his wife, who had wide shoulders, made even wider by what was probably padding, his shoulders were narrow, and I could see from his tight skinned, tanned face that he didn't have an ounce of fat on his body.

"Hello, children," Mrs. Degner said, with a soft, almost angelic voice. "I'm so glad to meet you. Have you been waiting for a long time?"

I assumed she meant waiting in my room, but she could have just as well meant waiting for a new mom and dad.

Bending over ever so slightly, she added, "How would the two of you like to go on a picnic with us?"

"That would be fun," I heard my sister say. I'd totally forgotten she was standing next to me.

"Where would you like to go? Do you have a favorite place?" Mrs. Degner asked.

"Can we go to Chester Bowl?" I asked.

"I'm not sure where Chester Bowl is, but if it's close I think that would be fine."

"It's just up the hill," Mrs. Hemphill said. "Terry can show you the way."

"Well, it's Chester Bowl then," Mrs. Degner said, standing up straight, a tender smile spreading across her face. "We will have to go to a grocery store first." She looked at Mrs. Hemphill. "Is there a place nearby where we can buy some food?"

"There's a convenience store a block and a half away and Terry knows how to get there, too, don't you?"

Feeling important, I nodded in agreement. It was the store across from the Fourth Street Bridge. The bridge where I got my tongue stuck two years earlier, and the man who owned the convenience store was the one who had rescued me.

Jean and I walked with Mr. and Mrs. Degner out the side door and down the steps to a parked car. It was light blue car with a white top.

"Is this your car? I asked, in wonderment. I'd never ridden in a car as new as this one and the very thought of it filled me with excitement.

"No, I'm sorry," Mrs. Degner replied. "It belongs to my sister and her husband. We're just using it for the time we're up here."

"What kind of car do you have?" I asked.

"Well, we don't have a car. We have a truck, but we thought you and your sister would be more comfortable riding in a car. It's a long drive to our house."

I remember thinking that, due to the way she said it, she assumed we were going with them.

Turning to her husband, she asked, "Honey, what kind of car is this?"

"It's an Oldsmobile," he replied. I would later learn it was a 1953 Oldsmobile 88. A luxury car back in the early 1950s.

Instead of putting us in the back seat, our mother insisted we sit up front with them. When I got in, it smelled fresh.

"OK, where do we go from here?" Mrs. Degner said, good-naturedly.

Moving forward in the seat and stretching to see out the front window, I pointed and said, "You need to go there."

Mr. Degner, who had said very little, drove out of the parking lot and down the street.

"You go to the right, there," I almost shouted as we approached the first intersection. Not long after making the turn, I pointed at a store. "There it is!"

He drove past, made a U-turn, and then parked in front of the store.

Once inside, Mrs. Degner bent over and said in that soft voice of hers, "You children pick out what you would like to eat."

"Can we have anything we want?" I asked.

"Well, within reason," she replied.

It didn't take long for me to spot a package of Twinkies. "Can I have this?" I picked it up and showed her.

"Is that all you want? I think you should pick out something more substantial, don't you?"

"But I want this," I said dryly.

"I'm not saying you can't have it. I just think you need something more substantial. How about some potato chips and lunchmeat?"

"Could we have a peanut butter and jelly sandwich?" I asked.

"Yes, I guess we could do that, if that's what you really like."

"And this," I said, holding up the Twinkies again.

"Yes, and that."

"Now, what would you like to drink?"

"Can we have pop?" I asked eagerly. No one ever gave us pop.

"What kind would you like?"

"Coca-Cola," I answered.

"Jean, what kind of pop would you like?"

"I like Coca-Cola, too," she answered mildly.

Again, following my directions, Mr. Degner drove us to Chester Bowl and parked by the same picnic tables I'd seen when I ran away. Because it'd happened just the day before, the scene felt surreal.

Mrs. Degner asked where we would like to sit, and instead of choosing the first picnic table we came to, I chose the one where the couple had been sitting when I stopped to ask for directions. The table was empty today, as were the other three, but like yesterday, the sun shone brightly and the flow of the creek was barely audible.

As we ate, my mind kept drifting off. I saw in the distance the point where I had crossed the creek, the old bobsled run I'd used as a guide to find St. Scholastica, and the woods where I'd almost gotten lost. I wondered what my mother was doing. Was she cleaning up after the noon meal, or was she walking in the graveyard reading the tombstones?

I'll come back to find her when I get older, I thought. I'd made my mother that promise and I would keep it.

Other than that, I don't remember much about the picnic. I do remember Mrs. Degner telling us some things about their farm. She mentioned their dog, Blackie, and their cows, chickens, and pigs.

I asked her if they had a horse and she answered, "No, but

there's a horse in the pasture across the road from our house."

My spirits brightened. *Was that the horse in my dreams?*

"Did they tell you about our brother?" Jean suddenly asked, interrupting my thoughts.

"No, no one mentioned a brother," Mrs. Degner said. "What's his name?"

"Larry," my sister answered, "but he's already adopted. He went to live with his new mom and dad last week."

In truth, it was the week before, but I kept my mouth shut.

"Oh, I'm sorry to hear that. We would've been happy to take him, too, but no one told us you had another brother. I wonder why they did that?"

Years later, our adopted mother told us that when she asked why they had not been informed about our brother, the social worker had said they felt it best to separate us brothers because we were too competitive. But what she never told me is that I, too, had been a throw-in. Initially, they'd requested a girl, but when Miss Lee asked if they would consider her older brother, Mrs. Degner jumped at the opportunity.

After the picnic, Mrs. Hemphill took my sister and me aside and asked us if we liked our new parents. She didn't call them by name, she used the adjective "new" as if they were already our parents. We both said yes.

I suppose I could've said no, but what other options did I have? I couldn't stay at the orphanage forever, and I didn't want to be separated from my sister. Besides, I knew in my heart that my mother was out of the picture.

The official adoption took place on July 14, 1953. All of us, including our new parents, gathered in the superintendent's office. Without fanfare, the social worker looked at my sister and me and asked, "Would the two of you like to go and live with Mr. and Mrs. Degner on their farm?"

I don't recall if my sister said something. All I remember is nodding and that was it.

The superintendent reached over and picked up one of two Bibles sitting on a table next to her desk. Then, she opened a desk drawer, pulled out a pair of scissors, and in a light-hearted manner, said, "This is Terry's Bible. To make this official, I'll cut his last name out of the first page." With that, she proceeded to cut out my last name—I still have that Bible. Then, she did the same with Jean's and handed them to our new parents.

After signing a paper and hearing some congratulatory words from Mrs. Hemphill and Miss Lee, we left the orphanage for our new life. There was no send-off from the other children, and the staff was nowhere in sight. Holding hands, my sister and I walked out the front door and into the unknown.

Front steps of the Children's Home in Duluth MN

CHAPTER 2

A New World Awaits

July 14, 1953

The Oldsmobile was parked next to the curb when we exited the Children's Home, and sitting in the front seat were two people I'd never seen before. I couldn't make out the man's face in the driver's seat, but the woman sitting on the passenger side gave me an inviting smile.

When the four of us reached the car, Mr. Degner opened the rear door.

"I know it's going to get a bit crowded, but why don't the two of you get in first and I'll sit next to the door on this side, and your dad can sit on the other side," Mrs. Degner suggested.

Jean and I scooted in, followed by our new mother. Our new dad walked to the other side of the car and got in next to Jean.

"Children, this is my sister, Alice, and her husband, Bud. Alice and Bud, this is Terry and Jean. They'll be coming with us to the farm."

She may have told us why they were there, but it didn't register at the time. Later, I would learn that our adopted mother had asked her sister to come along for support.

Alice, the youngest of five Ash girls, was affable and did most of the talking during the trip. No, that's not true—except for the few words our new mother said, she did all the talking.

Despite Alice's efforts to entertain us, however, the drive to our new home gradually turned into a grueling affair. We stopped at least twice: once to let me puke, and another time to eat, but for the most part it was nonstop driving. Even Alice became silent as daylight turned to darkness.

What would normally take something like five hours, ended up taking eight hours, and with no moon in the sky that night, the only visual diversion available were miles of ditches and flat countryside.

"It won't be long now," our new mom finally said.

Bud turned off the highway onto a dirt road. Five minutes later, he slowed and took a left and there, lit up by the headlights, would be my home for the next eleven years.

"Oh my, the hired man forgot to turn on the yard light. That's too bad," our new mom said.

"He probably finished the chores before it was dark," our new dad piped in.

I thought about asking them who they were talking about, but I was too exhausted. All I wanted to do was crawl into a bed and sleep.

The headlights lit up a white, two-story house with an attached, single-story structures at the front and another one at the back. As the car straightened, I spotted another white, rectangular, single-story building to the left of the house and the partial outline of a red barn to the left of that.

Bud drove over to a hedge, turned to the right, and came to a stop, the lights now pointing at a grove of large trees through which I could make out a ridge and another grove of trees.

"We'll wait here until you get into the house," Bud said, "but we better not come in. It's getting late and I've got some chores to do before I can call it a day."

"I better run to the barn and check things out before I call it a day, too," Mr. Degner said and without saying another word, he got out and disappeared into the darkness.

"We'll be OK," our new mother said, as she opened her door. "As soon as we get into the house, the two of you leave."

After helping us out, she took our hands and led us toward the front steps, but before we got there, a black dog walked right up to me. Startled, I lifted my arms defensively, but as soon as I saw his tail wagging, I regained my composure and reached down to pet him.

"Is this Blackie?" I asked, scratching his ears.

"Yes! He loves children, so you don't need to worry about him biting."

Blackie joined us as we climbed the steps, but he stopped when our mother opened the front door. "We don't let Blackie in the house," she said, while my sister and I moved past her.

The entryway smelled like barn manure. Hanging on hooks on either side of a window overlooking the yard were over-hauls and coats. Several boots were sitting on a newspaper on the floor, caked with a yellowish, brown substance. I imme-diately assumed this was where the smell was coming from. I knew what manure smelled like from my days on Grandma and Grandpa's farm, so it didn't bother me, but the room was confining, making the smell even more potent.

"I hope you don't mind the smell," our new mother said,

as she opened another door. "This is where we keep our work clothes. In time, you'll get used to it."

She turned on a light and Jean and I stepped into what was obviously the kitchen. It was a plain looking kitchen, but uncluttered and roomy. There was an open door to my immediate left leading into what looked like a bathroom, and on the other side of the door sat a white stove. Butted up to the stove was a flat countertop and cabinets that disappeared into what looked like a pantry.

I stepped farther in and bumped against a chair. It was one of four that belonged to a small, square table. The table rested against the wall to my right and under a window that overlooked the farmyard.

Directly across from where I stood, an open doorway led into another room, and to the left of the doorway in the corner stood a refrigerator. To the left of the refrigerator and across from the kitchen table was another countertop with overhead cabinets.

What was it about yellow, I thought, looking at the walls. They, like the walls at the orphanage, were painted yellow. A brighter shade perhaps, but yellow nonetheless.

"What's that door for?" I asked, pointing at a door in the darkened pantry.

"Oh, that goes to the basement. Let's not go there now," Mrs. Degner replied. "Would you like something to eat or drink before I show you to your bedrooms?"

Both of us shook our heads. We'd had enough to eat during the drive and I didn't want anything to drink.

Do they know about my bed wetting problem? I wondered. *Did the people at the Children's Home tell them? And what would they do if I wet the bed? Would they spank me, or make me clean the sheets?*

"Can I go to the bathroom?" I asked.

"It's through this door," my new mother said, walking ahead and pointing to a curtain. "Behind that."

I walked in and heard the door close behind me. What I didn't know at the time, is they were told by the state adoption services in St. Paul that they would have to put in running water before they could qualify as adoptive parents, so the bathroom was less than a year old.

After relieving myself, I washed my hands and returned to the kitchen where we waited for Jean to use the bathroom.

When she did return, our new mother led us through the living room to a door at the far end. Next to it was another open door, which I assumed from its contents was where our new parents slept. We followed her up a steep set of stairs, and when we reached the top, she pointed at a curtain. "Your room is behind that curtain, Terry. One of these days we'll put up a wall, but for now the curtain will have to do."

The creaky stairs and the curtain reminded me of the two-toned black and brown wallpaper in Grandpa and Grandma Larson's farmhouse.

The first thing I noticed when my new mother pulled it aside was my new bed, its head against the far wall. Unlike the small beds at the orphanage, this looked like one an adult would sleep on; one I would have to climb into. A window looked out over the yard, and in the far corner against the wall sat a small dresser.

Linoleum tile rested on top of the floor, but instead of covering the entire room, it ended four inches from the walls, exposing gray floorboards. In several places, I saw brown smudges, which probably came from years of use.

The plastered walls were the same dirty yellow as those at the Children's Home, and the ceiling was shiny white with an uncovered light bulb in the center. There was one additional amenity, but it was at the end of the hallway. There, built into the corner, stood a small closet. It would serve as storage for winter clothes, but little else while I lived there.

"And this is your bedroom, Jean," our new mom said, pointing at an open door.

I followed them and stood in the doorway as Jean surveyed her new bedroom. It was more spacious than my room. A standard bed sat against the inside wall, along with a full-sized dresser and a large closet. Her window faced the road we had come in on, and to the left of the window there was a full-length mirror.

"What's that door for?" my sister asked.

Stepping into the room, I saw an Alice in Wonderland kind of door to the right of her bed.

"That's storage space," our new mother said. "We'll look at that some other time."

Brown wallpaper with ornate black vertical stripes covered the walls. Like my room, the ceiling was painted a shiny white, and a nondescript, light colored, Linoleum covered the floor, but I didn't see any worn spots or floorboards around the edges. Another detail, one that would become more important in the winter, was the ornate floor vent in her room, which circled around a pipe that came up from a heater in the living room.

As I would later learn, my bedroom did not have a vent. To heat my bedroom, it was necessary to leave the downstairs door open, an arrangement like the one at Grandpa and Grandma's house—the one where my brother and I got scarlet fever.

There would be many winter nights when I would return

home late to find the door closed. Ascending the stairs, I would see my breath, like a cloud, suspended in the air. Fortunately, I did not get scarlet fever again, because unlike the army cot at Grandpa and Grandma's, I had a mattress underneath me, and by rolling up into a ball, I could retain enough body heat to stay warm until the heat from downstairs found its way into my room.

"Well, I'm sure you're tired from that long trip. Do you need any help, or can you get undressed by yourself?" my new mother asked. I shook my head and returned to my bedroom.

As I closed the curtain behind me, I heard her say, "I'll come in there in a few minutes to say goodnight, Terry."

Taking everything but my underwear off, I crawled into bed and pulled the sheets up to my chin. Then, as I waited for my new mother, my mind raced over the events of the day; the adoption and the long drive to this strange new place in the middle of nowhere with people who I didn't know. *What's going to happen to me? They're not my real parents.* With gritted teeth, I vowed that I wouldn't let them hurt me—I would be a man.

"Are you all set?" my new mom asked as she entered.

"Yes," I said, concerned that she might even try to kiss me, but to my relief she didn't. She said something about seeing me in the morning, and then she walked out, turning off the lights before descending the stairs.

As I lay there in the dark, it hit me again: *What if I have to go to the bathroom?*

Our new home was larger and it had more comforts than our grandpa and grandma's house, but at Grandpa and Grandma's there was a pail in my bedroom, and at the orphanage the bathroom was attached to the bedroom. The only bathroom here was downstairs. That meant walking in the dark in a strange house past people I didn't know. *What if I wet the bed?*

Feeling completely lost and alone in a strange new world—one that I wasn't prepared to be a part of as my new parents would soon find out—I fell into a restless sleep.

Photo of the Degner family taken during the trip from Duluth, MN to Wendell, MN in 1953

CHAPTER 3

You're Not My Real Mom and Dad

July 15, 1953

I tossed and turned throughout the night, worrying about wetting the bed. The matrons at the orphanage had been vigilant about reminding me not to drink anything after the evening meal, and it had begun to pay off—somewhat, anyway. I still couldn't help myself when I came in after playing. Running to the drinking fountain was instinctive, especially when the other kids did the same thing. For that reason and because of the newness of my situation, I did not drink anything after arriving at the farm, and to my relief, when I awoke in the morning, the bed was dry.

"Rise and shine," I suddenly heard our new mother shout from the bottom of the steps. "Breakfast is ready and we have a busy day ahead of us."

I put on the clothes from the day before. I had brought two pair of pants, two shirts, and the tee shirt I got from the Duluth Dukes baseball team, along with several pairs of underwear, some socks, and my square toed Buster Brown shoes.

As I reached down to put them on, I heard my sister scurry by on the other side of the curtain. Then, I heard her start down the stairs. Not wanting to be left out, I tied my shoes and bolted.

The first thing that hit me as I stepped into the kitchen was the overpowering smell of grease. I felt like I had stepped into a shower of fat.

"How do you like your eggs?" my new mother asked, as I sat down on the chair next to my sister.

Our new mother was standing next to the stove, a spatula in her hands. "How do you like your eggs?" she asked again.

"I like it so the yellow isn't runny," I replied.

When she was finished, she put two on a plate—along with toast—and brought it to where I was sitting. "I'm sorry, the toast got a little burnt," she said, setting the plate on the table in front of me.

Burnt to a crisp was a more accurate description, and the eggs were overcooked. The only thing that looked normal was the jam, and from what I could see, it came from a store-bought jar.

"Oh, I almost forgot, here's the bacon," she said, handing the plate to Jean, who then passed it to me.

"Did they give you bacon at the orphanage?" she asked.

"Grandma did, but we didn't have it at the orphanage," I answered.

"Well, this might taste a little different than your grandma's bacon. I ran out of smoked bacon, so I had to use salt pork. It comes from the same place on the pig, but it's not cured." With that, she helped herself to a piece.

If you've never had salt port, you haven't missed a thing. It's what they use in cans of beans to give it texture and flavor, but it does not taste like regular bacon. It's tasteless and it feels like you're chewing on pure fat.

I took one bite and spit it out. "Yuck. I don't like it."

"I'm sorry. You don't have to eat it. I didn't have anything else," she said, concern on her face.

I ate the over-fried eggs and the burnt toast, washing it down with milk that almost tasted like cream. As it turns out, it was whole milk straight from the cows.

Looking back, there are few, if any, negative things I can say about my adopted mother but, to be blunt, cooking and baking were not her favorite activities. As she once told me, "I'm afraid I can burn water," and time would prove her right on that score.

After we finished eating, our new mother said, "Dad and I would like to talk to the both of you about chores. Did you have chores at the orphanage?"

"Yes." I answered. "I had to scrub the steps."

"I helped take care of the babies," my sister piped in.

"Well, your dad and I think it's important for you to have some chores and we thought it would be nice if you worked together, at least to begin with. You could start by washing and drying the dishes, and after you're done with that, I'll show you how to wash and candle eggs. How would that be?"

Without hesitation, I asked, "How much are you going to pay me?"

"Pay you? What do you mean?" she asked in surprise.

"The orphanage gave me money for scrubbing the steps," I replied.

Our new mom and dad looked at each other, and then she said, "We'll have to think about that and get back to you."

As she spoke those words, a car drove into the yard.

"It's the Brutlags," our new dad said.

"Well, isn't that a nice surprise," our new mother pitched in. "It's our neighbors, Erv and Grace Brutlag. You'll want to meet them because they have two boys about your age. I told them all about the adoption, so they're excited to meet you." They both got up and motioned for us to follow as they headed for the door.

The introduction was short and awkward. Our new mother introduced us to the adults and they in turn introduced us to their sons. Paul, the oldest son, was our age, and Larry was a couple years younger. Erv and Grace seemed truly interested in the adoption. In a strange way, I think they wanted to see what an orphan looked and sounded like. It was as if we were from another planet.

They asked us several questions about the orphanage, most of which our new mother answered, and then Erv asked if we knew what happened to our "real" parents. It wasn't done maliciously, but in a way, it was a slap in the face and I think his wife saw it that way because she immediately said, "Erv, I don't think that's an appropriate question."

They told us they lived on a farm about two miles away. Then they told us that their boys loved to make forts in the haymow with the bales, and they asked if we would like to come over after things settled down to make forts in their haymow. It sounded fun, but I didn't understand what they were talking about because I had never seen a bale. Grandpa Larson had stored loose hay in his barn, but not bales.

The conversation shifted to the adults while my sister and I were caught in a staring contest with the Brutlag boys. I do not recall any words being spoken between the four of us, and we certainly didn't run off to play, but over the years we became friends, as we are even to this day.

When they finally left, our new dad said he had more chores to do before he could get into the field, and we walked back to the house with our new mother.

For the remainder of that morning, Jean and I were put to work. First, we washed and dried the dishes, and then our mother took us out to the chicken coop to gather eggs. I was familiar with chickens, but I had never gathered eggs.

When we entered the coop, the chickens scattered, making high-pitched clucking sounds, some of them even making a feeble attempt at flight, as feathers, straw, and dust blew around us. I coughed and gagged as the taste of the dust settled on my tongue.

The chickens were everywhere. Many were perched on wooden slats that ran the length of the building, but most were milling around troughs filled with the crushed grain I'd seen in the entry. Mounted along the wall on both ends of the building were hundreds of boxes.

"What are those?" I asked, pointing at the boxes.

"Those are nests and that's where the eggs are," our new mom said. "Come with me, I'll show you how to gather them."

I watched as she stuck her hand inside, took out an egg, and put it into the bucket she was carrying. "Now you try it, Terry," she said, pointing at the next box.

I started to put my hand inside, but quickly pulled it back when a chicken stuck its head out and made a pecking motion. "The chicken's still in there," I yelped, keeping my hand a safe distance away.

My new mother smiled and stuck her hand into the nest.

The bird pecked at her a couple of times and then it walked out and flew to the floor, squawking. "You'll get used to it," she said. "It doesn't hurt, but I can understand you getting scared the first time." She must have decided not to push it because she gathered the rest of the eggs herself. I watched, but after a while I decided I'd had enough of the dust, so I went outside to wait while Jean stayed.

When they finally came out, our new mom was carrying two buckets filled with eggs. We walked back to the house together and then she showed us how to wash and candle. Each egg had to be washed by hand, rinsed, and then dried. Some had gobs of chicken manure stuck to them, but most looked clean.

Our new mom told us to wash all the eggs even if they looked clean because they probably had a micro something or other on the shell. Based on the taste test I got while I was in the chicken coop, she was probably right. Then, she showed us how to hold the egg in front of a light to look for blood in the yoke.

"People who buy eggs don't want to break an egg open and find blood inside," she explained, "so it's important to find those eggs before we take them to town."

"Blood spots," she later told me, "are a result of a ruptured blood vessel during the formation of the egg. They are not harmful to eat, but it doesn't look very appetizing."

Following her instructions, my sister and I washed and candled each egg. Then we put it into a large cardboard box with layers of grooved pockets like you see in the grocery store. The bloodied eggs were placed in a bucket and later thrown out. There weren't many, maybe one out of every fifty or so. It was easy work, but tedious and boring.

After the noon meal, our new mother addressed the issue of money. "Dad and I have given some thought to paying you for the chores you do around the house and we feel it would be OK. We'll have to work out the amount—"

"I got fifty cents an hour at the orphanage," I said, interrupting her.

"Well, that might work, but what I was about to say is that we'll pay you, but you'll have to pay us for Room and Board."

I'm sure I'd never heard the catchphrase Room and Board, but I knew what pay meant, and when you combine those words it forms a clear meaning, even for this soon-to-be eight-year-old. I looked at her, and then I said something I've always regretted.

"You're not my real mom and dad, so there." I didn't shout it. Instead, I squinted my eyes and I spit it out.

My parents were stunned and for a few seconds, silence filled the room. Finally, my new dad pointed his finger toward the door to the living room and in a stern voice said, "Go to your room right now, young man. We will not have any talk like that around this house."

I got up, but instinctively, I turned back and spat, "I'm not a cow. You can't buy me."

Where that came from, I don't know. It's not something most seven-year-olds would even understand, let alone say, but I said it nonetheless.

His finger shaking and his face now red, he pointed toward the living room door again. "Go to your room young man and don't come down until we tell you to. Is that understood?"

I turned and ran through the living room and up the stairs. Reaching the top, I pulled aside the curtain and angrily threw myself onto the bed.

Looking back, it wasn't about money; it was about control. They had outwitted me with the Room and Board comment, and I had responded inappropriately—and I knew it.

I lay in bed sulking, and then somewhere around four o'clock, I heard my mother's calm voice at the bottom of the stairs.

"Terry, my sister Evelyn and her family are coming to visit us in a little while, so why don't you come down. If you want to talk about what happened, we can do that before they get here."

I didn't want to talk about what had happened, and the thought of meeting complete strangers made the situation even worse, so I stayed in the bedroom. When I heard the dog barking and the sounds of a car on gravel, I knew they'd arrived. I also realized it would be wrong for me to stay in my room while they were here, so with some reluctance I walked down the stairs, timing my entrance into the kitchen just as the entire Reeser family walked in.

The Reesers had four daughters; Bonnie, Carlyon, Kitty, and Ilene, in that order. Bonnie was two years older than me, and Kitty two years younger, putting Carlyon in my age bracket, but it was Kitty who stuck out the most. She had a winning smile and the most energetic and alluring personality of all the girls. Ilene, two at the time, was the youngest.

They lived in Fergus Falls, which was about twenty-four miles from the farm. With approximately thirteen thousand inhabitants, Fergus was the largest town in the area. Evelyn was a stay-at-home mother. Jim, her husband, was a mechanic by trade.

I remember very little about their visit, other than the noise of girls playing. There were no boys, so I kept to myself, and

even if there had been, I most likely wouldn't have been as social as my sister. She has always been able to make friends easily.

After the Reesers left, my mother sat me down at the kitch-
en table and told me not to worry about what had happened
that morning. She said she would forget, and she asked me to
do the same.

No one had ever spoken to me like that before. She said
it with so much warmth and kindness—a kindness, I would
come to learn, that was well-known and loved by everyone in
the community.

I'd like to say I adopted her as my mother at that very moment, and that I never hurt her again, but that would be a lie.
Before that journey could even begin, however, I would need to
explore my new home and the surrounding community.

CHAPTER 4
Glimpses of the Future

July 16, 1953

"Rise and shine. It's time for breakfast," I heard my mother shout from the bottom of the steps. I heard noises coming from Jean's bedroom and shortly thereafter, I saw the curtain flutter as she ran by.

Rolling over, I clutched the pillow and groaned inwardly, shutting my eyes and biting my lip. I'd been awake for the past fifteen minutes. I was lying on my side, my legs curled to avoid a large wet spot in the center of the bed.

Why did I have that stupid glass of water last night?

"Terry, did you hear me?" Mom shouted again.

"Yes. I'm coming. I need to find my pants." When I heard her walk away from the bottom of the staircase, I lifted the covers and gingerly moved to avoid the wet spot. I took my underwear off and tucked it between the top mattress and the innerspring. Then, I put on my clothes, and after covering the wet spot with my blanket, I slowly walked downstairs to face the day.

"Good morning, Terry," my mother said cheerfully. "How did you sleep last night?"

"Fine." Actually, I'd slept like a log, which was a big part of my problem. *If only I could wake up when I felt the urge to pee,*

"The hired man is coming this morning," Mom said. "He'll be here any minute so eat up."

"Who is he?"

"You've heard us talk about the hired man before."

She said it as if there had been a long conversation about him, but the only thing I could remember was someone forgetting to turn on the yard light when we first arrived.

"What does he do?" I asked.

"Well, he helps Dad around the farm and he's become like family to us. I'm sure you'll like him."

After the meal, Jean and I gathered the dirty dishes from the kitchen and took them to the sink—she washed and I dried. It was an arrangement we'd agreed to at the start, and it continued until my outdoor chores took up all of my time.

As we were finishing up, I heard the roar of an engine. Looking out the kitchen window, I saw a young man astride a motorcycle drive by and disappear.

"OK, the hired man's here. Let's go out and greet him," our mother said. "I'm sure he's just as excited to meet you as you are to meet him."

Actually, I was more excited to see the motorcycle. We scurried out of the house and over to where he'd parked his bike. As I later learned, it was a red and white Indian Chief motorcycle and by the looks of it, it wasn't new. The saddlebags gave it away. They weren't frayed or damaged, but I could tell from the look of the leather that they'd been in the elements for some time. I'd never been that close to a motorcycle before and I got the distinct impression that seeing the hired man on the motorcycle might have been a first for my parents.

He was much younger than I'd expected; not that I'd thought anything about age, but for some reason, I had envisioned a much older man. As it turned out, he was fifteen. He was fit and trim and good-looking, and I could tell from the way he talked with my parents that they had something special going on, especially with my father who seemed taken by him.

I later learned that the hired man's parents had owned a farm about two miles from ours. At first, he would come over during the threshing season to help out, but after his father underwent surgery for a brain tumor and moved into town, he had moved in with our parents.

He slept in what would become Jean's room, and when talks about adoption turned serious, our father built an addition to the house specifically for him. The addition faced the road and was accessed through the living room, but he didn't like it because there were too many windows. For that reason, he moved to the small town of Campbell to be with his mother, his father having moved to the Twin Cities.

The hired man had parked the motorcycle under the yard light and it stayed there for the rest of the day while both he and our dad worked in the fields. Meanwhile, Jean and I went back into the house to finish our chores. While we were washing dishes, our mother told us that she was going out to the garden to get some vegetables for dinner. I asked if I could go with her and she said, "As soon as you and Jean are done with the dishes you can come out, Terry, and help me in the garden, but you finish up with the dishes first."

As soon as we were done, I ran outside. The garden was behind the shrubbery I'd seen the night before. Turns out, the shrubs, ten all told, were lilac bushes. They had obviously been planted many years earlier as each bush stood a good seven feet in height and, from what I could tell, at least six feet in diameter.

Directly behind the bushes, two clothesline poles along with five attached wire lines ran parallel to the lilac bushes and behind that, sat the garden.

At the farmyard end of the garden, an old black car was parked next to what looked like a large gas tank sitting atop a metal frame. The tires on the old car were flat and the grass and weeds surrounding it almost came up to the door handle.

"My grandpa had a car like that," I said to my mother, who was pulling weeds.

"Did he? It's an old Model A and we haven't driven it for a long time. I don't even know if it still runs."

"What's that thing?" I asked, pointing at the tank.

"That's a gas tank."

"How come you have a big gas tank?"

"Because we can't run into town every time the tractors need to be refueled."

I'd seen two tractors sitting in the yard that morning. The hired man had taken the thinner of the two and Dad drove off with the other one. The one the hired man drove was faded red, while the other one was a dark, dirty red. They were both the same height, but the bulky one looked like it could pull a heavier load.

I would later learn that the thinner tractor was a Farmall H, and the bulkier one was a Massey-Harris 44.

"How do you get it?"

"Get what?" my mother asked.

"Gas."

"Oh, that. You drive the tractor up to the tank and—"

"No, no! I mean, how does the gas get into the tank?"

"Oh, that! I thought you meant, how do we fill the tractor. We call the gas company in town and then they send out a truck full of gas and a man fills the tank. It's as simple as that."

Changing the subject, I pointed at a jumbled bunch of loose boards next to the garden and asked, "How come you have those?"

It was a large pile, and many of the boards still had nails sticking out of them. Mixed within the boards were old doors and even an old window or two; the glass cracked and in some cases, even missing.

"Oh, I wish they weren't there. I know it doesn't look good, but Dad believes there will come a day when he'll need them to repair something. So, for the time being we'll have to put up with the mess." And with that, she went to her knees and started to pull some carrots.

She didn't ask me to help, so, with nothing to do, I stood there, evaluating my new surroundings. Looking west, my eyes followed a path of trees at the far end that wound down toward a gradual embankment. It circled around the wood pile and kept going past a high fenced-in yard in the back of the chicken coop. It ended at a much lower fence, behind which stood two cows; their ankles deep in mud.

A path wide enough for a tractor ran to the left of the wood pile and through the trees, disappearing around a bend. It wasn't a forest, per say, but it was just big enough to partially obstruct my view of the fields to the south of where I was standing.

"Can I go over there?" I asked, pointing at the trees at the far end of the lilac bushes.

"I don't think that would be a good idea," she said, standing up and brushing strands of hair out of her face. "There's a lot of poison ivy in the woods this time of year."

"Can I go in the barn?"

"I guess that would be OK. The cows are out now, but be careful and don't go into the haymow. Not until someone goes with you."

I quickly walked past the front of the chicken coop and headed for the barn. Like most of the barns I had seen, it was painted red and, like the orphanage, it had a gabled roof.

I would later learn that it was a typical early twentieth century structure designed and manufactured by, of all companies, Sears & Roebuck. That's right; it came right out of the Sears catalog. The materials were pre-cut and then shipped with instructions, leaving the actual assembly up to the farmer.

I opened the door to the barn and stepped inside. It was dark and dingy and it smelled like manure. The only light came from six small windows, and from cracks in two large sliding doors at the far end. Long, dirt-filled cobwebs hung from the ceiling everywhere, some extending down a foot or two.

On the left side, running the length of the building, I saw a bunch of upright metal frames hanging from a wooden beam. All told, there were twelve metal frames with a passageway at the midpoint. Called stanchions, I would soon learn they were used to keep the cows anchored during the milking process.

On the righ side of the barn and under the windows were three calf pens. To my immediate right an open door led into a small room. Poking my head in, I saw some milk pails with strange-looking cups hanging on the side, and a large shiny metal container that looked like an oversized freezer. I would later learn that the pails with the cups were the milking ma-chines and the large container kept the milk cool.

Seeing a ladder on the other side of the stanchions, I care-fully stepped over the straw-filled gutter until I stood at the base of the ladder. Looking up, I saw an open hole, which ap-peared to be a passageway to the haymow.

Against my mother's wishes, I climbed to the top and stuck my head into a large room. Loose hay lay on the floor in the middle, and on both ends of the haymow, piled halfway to the top of the ceiling, were hundreds, if not thousands, of what Mr. Brutlag had called hay bales. I didn't go any farther that day, but over the next eleven years I would get to know every inch of that haymow.

I left the barn and, without asking for permission, headed toward what must be the pig barn. I say that because I could see five or six sows and up to twenty-five piglets wallowing in mud. In addition, there were pigs going in and out of an opening on the side of the building.

The structure certainly didn't look like a pig barn, it looked more like a church. I say that because a bell tower, or what looked like a bell tower, protruded out of the roof at the front end. In addition, the building was painted white and a row of windows ran the length of the structure.

I would later learn that the pig barn had at one time been a one-room schoolhouse, which our parents had purchased and moved to the farm.

Upon opening the front door, I heard what sounded like hundreds of little feet scurrying about, but I didn't see any pigs. I hesitated for a second until the noise had settled, and then I stepped into what looked like a storage room. To my right, three five-gallon pails rested randomly on the floor. To my left was a boarded-up enclosure, filled to the brim with ground up corn. I cautiously walked to an inner second door and opened it.

What I assumed had once been the church's worship area (nave) was filled with pigs on either side of a narrow isle. The wood flooring had been torn out and replaced with cement, but everything else resembled a school. Satisfied, I closed the door and left the way I'd entered.

Stepping back into the sunlight, I looked to see Mom still on her knees, pulling something out of the ground. She suddenly looked in my direction and waved in a manner suggesting a lack of concern, so I kept going.

When I had first approached the pig barn, I'd seen a path to the left. Now, as I looked down it, I could see that it slopped down toward a pond, behind which was the road running past the farm. A small red building stood on my left and a corn crib to my right.

I walked toward the pond and stopped when I got to the red building. I'd half expected to see a blank wall, but instead I saw an open portico, within which stood two farm implements.

Upon reaching the pond, I saw a culvert running under the road from which water flowed. The water in the small pond then emptied into a creek that ran through my parents' farm. When I say small, I mean small. At most, the pond was twenty feet in diameter. It was perfectly round, and it even had a sandy beach.

Wouldn't it be great if it was deep enough to swim in, I thought.

I stood at the edge for maybe five or ten minutes, staring at the water. I even thought about taking my shoes off and wading in, but I couldn't see the bottom, so I gave up on the idea and left.

From the pond, the path ran parallel to the road and toward the farmhouse. I couldn't see the house because of the many trees. In addition, the pond had to be a good twenty feet below the level of the yard.

As I began to walk up the steep grade, I noticed for the first time lots of junk lying at the foot of the trees to my left. I saw a bedspring, the metal legs of an old table, a coach, some metal chairs, and an old tractor seat…just to mention a few.

When I reached the top of the grade, I looked to see if Mom was still in the garden and not seeing her, I returned to the house.

"Hi, did you enjoy your little tour?" she asked as I walked into the kitchen.

Without answering, I asked, "Can I swim in the pond?"

"I thought you might ask that," she replied. "You can, but I'm not sure you'll like it because the bottom is muddy and there might be some blood suckers in there."

She didn't have to say another word. I knew from experience about blood suckers and I didn't want to have anything to do with them, so any thoughts of swimming in the pond went out of my mind for good.

"Where's all the noise coming from when you go into the pig barn?" I asked.

"It's the pigs," she replied.

"No, no, the noise when you first get in," I said, somewhat frustrated that she didn't understand.

"Oh, those are rats. I don't know how many there are, but they like to eat the feed in the entryway."

During the years I lived on the farm, I never heard or saw a rat in any building other than the pig barn. I would, on rare occasions, see a mouse scurrying about, but the wild cats took care of them. For some reason, these same cats didn't go near the pig barn.

The hired man left on his motorcycle that evening without saying goodbye. At least, he didn't say goodbye to me. In fact, over the course of that first summer, he pretty much ignored me. If anything, he seemed annoyed whenever I happened to be in his presence. He socialized with Mom and Dad and with Jean on a regular basis, but not with me. It wouldn't be until the end of summer that I would come to understand why.

CHAPTER 5

A Dream Come True

July 17, 1953

I slept in the center of the bed that night, as the accident from the night before was still damp and smelled of urine. I hadn't said anything to my mother. I didn't know how.

Maybe I could wash the sheets without Mom finding out, I thought. *If I wash them in the bathroom sink while she's picking eggs, and hang them out to dry, maybe she won't notice. Then, I could sneak them in when she wasn't looking.*

I rolled onto my side, curled into a ball, and hugged my other pillow, a habit I had started in the orphanage. *What was I going to do? I have to stop drinking after supper—I just have to*, I told myself.

When I awoke the next morning, the only reminder of the accident was a yellow stain, as the sheets had dried during the night. I crawled out of bed and quickly pulled on my pants, but as I reached over to grab my shirt off the back of the chair, something caught my eye. Through the window, I saw the figure of a man walking down the road toward our farm. Aside from the fact that he was walking in the middle of a deserted dirt road at six-thirty in the morning, what made the scene stand out even more was his gait. His arms were moving faster than his legs and his feet never left the ground, as evidenced by the cloud of dust swirling around his ankles.

Running downstairs, I found both my mom and dad sitting at the kitchen table; coffee cups in their hands.

"There's a man walking down the road," I said, "and he's walking really slow."

"Oh, that's just our neighbor, Mr. Bruster," Mom said, matter-of-factly. "He comes once a week during the summer to have coffee with us. Sit down and eat your breakfast and when he comes in we'll introduce you."

It took the man another twenty minutes to walk the third of a mile to our farm, or at least it seemed like twenty minutes because I was already done with breakfast by the time he knocked on the door.

That's how I met Mr. Bruster, and for the rest of that summer and part of the next, he would make the once-a-week trip from his place to spend an hour with my parents. Mom and Dad would have their coffee, and Mr. Bruster would have a cup of hot water. Then, after they talked about the weather and the state of the crops, he would shuffle back to his farm and a life of solitude.

Mr. Bruster was in his nineties when I met him, and he died the following year. I don't believe I've ever come across anyone like him, and I probably never will. I can't say that I got to know him well, but I did know him well enough to realize that he was someone who preferred to live in the past.

His wife had passed away several years before our arrival, and his children were grown and living elsewhere. The only connection he had to the outside world was my parents and a daughter who would drive out from Fergus Falls once a week to bring him groceries.

Imagine for a second, being in your nineties and living alone, not in town but in the country, getting by without electricity or running water. He didn't have an indoor toilet, a shower, or a refrigerator, and he used wood for cooking and heat during the winter. To get the wood, he had to find suitable trees; usually dead ones because live trees need to dry out before they can be used as firewood, and that often takes at least a year. Then he had to haul the wood back to his house and cut it into usable lengths for burning.

In his prime, Mr. Bruster had owned horses, which he used for extricating gravel from his property. He then sold the gravel to the county and they used it to build roads. Because his land sat entirely on the lakeshore of Lake Agassiz, the land was ideally suited for that purpose, but not useful for much else.

At one time, Lake Agassiz was the largest body of fresh water in the world. In fact, all the fresh water lakes in the world today could easily fit into the basin left by that great lake. The only thing left of it are the flatlands of western Minnesota, almost all of North and South Dakota, a good chunk of Central Canada, and the Red River (which flows north into Hudson Bay).

By the time we arrived, what had been Mr. Bruster's gravel pit was now a small forest, covering up the past he'd once known. I've always treasured the love our parents showed this senior and, in appreciation, he gave Jean and me a buggy—not a toy buggy, but the real thing. Unfortunately, we stored it in the granary, which later burned, taking what could have been a wonderful museum gift with it.

Mr. Bruster lived on the north side of the road of that ran past our place and the river that ran through our farmland flowed south from his land and land owned the Wiggins. Mr. Bruster's land was on the west side of the river and the Wiggins on the east side.

About a half mile northeast of the river stood the remains of what had at one time been the small village of Hereford. There was nothing left of the town by the time we arrived; its buildings, except for a church and graveyard, had long since been torn down for scrap, leaving only a few foundations and one rusting 1930s automobile. The village had been established in 1887, and at its height it boasted two grain elevators, a coal shed, a blacksmith shop, a general store, a lumber yard, a train depot, the church, and even a cement block factory.

Someone, most likely my mother, told me the lumber in the junk pile next to the clothesline came from Hereford, but not the pig barn. Its original site had been about two miles east of our farm.

With all that said, after Mr. Bruster left on the day I first met him, I walked outside with my parents to say goodbye and as I observed him shuffling down our driveway, something else grabbed my attention. Across the road, in the wooded pasture boarding the creek, stood a beautiful horse. It was full grown, its main a dirty blond, its hide a light tan.

I watched as it stuck its head under the fence to get at the long grass in the ditch, and then he lifted his head and stared at me as he munched. It looked just like the horse in the dream I had at the orphanage. In the dream, I was standing on a ridge next to a horse overlooking a vast prairie. Mr. Bruster lived on that ridge.

"Mom, look there's a horse across the road. Can I go over and pet him?"

"Of course you can," she said, "but I'm not sure he'll let you."

"Is it Mr. Bruster's horse?"

"No, it belongs to the Wiggins."

"Where do they live?" I asked.

"They live about two miles south of us. I don't know why they even bother to keep him because they don't seem to ever ride him."

"What kind of horse is it?"

"It's a stallion. I think they call it a palomino, but I could be mistaken."

"Do you think they would let me ride him?" I asked.

"We don't have a saddle and even if we did, I don't think you could catch him."

She was right, of course; whenever I tried to get close, he would saunter off. I tried giving him an apple, but that didn't work. He was independent and he had everything—good grazing land and water from the creek.

The Wiggins would house him during the winter, but in the summer, they pastured him next to the creek. Over the years he created a path that would one day take me to a place I shall never forget—a place that helped shape my future.

CHAPTER 6

A One-Stop Town

July 18, 1953

On Saturday morning, I again awoke to Mom yelling, "It's time to rise and shine," but this time she added, "we have lots to do today, so let's get a good start."

"What do you mean?" I asked.

"Dad's taking us into town this morning to pick up some things and then this afternoon I want to get washing done, so when you come down, please bring your sheets and anything else that needs washing."

A sick feeling came over me as I climbed out of bed. I hadn't wet the bed again, but the sheets were stained and so was the mattress. *Maybe,* I thought, *she'll wash my sheets with all the other clothes and she won't see the stains on the sheets or the mattress.*

I took the sheets off the bed and rolled them into a ball. When I walked into the kitchen, Mom pointed at a basket in the pantry and said, "Throw your sheets and clothes into the basket over there. I'll get at them this afternoon."

I threw them into the basket and sighed with relief.

After breakfast and the morning chores, Dad drove us to the small town of Wendell. We'd driven through the town on the day of the adoption, but it was dark and I was tired, so I had no memory of it.

The drive was a short, four-mile trip, but it took forever—or at least that's how it seemed. After a two-mile ride on the dirt road that ran past our place, Dad took a left and drove another two miles north on a paved road, which took us to the outskirts of town.

There are municipalities in the state of Minnesota smaller then Wendell, but if you compare it to other towns with one stop sign, it's right up there in size. Today the town has around one hundred and seventy residents, but in the early 1950s, the population was a whopping two-hundred and fifty. In those days, the town prided itself on having a bank, a grade school, a baseball field, two bars, two gas stations, a general store, two restaurants, an International Harvester Dealership, a blacksmith shop, a barbershop, an insurance agent, an American Legion, a dance hall, a park, and even a drive-in theater.

The park was an empty lot between the dance hall and one of the bars. A small octagonal bandstand and four horseshoe arenas took up most of the space. The drive-in theater was in an empty lot to the left of the dance hall and across the street from the grade school. Because I'd never seen a drive-in, the significance of a rather small, somewhat white screen sticking out of the ground didn't register. Our parents would end up taking us there once to watch an Abbott & Costello movie. Not long after that, the Farmers Coop built a gas station on the site.

According to town gossip, Wendell's baseball team had been

a dynamic force in the late nineteenth and the first half of the twentieth century. The team had a long-standing reputation for winning against the bigger towns in the area. Later, when I attended junior high and high school in the nearby town of Elbow Lake, I would observe that many of the stars on the football, basketball, wrestling, track, and baseball teams had come from the town of Wendell and the surrounding farm community—including myself, I might add.

Most of the people who ask me today where I grew up don't have a clue about where Wendell is or how big the town is. But, in 1972, on the very day of the Symbionese Liberation Army shootout in Los Angles, I was having a nightcap in West L.A. and sitting next to me was a Chase Manhattan executive from New York. When he asked me where I was from and I told him, the first thing that sprang out of his mouth was, "Donavan Olson." I couldn't believe my ears. He had just named the one and only banker in Wendell.

He went on to explain that he'd recently traveled through Minnesota, setting up a new program offered by Chase Manhattan called a "credit card."

Before we had left the farm, Mom had mentioned the need for groceries—specifically bacon—but as we neared town she brought up the subject of clothes. As she put it, "While we're in town, we'll get you kids some nice clothes for church tomorrow."

It was, I believed, her polite way of saying we looked like orphans. I still have some of those clothes, and they do look like they came from Salvation Army. Besides being leftovers, the tags were missing. The first thing a clothing store did when they donated leftovers was tear off the tags. That way, the beneficiary couldn't resell them.

Upon arrival, Dad slowly drove across a railroad track, past the grain elevators, a few houses, and the grade school before finally coming to a stop in front of the general store. As we started to climb out of the truck, Dad said, "I have to do something at the bank so I'm going to drop you off and then I'll stop by later to pick you up."

Why he felt the need to drive to the bank was odd because it was just across the street, but that's what he did. We got out and I watched as he drove five car lengths to the only stop sign in town. There, he took a left and parked in front of a two-story, dark brick building.

Turning, I followed Mom and Jean into what was called, The Dybdal, Pikop, Skinnemoen dry goods and grocery store. The store was something out of the nineteenth century. It had everything; groceries, furniture, guns, and clothing. In the center stood an old wood burning heater with several spittoons sitting on the floor next to it. Corrugated tin, which was dirty yellow in color, covered both the walls and ceiling, and the wooden floorboards showed years of wear.

This was my first shopping spree. Mom bought me two shirts, two pairs of pants, underwear, socks, and even a pair of boots. I wanted boots that looked like the ones I'd worn at the orphanage, minus the holes in the soles, of course, but I couldn't find any black ones that fit, so I settled on a brown pair.

"Can I have the kind of overhauls Dad has?" I asked.

"You mean the ones with the straps?"

I nodded.

"Those are called bib overhauls, but I'm not sure if they have them for little boys. We can look."

We searched through the few stacks of jeans they had but there were no bib overhauls for kids, so I ended up getting my first pair of blue jeans.

"Can I try them on?" I asked, excitedly.

"I'm afraid they don't have a dressing room here, but I think these will work. They might be a tad bit big on you, but you'll grow into them.

Dad was waiting as we exited the store.

"Did you get bacon?" I asked Mom as we started to get into the truck.

"Oh my, I forgot what we came for," and with that, she ran back into the store while Jean and I climbed into the cab with Dad.

Mom was right about the "tad bit big," and since stores in those days didn't have a return policy, I had to use a belt to keep them from falling down, but over the course of the summer, I would grow into them.

That evening, Mom pulled me aside and said, "Terry, I see where you had an accident."

My heart almost came to a stop.

"I didn't mean to," I said in a pleading voice.

"I know you didn't mean to, but maybe we should do something special, so it doesn't happen again."

"What do you mean?"

"Well, would it help if we put plastic under your sheet? That way, if you have an accident in the future it won't stain the mattress," and with those words I immediately knew how she had found out. She didn't see the stain on the sheet, she saw the stain on the mattress when she made my bed. In my scheming, I hadn't given that any thought.

"I won't wet the bed again. I promise."

"Well, we can try it for a while, but if it happens again, we'll have to do something about it because you don't want to sleep on a stained mattress, do you?" And with those words, the conversation ended.

I went to bed that night determined not to wet the bed anymore, but unfortunately it was a promise I couldn't keep.

The Dybdal, Pikop, Skinnemoen dry goods and grocery store. Photo scanned from the Prairie Village. Published by the Wendell Centennial Committee and edited by Don S. Lilleboe.

CHAPTER 7

The Church Community

July 19, 1953

"Rise and shine. You'll have to hurry this morning because we're going to church, and afterwards we're going to my parents' for dinner. Terry, do you want to take a bath first, or would you prefer Jean take hers?" Mom asked.

"I don't care," I answered.

"Well, then Jean, you take your bath first. Bring the Sunday clothes I bought for you yesterday and Terry, while your sister's bathing, you can eat breakfast."

Breakfast, as had been the case all week, wasn't anything to brag about, but at least we had real bacon this time. It was burnt to a crisp, but it tasted like bacon and that's what counted.

After Jean came out of the bathroom, I went in and, using her water, took my first bath in our new home. It wasn't the same as taking a bath in the pool at the orphanage, but that was a community bathtub; this was a small, one-person tub.

"Can I have more hot water?" I yelled, as I settled into the slightly soiled and now lukewarm water.

"You can try," Mom shouted back from the kitchen. "Do you need my help?"

"No, I can do it by myself," I said, not wanting her to see me naked.

"Just use the hot water. It's the knob to the left, but please don't use too much because it hasn't rained for some time and I'm afraid the cistern might be drying up."

"What cistern?" I asked, having not heard the term before.

"The cistern by the front steps," she answered, sounding somewhat closer.

"You mean the cement thing in the ground?"

"Yes. You might know it as a water reservoir. When it rains, the water from the roof goes into the cistern and that's what we use for drinking and washing. We have a well by the barn, but we don't have one for the house. Maybe someday, but not now."

I'd seen the cistern when we first arrived, but its meaning hadn't registered. It should have, or at least the sight of it should've made me think because there was something familiar about it. Directly in the center of the ten by ten-foot slab of cement was a manhole cover. I'd seen these metal doors to the underworld in Duluth, so I should've guessed there was a cavity beneath the slab, but I'd been so overwhelmed with all the other new sights and sounds that this one passed right by me. I also knew what a reservoir was because I used to play on the top of one when I lived in the orphanage. In a way, this cistern was a miniature version of it.

When I'd finished bathing, I returned to the kitchen in my new duds to find Dad sitting at the table.

"Are you done?" he asked.

"Yes."

He brushed by me and into the bathroom, then washed himself in the sink. He changed into his suit, the same suit, I would later learn, he had worn on my parents' wedding day.

When he was ready, we crowded into the family's rusty, dirty, light blue 1949 pickup truck. The smell of his Old Spice aftershave, mixed with the odor of the barn, filled the cab. It's a smell that will forever remind me of my adopted father.

Fifteen minutes and six miles later, we arrived at the Lawrence Presbyterian Church. I can still picture the first time I saw it. When our pickup reached the top of a ridge, our mother pointed and said, "There it is."

Looking out the front window, I saw a small, white building sitting in the middle of nowhere. As some members of the church liked to say, "It's in the middle of God's country," but to me, it looked like nowhere.

Imagine for a second, a drained Atlantic Ocean. What would you see from the shoreline? You would see miles and miles of endless, flat land gradually sloping downward and disappearing over the horizon. Now imagine a small, white church sitting on the ocean floor not far from that shoreline. That's the view I got from the pickup that morning. The ridge we topped was the lakeshore of Lake Agassiz, and the flat land was what was left of that once great lake.

I also have a vivid memory of the reception we got. I especially remember the warm welcome as we stepped into the vestibule. There are welcomes, and then there are welcomes that come from the heart—this was one of those moments. What I didn't know at the time is just how important that small church community would come to mean to me. It's not an easy thing to describe because it's not tangible; you can't see or touch it. It's a heartwarming, genuine love that gradually and subconsciously changes your very essence. Some people call it role modeling. I call it soul modeling because that's what my parents and that small community did for me.

After the service, our mother introduced us to her parents. Her father, Walter Ash, was a short, stout man with bushy eyebrows that curled up at the corners. He'd most likely shaved that morning, but you wouldn't have known it from the stubble covering his face. Her mother, Della Ash, was one of the shortest women in church. Besides being vertically challenged, she was slim, flat-chested, and ordinary in appearance. She had a shape edge to her voice, while Walter had a gentle, persuasive way of speaking. It was obvious even to me that our mother got her manners from her father.

After the introductions, our mother escorted us to Sunday school. As soon as we stepped inside the room, the teacher stopped what she was doing and said, "Well here they are. We've been waiting for you."

"Good morning, Shirley," our mother said. "I'm sorry we're late. I had to introduce the children to my parents. Children, this is Mrs. Jandt. She's your new Sunday school teacher."

Bending over, Mrs. Jandt said, "Hi, children. We're so happy to have you in our class."

Pointing at the other kids sitting around the table, she said, "This is Neil, Lena, and Walter. Say hi, kids."

In unison, they greeted us and then the teacher motioned for us to take the two remaining chairs.

"Do you want to stay here with the children, Winifred?"

"No, I've got some things to do, but I'll return later to pick them up." Waving at us, Mom said, "Have fun, kids." Then she disappeared.

Other than scribbling in a coloring book, I don't remember anything about what we studied that day, and the only reason I remember the coloring book is because I was always terrible at coloring. I couldn't keep the crayons within the lines and it was embarrassing.

Jean and I would spend the next eleven years getting to know all of them. The one exception was Walter. He was the minister's son, and he and his family would move to Texas the following year.

After Sunday school, we drove to the Ash farm for dinner. It was two miles southeast of the church, so the trip was short. Sunday dinner had been a family tradition for years, and it was one that would continue until the grandparents were too old, or just tired of cooking for all the grandchildren.

"There's Grandpa and Grandma's farm," Mom said, as Dad made a left hand turn off the gravel road onto a dirt road. I looked in the direction she was pointing, but the only thing I could see was what looked like the upper part of a farmhouse, which had to be a good three-quarters of a mile away.

As we neared the farmstead, more buildings appeared and the house became fully visible.

"Is that a lake?" I asked.

"Yes, that's Ash Lake. It's named after my grandfather, James, and his brother, Samuel. They were one of the first settlers in the area. Well, that's not completely true, Samuel was the first Ash. A couple years after he arrived, he wrote a letter to my grandfather, encouraging him to come to Minnesota."

Continuing, she said, "My grandpa, James, and his wife, Mary, left Pennsylvania in 1876. They stopped in St. Paul to help celebrate the one-hundred-year anniversary of our country, then they came here and settled on the west side of the lake."

That was my introduction to the Ash side of the family, a family with an extensive and fascinating history. The first Ash, Daniel Henrich Esch, later changed to Ash, came to the new world from Germany in 1741. His father, Fredrick Wilhelm Esch, was, as the historical documents state: "apothecary, counselor's relative, and members of executive staff in the court of Hesse-Kassel," and Daniel was his apprentice.

Shortly after Daniel's arrival in the new world, he married Elizabeth Kerlin, daughter of John Kerlin—a member of the Society of Friends (Quaker). They had one son, Joseph, before Daniel returned to Germany to settle the family estate. On the return voyage, his ship was lost at sea and the art of preparing medicines was lost to his descendants.

Joseph Ash went on to fight in the Revolutionary War. Later he married a Rachel Whitaker and they had thirteen children who thrived in Pennsylvania as carpenters and farmers. Their one claim to fame is that in the early 1800s they replaced the original wood braces holding up the Liberty Bell. There are two canes made from that wood floating around in the family.

Many of Daniel's children now reside in the Society of Friends gravesite, in West Caln Township in Pennsylvania, and the original family home still sits on Ash Street.

Little is known about Grandma's side of the family. Her last name was Bullis. She grew up on a farm not far from the church, but the family history ends there. Publishers say that only about thirty percent of the population read regularly, so it's no surprise that most families in the United States don't have a family tree, let alone knowledge of their past. The Ash family, on the other hand, was proud of their past and they kept it alive.

Walter and Della Ash were married in 1907 and, despite being the youngest of five children, Walter took over the family farm; I would later learn this was not to his liking. They spent their entire life anchored to the small community they grew up in, and over the years Della gave birth to five daughters. All told, they ended up with sixteen grandchildren, ten of them living close by. The remaining six were too far away to spend every weekend at the farm, but when they showed up for special holidays, their little farmhouse was crowded.

The Sunday dinners were a welcome reprieve from our mother's cooking, and playing outdoors with all my new cousins was a real treat, especially since I was the oldest boy and second oldest in the crowd. Not that I'm bragging, well maybe just a little, but I must admit I did love to show off my athletic skills.

That first week would turn out to be a precursor of things to come. As for the bed wetting, Mom never did make a big deal about it, and over time my diligence at staying away from water in the evening would pay off.

Lawrence Presbyterian Church

CHAPTER 8
A Butter Paddle

Summer 1953

For the remainder of that first summer, Jean and I learned what it was like to stay busy six days a week. Our adoptive parents ran one of the larger farms in the area. They owned two hundred and eighty acres, and they rented a quarter section (160 acres) from the retired father of the hired man. All told, we farmed four hundred and forty acres. Nothing by today's standards, but it was a good-sized farm back in the days when farmers used two and three-bottom plows. We also had twelve milk cows, ten sows, along with their many piglets, and a thousand chickens.

I remember asking my father once what kind of farm we had, and he said, "It's a farm-farm."

What he meant is that with the land and the livestock, vacations were out of the question. The four days in Duluth were the most time he had spent away from the farm and, as things would turn out, it was four days more than I would get while I lived with my adoptive parents.

A typical day consisted of washing and drying the dishes after each meal. In the morning, we would go out to the chicken coop and help Mom pick the eggs. Then, Jean and I would sit on small stools in the middle of the kitchen and wash, candle, and pack the eggs in cartons. We didn't have an egg washer, so we had to wash each one by hand.

When I wasn't in the kitchen, I was in the garden with my mother or following my father around the farm. I would often walk out to the pasture with him to bring in the cows for milking, help feed the pigs, and spread straw in the gutters. If the five-gallon, galvanized milk pail was empty, my father would ask me to bring it to where he was disconnecting the milking machine from the cow's udders. I would lift the lid off the pail and he would pour the milk inside, then I'd put the lid back on. Sounds easy, but with one dump from the milking machine, I had to leave the pail where it sat because I wasn't big enough or strong enough to carry it to the next stanchion, let alone the cooler.

Free time wasn't what it is today for children. When I was lucky enough to have a few minutes to kill, I didn't run to the house and turn on the TV because we didn't have one; we didn't even have a radio. Instead, I would go down by the creek, poke around the junk pile, or climb one of the many trees on the farm—anything to keep my body and mind active.

What I didn't do during this period of my life was behave like a son. I do not mean to imply there was actual misbehavior, but rather an indifference. By indifference I mean that I looked upon my adopted parents as I had the staff at the orphanage. They were not my parents, but caretakers. Some extended family members interpreted my mindset and outlook on life as an act of misbehavior, and they reacted accordingly. This, I believe, was due to the pain they saw my mother going through during this adjustment period. To them, it was me who should've been doing the adjusting, not their daughter or sister.

What they failed to consider was my background. A child's outlook on the world is made happy or unhappy, easy or difficult, in accordance with their early upbringing. A person's entire life is enormously influenced by what happened during their first five years.

When my wife and I recently purchased a new puppy, I told the dog trainer it wasn't the puppy she was training, it was us and she smiled in agreement.

I bring this up because of an incident that took place during that first summer. My mother decided, for whatever reason, to spank me with a butter paddle. I hadn't forgotten the incident, but I also hadn't given it much thought until one recent afternoon. I was getting ready to depart from one of my many visits to her assisted living quarters when she suddenly said, "Before you leave, Terry, I want you to take down the butter paddle hanging over the stove and take it home with you."

"Why?" I asked in astonishment. It had been hanging over the stove in her previous homes for as long as I could remember.

"Because that's the paddle I was about to spank you with when Wally came in and took it out of my hands."

"You mean you put it above the stove to remind yourself of that?"

"Yes," she said in her soft voice. "I've always regretted what I was about to do and I've kept it as a reminder, but now I want you to take it home with you."

I do not recall what I had done or said to deserve the spanking, and she doesn't remember, either. It certainly didn't match the personality I've come to know and love in my mother. The only thing I do remember is bending over her knees and thinking to myself, Don't struggle or try to get away. Let her do it and get it over with.

What I couldn't fathom or even think about at the young age of eight was the emotional suffering I was putting this wonderful woman through.

Over the course of the first year, I would be reminded on at least two occasions of my not-so-secure status in the family. The warning came not from my mother, but from the social worker that dropped in from time to time to see how things were going.

"If you don't behave yourself, you could end up back to the orphanage," she would say to me, but she never mentioned what I'd done.

So, what had I done to deserve the paddle? Was it something I said or did? Was it something I didn't do?

Yes, I had said some hurtful things that first day, but at no time had I done anything with malicious intent. Nor did I strike or hit anyone.

The answer is very simple: it came to me when I was watching my own three daughters raise their children. Like my daughters, my adopted mother had dreamt from an early age of becoming a mother. She was one of five girls, and all of them had children except for her. All she wanted was to feel needed and loved as a mother and not, as I wrote before, as a staff member. I not only disregarded her as my mother, but my very aura said, "You're not my real mom."

Why? Because I had a real mother and I wasn't a child anymore. I had been making decisions on my own since the age of four and survival, not love, was my driving force. It was, I now believe, this survival instinct that drove my adopted mother to flee to her parents' home on more than one occasion. She felt like she was failing. When I asked my dad one day why she wasn't at home, he said, "Your mother is frustrated and doesn't know what to do with you."

I now have the butter paddle hanging in my house as a loving reminder of what she must've gone through during those early years.

The Butter Paddle

CHAPTER 9

You're NOT Wanted

Summer 1953 continued....

"You know where boys like you end up, don't you?" the hired man said tersely at the dinner table one day.

"What did I do?" I asked.

"They end up in Stillwater at the detention center, and that's where you'll end up if you don't behave yourself."

"Don't tell him that," my mother cut in. "That isn't nice. I'm sure he won't be going to any detention center."

The subject was dropped, but not the anger.

What had I ever done to him? I couldn't help but wonder. I hadn't been in his company that much during the summer, but when we had been together, he had ignored me. Mom would often take his noon meal out to the field for him to eat and on those rare occasions when he did come in for dinner, he would talk good naturedly with my parents and goof around with my sister but never with me. Only once did he say anything to me—and that was the detention center threat.

Then, shortly after my eighth birthday, an incident occurred that neither one of us has ever forgotten; one that is difficult to write about, but one that may explain why he seemed to dislike me so much.

It was a beautiful, late August afternoon when I stepped out of the house and spotted the hired man lying on his back under the corn picker. The machine was parked in an unusual spot. Instead of next to the light pole, it stood next to the barn and not far from the water tank. Out of curiosity, I walked out to where it was located and looked down.

"What are you doing?" I asked.

"I'm cleaning the corn picker, can't you see," he said in a don't bother me tone.

"How come?" I asked, ignoring it.

"Because Harry didn't bother to clean it, and your dad wants it cleaned before we use it."

Harry was my father's younger brother. He lived on the home place about fifteen miles north of Wendell and evidently he had borrowed the picker.

Without giving my next action much thought, I kicked the soul of his boot. I'm not sure why I did it. I know it wasn't in anger and it certainly wasn't a hard kick—it was more of a tap. If anything, it was my way of getting attention, but he obviously didn't see it that way.

"Stop that!" he yelled. "Do that again and you'll wish you hadn't. Get out of here so I can do my work."

A few seconds went by and then—again, not in anger but as a joke—I tapped my foot lightly on the side of his boot. In fact, I remember having a smile on my face and thinking, *OK, I won't kick the sole of your boot this time, I'll tap the side of it.*

In a rush of anger, he pulled himself from under the corn

picker and stood up. "I told you to stop it," he said, his teeth clenched. Then, without warning, he grabbed me, picked me up, turned me upside down, and carried me over to the cow's water tank.

"What did I do?" I shouted.

"I told you to stop, you little shit, and now you'll get what you deserve." And with that he shoved my head under the water.

I tried desperately to come up for air, but with his hand on my chest, he kept me submerged.

A few seconds later, he pulled my head out and yelled, "Are you going to behave yourself?"

Squirming and kicking, I yelled, "I didn't do anything wrong."

Again, he dunked me and held me under.

When he pulled me back out, I yelled, "I didn't do anything."

I don't know how long he left me under, but I do know I was gagging for air when he pulled me out, and then on a fourth dunking, he left my head under the water a lot longer— much longer than the previous three times.

I was gasping and fighting for air and my lungs were beginning to fill with water.

He didn't bother to ask me if I was going to behave myself after the fourth dunking, and I didn't say anything. He tipped me right side up and put me on the ground. Without, hesitating, I ran toward the house, still gasping for air and spitting up water. For the first time in my life, I was truly frightened.

As I was preparing to write this book, I called the hired man to get some dates and to find out the model of his motorcycle. Not long into the question and answer session, he brought up the dunking incident. I had not intended to ask him about the event, but it must've weighed heavily on his conscience because he just started talking about it. I listened and when he finished telling me his version of what happened and why, I realized that he had given me the answer to a question that had bothered me for years. Why did he dislike me so much?

During the interview he told me that if he had dunked me a fifth time, it would've been disastrous for everyone. According to him, it was then that he made the decision to leave and not come back—a good choice given the circumstances.

However, what really intrigued me were his excuses for why he did it. He told me that I had used foul language around my parents, I didn't behave myself, and I refused to work. To my knowledge, the hired man could not have witnessed any of these so-called misdeeds because they didn't happen.

As for the swearing, I did swear from time to time, but I never swore at my parents—ever. My sister may have heard me swear when I would accidently drop an egg on the floor, but according to my mother, she never heard me swear. My father heard me swear once, but it was when I was much older.

My father may have told the hired man about some of my not-so-good moments, like when I told my parents they weren't my real parents; that's a real possibility. But there's an alternative answer that encompasses all of the so-called transgressions he mentioned.

Over the years, the hired man kept in touch with members of our family. Had one or more of them innocently told him about things that had happened over the years, and did he use bits and pieces of those conversations as an excuse for his actions? I believe, based on what he told me, that this was the most likely scenario.

However, there is another possibility. My parents had discussed adopting a daughter and I had been a throw in—an interloper. Did my sudden and unexpected appearance upset the hired man's dreams?

Walter and Winifred were like family to him, and there was a strong bond between him and my father. On top of that, he had farming in his blood. Did he have dreams about taking over the farm someday?

I can't speak to that with any substantive knowledge, but I have always had this feeling that I came between him and my parents. He certainly would've made a good farmer, and maybe a better son, for that matter.

The hired man left the next day for school. It was a private high school in Morris, Minnesota, with a focus on agriculture. To my knowledge, he never returned to farming, but he has always stayed in touch with my parents and my sister. As for our relationship, we exchange greetings whenever he drops in for a visit, but that's as far as it goes.

CHAPTER 10
A Teacher's Gift

Second Grade

"When the student is ready, the teacher appears." I suspect this quote goes much further back than Tibetan or Buddhist teachings, but its meaning is just as relevant today. That's what happened to me during the school year of 1953.

There are people in everyone's life who make a difference, and over the years I've had my share. It can be a simple act of kindness from a stranger, a mentor imparting wisdom, or the act of adopting two orphaned children.

Then there are those special times when a non-family member goes far beyond expectations to prepare a child for the future. For me, that person was Mrs. Patricia Kavney.

I met Mrs. Kavney the week before the start of school in 1953 when Mom took my sister and me to Wendell. She was sitting at her desk talking to another set of parents when we first arrived, and upon seeing this, Mom said, "Mrs. Kavney is busy now, so we'll wait in the hallway until she's done."

"Who's my teacher?" I asked, looking down the hall.

"What do you mean? Mrs. Kavney is your new teacher."

"But this is the second grade," I said, looking at the number placard next to the door.

"I'm sorry, Terry. We should've talked about this before, but your teacher in Duluth recommended that you take second grade over again."

"What?" I whined. "Why?"

"Because she felt you needed more work on reading and writing before you go to the next level, and the school principal agrees."

My heart sank. I didn't know what to say. Yes, I'd felt like a complete dunce the year before, but to be in the same grade as my sister was unsettling, to say the least.

"How come my sister doesn't have to take first grade again? She doesn't know how to read," I said, feeling sorry for myself.

"It might be nice if you and your sister go through school together. You can be her protector. Wouldn't that be nice? Besides, I don't think you will like being behind the other boys and girls." Bending over and taking my hands in hers, she continued, "I think you'll like your new teacher Terry, and before long you'll be reading and writing with the rest of the children."

I could tell from the tone of her voice that I didn't have a choice. I also knew deep down she was right. I recalled how frustrated I'd been in school the year before. How the other students would snicker when I tried to read and how, in frustration, I would sit in my seat and stare out the window, hoping the teacher wouldn't call on me.

After the other parents left, Mom walked with us into the classroom and introduced us to our new teacher. Mrs. Kavney was of medium height, trim, and pleasant-looking and, as I would quickly find out, a dedicated teacher. She wasn't gushy or overly sensitive, but serious in a congenial way.

After asking us a few basic questions, she said, "Why don't you children sit down in one of the desks while I talk to your mother."

We did as she asked and waited impatiently as they talked. I couldn't hear their conversation because they kept their voices low, but it stands to reason they were discussing my growth record from the previous year. Duluth Public School recorded a child's emotional, social, and educational progress in kindergarten, first, and second grade.

In my growth record, it stated:

Language Arts: Terry has a limited sight vocabulary and is unable to attack many new words independently because of his lack of phonetic understanding and application. By repeating the second grade next year, Terry will learn these skills and read with understanding and enjoyment.

Arithmetic: Uses numbers with understanding, but needs more drill on the number facts for the grade.

Social Living: Learning to be kind and cooperative and gain happiness in his school and community.

After they were through talking Mom took us on a tour of the school. Built in 1910, this school was by far the largest building in town. Several years before our arrival, the rural, one-room schools in the surrounding area had closed. To accommodate for the influx of new students the city added space to the front of the old structure. The first and second grade classrooms were in the new addition, and grades three and four, along with a small library, were on the first floor of the old structure. The principal's office and the fifth and sixth grade classrooms were on the second floor, and the lunchroom and auditorium were in the basement.

When we returned home, Dad had a new chore waiting— one that would keep all of us busy for the rest of that day and right up to the start of school, so I didn't have time to mope.

At the dinner table, he said, "We'll have to do something about a different corn picker next year. There's still a lot on the stocks and too many ears lying on the ground."

"Do you think it would be worth it if we all went out to the field to see how many ears we can save?" our mother asked.

"Wouldn't hurt," Dad said, "but, if we're going to do that, we'll need to shuck it."

I didn't know what shuck meant, but it didn't take long for me to find out. With Mom driving, Dad, Jean, and I climbed on the wagon and we headed out to the cornfield.

"How many rows do you think we can cover?" Mom shout-ed from the seat of the Farmall.

"Let's see," Dad said, pausing to consider the question. "If each of us covers four rows, that should make it go faster."

"Where do I go?" I asked, overwhelmed by the sheer mag-nitude of what he was asking me to do. From where I was standing, I couldn't see the end of the row and from what I understood, we had to walk up and down until we covered the entire field. *How many more fields of corn are there?*

"Terry, why don't you walk on the right side of the wagon. Jean, you can walk on the left. I'll get everything behind the wagon."

Still confused, I asked. "What do I do?"

"Walk beside the wagon and look for ears of corn on the ground and on the sock. If you see one, pick it up or pull it off the stock, shuck it, and throw it in the wagon."

"What does shuck mean?" I asked.

"Here, I'll show you," he said, yanking off a cob that was still on a stock. He pulled back the husk, and then he threw it into the wagon. "You don't have to pull the husk completely off, but you do have to expose the corn."

For the rest of the day and that entire weekend, we walked up and down the field, stripping corn from the stocks and ground. The work was tedious. By the end of the first day, my legs were killing me and my hands and face were cut up due to the sharp edges on the husks, and from brushing up against leaves still on the stocks. All I wanted to do was crawl into bed, and when I finally did, I slept like a log.

We took Sunday morning off, but we returned to the fields in the afternoon and worked until it was time for milking. I certainly didn't have to worry about wetting the bed because I doubt there was an ounce of water left in my body by the time I hit the sack.

The start of school on Monday turned out to be a relief. After breakfast Mom walked Jean and me to the end of the driveway to catch the bus. Going to school in a bus was a new experience for both of us—we'd always walked in the past.

The driver's name was Mores Bossen, a farmer from north of Wendell. Mores would be my driver for the greater share of my time in school. He would not only put up with some of my faults, but he would also play an important role in my development.

As it turned out, we were the next to last ones to be picked up, which also meant we were the next to last to be dropped off.

The drive to school took about twenty minutes, while the drive home took approximately an hour. When we got older, we would often ask the driver to let us off at a crossroads, which was only three-quarters of a mile from our farm. Then we'd walk to save time.

With one exception, the first day of school was uneventful. The one exception took place right after the bell for the noon meal rang,

"Terry, would you come up here, please? This won't take long," said Mrs. Kavney, in a soft but commanding voice.

I walked up to her desk and when I reached the front, she motioned me around to where she sat.

"I think you have some catching up to do in both English and math, but I'm more concerned about English, especially reading. I'm willing to work with you, but it will require some sacrifice on your part. How much and how fast you learn is up to you."

"What do you mean?" I asked, troubled.

"Would you be willing to give up recess, at least for a while? I'm thinking it might take up to six months. Are you willing to do that?"

I didn't answer her. I was confused and hurt by the idea that I was not only taking second grade over, but based on what she'd just said, I was behind first graders. I also didn't know if she was giving me a choice, or if this was a demand.

"Well, this is obviously something you need some time to think about," she gently said. "Go to lunch and when you're done eating, why don't you come back to the classroom and we'll talk about it some more. Would you be willing to do that?"

I nodded and focused my attention on the last student walking out of the classroom.

"I know, it's time for lunch," she said. "Do you know where to go?"

"I think so," I said, hesitantly.

"The lunchroom is in the basement. Just follow the other students and when you're done, come back here."

I left and found some other students in the hallway and followed them downstairs.

For the next six months, I would eat and then go back to class for a half hour of instruction. Mrs. Kavney would eat lunch at her desk, and then spend the rest of her free time working with me. I don't remember spending very much time on math, but I have a clear memory of how she approached English.

I had two major problems. The first, I didn't understand punctuation. I didn't know when to stop or start a sentence, or how to use the comma for emphasis. I would go from one sentence to the next without stopping.

Second, I didn't understand syllables, vowels, or consonants—nor did I understand how to apply them. In order to help me with these areas, she had me read out loud. Whenever I failed to stop for a period or pause for a comma, she would have me reread the sentence until it made sense. When I ran into a word I couldn't pronounce, she would help me break it down until it became second nature.

But, here's what really made the difference: she had me read stories out loud from beginning to end. Not Dick and Jane stories, mind you, but adult stories. Stories with a plot that caught and kept my attention.

For a good month or two, I was frustrated and aggravated. This is when Mom really found out just how infuriated I could get. Hearing my frustration one day, she came upstairs and said, "Terry, let me see if I can help. What are you working on?"

"I don't understand this question. It's stupid. It's a stupid question."

"Let me look and I'll see if I can make sense of it. Which question is it?" she asked, moving closer to where I was sitting. Prior to the start of school, Mom and Dad had given me a chair and a small table to work on.

"This one," I said, pointing.

She took a few seconds to read the question before speaking. "Well, that's a tough one, but I think it means…." Without giving me the answer, she went on to explain what she thought the question meant. But instead of soothing me, it made me even more furious.

"I hate this!" I shouted, throwing my pencil onto the floor and stomping my foot.

"Well, Terry, if you're going to act like that, I'm afraid I can't be of any help."

And with that, she walked out of my room and down the stairs.

I wish I could say I regretted my outburst and that I immediately apologized, but I wasn't done. I stood up, grabbed the chair, and walked to the head of the staircase. Looking down, I saw my mother at the bottom. I raised the chair over my head, but a little voice inside told me to wait until she was clear of the steps. Then, I threw it down the stairs. It landed harmlessly at the bottom.

Fortunately, she didn't tell my father about what had happened that day. I think she knew that if she had, he would've insisted on sending me back to the orphanage—I'm almost certain of it.

***

As the weeks and months went by, my confidence in reading and math began to improve. More and more I found myself raising my hand in class.

Then, not long after the New Year, Mrs. Kavney called me to her desk.

"Terry," she said, "I think you've come a long way. Your math might still need some improvement, but you're reading has improved dramatically. I think we're through. Would you like to go out and play with the other kids?"

From that time on, I went outdoors to play with the other kids after eating. I also felt at home in the classroom—frustration had been replaced by a healthy self-assurance.

Math has always been a boring subject for me, but not necessarily difficult. Reading, on the other hand, turned into a real love affair. On many a night, my mother would shout, "Terry, turn your light out and get to bed."

I would turn the light off, crawl into bed, pull the covers up over my head, and read with a flashlight until I fell asleep. I remember thinking, even as far back as third grade, that I'd completely missed out on the Dick and Jane phase of my life.

The first adult book I remember reading was John Bunyan's *Pilgrim's Progress.* I saw it sitting on an end table at Grandpa and Grandma Ash's house and, when I asked Grandpa if I could read it, he told me to take it home. From that time on, I've always had at least two, if not three, books open at any given time.

Unfortunately, Mrs. Kavney died before I had an opportunity to thank her. I owe her a great deal, and you can bet she'll be one of the first people I track down in the next life.

Wendell Grade School

Photo copied from the *Prairie Village*. A book edited by Don S. Lilleboe and published by the Wendell Centennial Committee in May, 1982.

CHAPTER 11

How Time Flies

Summer of 1954

Summer started before the end of the school year, or at least the work did. One Saturday morning during breakfast, Dad made an announcement.

"After you're done with your morning chores, we're all going out to the field to pick rocks."

The first thing that ran through my mind was walking up and down the fields the summer before, picking and husking corn.

"Why do we need to pick rocks?" I asked.

"The winter freeze and spring thaw pushes rocks to the surface every year, and this year is worse than it's been in the past. It has to be done before I start planting the crops."

For that entire weekend, we walked up and down the fields, picking up rocks the size of saucers; much larger in some cases. I threw most of the small and medium-sized rocks onto the stone bolt from a few feet away, but the larger ones were problematic. I would lug them over, but every once in a while, I'd run into a boulder. When that happened, I'd call on Dad and he'd hustle over and dispose of it.

A stone bolt is a roughly hewed platform or trailer, but unlike a trailer, it does not have wheels. Two logs, sharpened like a pencil at the front end, formed the underside of a platform. The logs were four feet apart and nailed together with boards. Mom would drive the tractor up and down the field, dragging the stone bolt behind, while Dad, Jean, and I walked alongside it. When it was full, Mom would pull over to an oak tree at the far end of the field. There, we would take the rocks off and throw them onto an already growing pile at the base of the tree. Some of those rocks were larger than even Dad could lift.

"Where did those big rocks come from?" I asked during one of our stops.

"I imagine they came from the fields. They were there when I bought the farm, so at one time there must've been lots of big rocks. I haven't found any that big since I started farming the land."

Geologically speaking, the land had been covered by the last ice age, so the rocks could've come from anywhere.

***

As soon as school let out, chores turned into full-time employment. I continued to dry the dishes after Jean washed them, but a technological investment at the beginning of summer reduced Mom's need for me substantially.

To make the egg washing go faster, our parents bought an egg agitator. So, instead of washing one egg at a time, Mom would put the basket into a bucket filled with soapy warm water. She would then turn on the agitator and, much like a washing machine, it would slowly rotate back and forth until the eggs were clean. We still had to check each one before putting it in the carton, but the investment cut my egg washing time to maybe an hour, two at the most.

Not long after the introduction of this new technology, the creamery in Wendell—that's where we sold the eggs—must've upgraded their capabilities because they told us we didn't have to candle the eggs anymore. And with that, my egg washing and candling skills had become obsolete. I was devastated, of course, but instead of rushing out to file for unemployment, Dad stepped in and gave me some new skills to work on. These included bringing the cows in from the pasture, walking the fence line, throwing hay down for the haymow, spreading straw in the gutters, feeding silage to the cows, slopping the pigs, and bailing.

Looking back, I sometimes wonder if it was fate or just plain dumb luck that landed me on a farm—and with that set of parents. I don't have an answer, but I can say with full certainty that I didn't have time to feel sorry for myself because Dad didn't let me sit still for a minute. I'd helped him bring in the cows from the pasture a few times the previous summer, and with that experience now behind me, the job became mine. After supper, I would cut across the field, find the lead cow, and yell, "Commm-bosssss, commm-bosssss."

Upon hearing those words, the lead cow would raise her head, turn and look at me, then slowly start walking toward the barn.

How did I know which one was the lead cow? Dad had pointed her out to me the year before. "See that cow with the bell hanging from her neck?" he'd said. "She's the lead cow, and once you get her going the others will follow."

Once out of curiosity, I yelled, "Come, Boss" just to see what would happen. To my amazement, she didn't even lift her head, but stretch the words out to "Commm-bossss," she would react and the rest of the cows would follow. All I had to do was walk behind the last cow at a leisurely pace and keep my eye on the ground to make sure I didn't step into a cow pie.

When the cows had gathered behind the barn, Dad would open the doors and they would instinctively walk to their stanchions, with me taking up the rear. I was amazed at how they knew which one was theirs. Every once in a while, one of the new cows would make a mistake and a scuffle would follow, but they always had a way of working things out. Any effort on my part to help would only have added to the confusion.

Walking the fence line with Dad was a make-work job, one that he hoped I would someday take over. Until then, I was responsible for following him with a can of staples. As we walked from one post to the next, Dad would look to see if a staple was missing or simply loose. If loose, he would pound it back in. If one had fallen out, he would lift the wire up to the height he wanted and secure it to the post with one of the staples from the can I held. It didn't require a lot of strength or endurance, but the experience did highlight Dad's one major weakness— he didn't know how to communicate on a personal level. Other than an occasional, "Bring the can here," or "Here, you try hitting it," that was the extent of our conversation. If there was ever an opportunity for us to bond, walking the fence line was it, but he never talked about his youth, his life experiences, or his ambitions, and I didn't think to ask.

Throwing hay down from the haymow is an exaggeration because at the age of eight, I still couldn't lift a bale. But I could push one, and that's what I did. I would push it to the opening in the center of the haymow and let it drop to the cement floor below. When we bailed, I did the same thing. With Mom driving, Dad would do the heavy lifting and stacking, while I labored to pull a bale away from the bailer and push it toward the back of the wagon where Dad would take over.

We baled alfalfa, grass, wheat, and flax straw. Dad sold the flax straw and the grass. The grass ended up in the slaughter houses for feed, the wheat straw we used in the barn for bedding, and the alfalfa for feed.

Alfalfa is a perennial flowering plant in the pea family. Along with corn fodder, or silage, it was the main source of food for the cows. With the right weather conditions, alfalfa will blossom three times a year.

I wasn't big enough to throw silage down from the silo, and because it was a confined space and Dad used a pitch fork, he discouraged me from being in the silo. While he did the milking, however, I would feed the cows. Using a pitchfork, I would throw the silage into a wheelbarrow and, starting at the far end of the barn, I would dump each load into a depression in the cement in front of the cows.

There were other jobs, like helping Dad slop the pigs and even holding down piglets while he castrated them. That last one was an out of the ordinary assignment. I held the piglet on his back, while Dad, using a simple pocket knife, sliced open the piglet's sack and cut out the testicle. One time, the blood of a piglet squirted into my eye.

***

Not long after the summer started, I did get a nice surprise.

My parents announced they were getting me my very own puppy.

"When will I get it?" I asked.

"Well, that depends," Mom said. "I heard Ruth Lacy mention at church last Sunday that one of her dogs gave birth to a batch of puppies, and it was time to find homes for them. You remember Ruth, don't you?"

I nodded my head, but in all honesty, I didn't remember her.

"Well, if you're willing to take care of a puppy, I'll call her to make an appointment so we can go over to their farm and pick one out. If they still have any, that is."

"What do you mean by take care of it?" I asked.

"Well, puppies need to be fed and they need extra attention."

"Can he be in the house?"

"We'll see. He can be in the house for a while, but when he gets older he'll have to stay outdoors like Blackie."

That was how a golden cocker spaniel by the name of Blupee came into my life. I chose him because of his nose. Unlike his brothers and sisters who had black noses, Blupee's was red and he had a longer snout and a bigger head.

Just as we were leaving, I asked Mrs. Lacy where the name Blupee came from. She told me it was the name of a dog on a popular television show. I never saw the show or the dog, but Blupee turned out to be my best friend.

****

Sundays continued to be an off day. After church, we would drive to Grandpa and Grandma Ash's farm for dinner. While the women prepared the food, the men would sit around talking, and the cousins would play. In the spring and summer months, we played croquet and badminton in the front yard, and during the winter we played hide-and-seek, board games, and some of us went ice-skating. We didn't have to go far to skate, because Grandma and Grandpa's front yard bordered on the shore of Ash Lake.

When the meal was ready, Grandpa would stand and say a prayer. When done, the passing of the food would begin, and the noise level would increase as everyone tried to be heard above everyone else.

It was during one of these family gatherings that I found Pilgrims Progress lying on one of Grandpa's living room end tables. I'm not sure if it was the picture on the front cover or the title that grabbed my attention, but I picked it up and, after paging through it, I brought it to Grandpa.

"Is this your book, Grandpa?"

"Yes," he answered. "It belonged to my father. I read it a long time ago and I ran across it the other day. I thought I might like to read it again."

"What's it about?" I asked.

"It's an allegory about one person's journey from this world into the next."

"What's a...what did you call it?" I asked.

"An allegory." He paused, rubbed his chin, and then he said, "Let's see, an allegory is a metaphor; no, that's not right. Let's just say it's a story about a man who overcomes all kinds of problems during his lifetime and, because he lives a life according to gospel, he goes to heaven after he dies."

"Can I read it?" I asked, intrigued by the heaven comment.

"Of course, you can. Take it home with you and I'll read it after you're done."

It wasn't about heaven, which was a big disappointment because I wanted to know what life was like there, but as I mentioned before, reading this book kickstarted me on a voracious journey; one I continue to this day.

After I'd finished reading it, I returned it to Grandpa. It was then I told him I'd started reading the Bible. I never told my mother or my father, but I did read it from cover to cover, a feat I accomplished before I was out of grade school.

In hindsight, reading the Bible by myself without supervision opened my eyes to the big picture. By this I mean, instead of being blindsided by a hand-picked passage from the New Testament followed by one from the Old Testament, I saw the forest without being overly influenced by a tree.

This has caused some conflicts over the years, especially with Bible study leaders and ministers, but it opened my eyes and led me down an interesting path.

The summer of 1954 was eventful for other reasons. Jean and I attended Bible school in our new community. I have no clear memories of those times other than the fact that it took place in the morning and it lasted for two weeks. Also, children from our sister church, Western Presbyterian, came to Lawrence, so there were more children of my age to play with. In fact, a boy from Western by the name of Byron Stock later became my best friend.

Another significant event took place in July. Each year on the Fourth, family members of Lawrence Presbyterian church would gather at a home, or in this case, at the Jeppson farm, to share food, hang out, and engage in recreational play. Jean and I had missed the event by some ten days the year before, so it was a new adventure for us.

The food was fantastic. There were rows of hot dishes and

corn on the cob. Additionally, the men cooked hot dogs and hamburgers over an outdoor grill. But, best of all, the pies were out of this world because the women who made them didn't skimp on sugar.

The fun and games started the moment we climbed out of the cab of our truck, but it didn't get serious until after the meal. That's when the men went out to the pasture to play softball and the younger children, including Jean and me, gathered to play tag and hide and seek.

Toward the end of the afternoon, Erving Jandt, a farmer and famous ball player on the Wendell Baseball team, walked up to me unexpectedly and said, "Terry, how would you like to play some softball with us?"

"Can I?" I asked. I'd been keeping my eye on the adult activities while we ran around the yard, and the very idea of playing with the men and older boys excited me.

"Of course. Go over to the pasture and I'll be there shortly." And with that he went about gathering some of the other boys and girls.

As it turned out, I didn't get to play softball, but the older players did let me take turns at hitting and running the bases and—surprise, surprise—whenever I hit the ball, I always made it to first base. The first time I made contact, the ball stopped halfway to the pitcher's mound. I was a third of the way to first base when the pitcher picked up the ball and threw it wildly over the first baseman's head.

By the time he retrieved the ball, I was standing on third.

"Terry, watch where you step when you're running," the third baseman said.

"Why?"

"Because if you swing out too far, there's a cow dropping

about halfway between here and home."

That was my introduction to softball, a game that would start me down the path of rebuilding my self-esteem.

July and August seemed to fly. Then, toward the end of summer, just as Dad finished combining, he asked me if I would like to participate in something I'd never heard of, something from out of the distant past.

"How would you like to come with me and help Harry with threshing?" Dad asked at the breakfast table. "You don't have to. You can stay here and get your chores done. It's up to you."

"What's threshing?" I asked.

"It's the way we used to do things," Dad said. "It's hard to explain…."

Mom cut in. "You saw Dad combining, right?"

I nodded.

"He pulled the combine through the field with the tractor. It picked up the swaths of grain, and then it separated the kernels from the straw. The grain went into a hopper and the straw came out the back end. Well, with threshing, the men go out to the field with wagons. They pick up bundles of grain, throw them onto the wagon, and when it's full, they bring it to a stationary machine called a threshing machine. They then throw the bundles of grain into the machine, which separates the kernels of grain from the straw. Threshing takes a lot more manpower."

"What's a bundle?" I asked.

"Oh my, you picked up on that, did you?" she said with a chuckle.

"When Uncle Harry swathed the grain, instead of laying it down in rows like your father does, the machine he uses ties the grain into small bundles. Later, Harry and his hired man go back to the field, pick up the bundles, and stack them vertically into small piles of maybe what, Wally, ten bundles?" Mom asked, looking at Dad for confirmation.

"Eight or ten," he said. "It really doesn't matter."

"That way," she continued, "if it rains, the grain won't rot."

"That's why I harvest right away," Dad said. cutting in. "If I didn't the grain would rot. Knowing my brother, he probably cut his several weeks ago,"

With that, he raised is eyebrows and looking at Mom. I could tell from his tone and the look he gave that there was more to this than he was saying.

Dad, I would gradually come to learn, saw his brother as an inconvenience. He felt obligated to help him, but Harry was undependable and lazy. He also spent a good share of time in the town bars, which probably explains why he was overweight and a lifelong bachelor.

Threshing was an experience I've never forgotten. I was a little boy in the company of ten men and one older boy. Two men worked the threshing machine, while the rest of us went out to the field to pick up the bundles.

They used a tractor instead of a steam engine to power the machine, and tractors to pull the wagons instead of horses, but essentially, the process remained the same. For two days, I walked alongside a hay wagon with Dad and when we came to a stack, I would pitch one bundle at a time onto the wagon. They weren't heavy, so throwing them onto the wagon wasn't difficult, even for me.

Pitching bundles into the mouth of the thresher, however, was a one-person job, and Dad didn't allow me to get close. "One misstep," he told me, "and you could end up being ground to a pulp." When the wagon was empty, it was back to the field and more walking.

It was around this time that Dad told me something rather profound. He said, "There are three kinds of farmers: those that have to have the latest and the greatest, those that wait until the technology proves itself, and then farmers like Harry, who remain stuck in the past."

He put Uncle Bud in the first category. When I asked him where he put himself, he said, "I guess I'm somewhere in between."

I remember thinking he hit that nail squarely on the head. Our implements were current, but they were on the verge of being out of date. Many of the neighbors had tractors big enough to pull four-bottom plows. Our 44 could pull a three-bottom plow, but not the H. It could barely handle a two-bottom.

I'm not sure how many hours I worked, and in truth it wasn't all work and no play, but the chores certainly took up most of the days in a week.

How did I feel about the life I now found myself in? I didn't have time to feel sorry for myself or to think about the past. Playing with my new cousins on Sundays and round-the-clock chores kept me busy and out of trouble.

CHAPTER 12

Fitting In

Third Grade

I turned nine the week before I started third grade. I mention this because most, if not all, of my classmates were eight years old, some even seven. Despite the age difference, I was still one of the runts. I don't know what my actual height and weight were because records weren't kept, but size didn't slow me down, especially in sports.

For years baseball had been taken seriously by the locals. Due to this fondness the town had built a nice-sized field behind the grade school. They even had a shed behind the seating area for serving snacks. Furthermore, the outfield fence was farther away from the infield than many of the others I would later play on in the surrounding towns. This was due to a local farmer who had a reputation for hitting long home runs. Thus, putting the outfield fence farther from the infield gave Wendell the advantage.

"How come we're walking to the grass, isn't that where we

play?" I asked, pointing in the direction of the infield.

"They don't let us play there," a classmate said.

"Why?"

"I don't know, they just don't. Besides, we can play more games in the outfield."

And therein lay the answer to my question.

Playing in the outfield allowed us to have up to three softball games going on simultaneously. One in left, one in center, and a third in right.

I don't recall who invited me to join in on the fun during the recess hour, but I do know that I played softball on that first day of school.

When everyone had gathered in the outfield, someone shouted, "Who's going to be the captains?"

And the process of choosing sides began.

Using a bat, the two captains took turns climbing the handle of the bat with their hands until one of them grabbed the knob. This gave him the right to choose first.

This unsupervised procedure would remain the same for the next four years. Indeed, the same went for the captains. They, too, remained the same; unless of course, they were sick, and then a substitute would take his place.

I waited impatiently as one boy after another was chosen. Finely, the captain, looked at me and instead of choosing me, asked, "What's your name?

"Terry," I said, looking around.

My ranking changed the following day. Not because I hit a home run or did something spectacular, but because I made it to first base at every opportunity and even scored once or twice. From that day forward, my name was almost always called near or close to the top. Never the first—that was reserved for the captain's best friends.

I played softball during recess at every opportunity. Sometimes we didn't have enough players to make up two teams, and at other times we had more players than we needed. Regardless, everyone got to play. So, it wasn't unusual to see four or five players standing in the outfield.

The third grade slipped by with little fanfare. The teacher, Miss Olson, was a heavyset woman with a serious side. The one thing that stands out is her spelling bees. At least once a week, she would tell the class to get up from their desks and stand against the wall. Then, starting with the student at the front of the line, she would ask them to spell a word. If they missed, she would tell them to sit down.

I remember standing against the wall for an hour or more, thinking to myself, *Give me a simple word like "the" and I'll misspell it intentionally.*

I know this might sound fanciful, but I wanted to tell her that she should have us sit during the spelling bee and stand when we misspelled a word; not the other way around. That would give each student a greater motive to learn the words.

I believe I reached the pinnacle of being the last one standing once, but I won't swear to it. I still don't know how the more resolute students learned to spell, because it's a discipline I've never worked on. Thanks to my love of reading, spell check, and the thesaurus, I have overcome most of my weaknesses from those early years. However, I must admit that I still struggle with homophones.

Once a week, Miss Olson would release us from class for what the school called "release time." It was this public school's way of getting around the constitutional issue of Separation of Church and State. Release time was really Bible study time. Not all students had to participate, but most would leave and walk to the one church in town, or to a private home for study.

Jean and I, along with our classmates Neil Jeppson and Leanne Hartman, would walk two blocks to Reverend Korselman's home; a parsonage owned by the members of the Lawrence Presbyterian Church. Reverend Korselman's youngest son, Walter, would also participate in Bible study, but he didn't always join us on the walk because he was in fourth grade and the teachers didn't always let the students out at the same time. I never did find out what the students who stayed behind did while we were gone.

Walter was a tall, gangly boy and like his father, he reminded me of pictures I'd seen of Abraham Lincoln. Due to age, his father looked more like the President, but Walter wasn't far removed. Over the course of the school year, he and I became friends and eventually started spending time together at church.

My memories of Bible study are vague, but an incident during the church service will forever stick in my mind. On the morning in question, Walter and I decided we wanted to sit together in the balcony during the service. It took some persuading, but our begging paid off. We found a seat in the front row, directly in front of the lectern.

As we were waiting for the service to begin, Walter asked, "Do you know how to make a paper plane?"

"No," I said, not sure what he even meant.

"Here, I'll show you."

He started to fold the paper program the usher had given him. When he was done, he said, "See, that's how you do it.

Now you try making one."

For the better part of the service, I tried to copy what he'd done and finally it came together; it looked like a limp blimp. The front of the plane was crooked and the wings had all kinds of folds in it, making it impossible for the paper to bunch together.

"Can I see yours?" I whispered.

"Yeah, here," he said, handing the plane to me.

I took it and looked it over. This was about the time that Reverend Korselman stood at the lectern and began to preach.

Holding Walter's plane in my hand, I leaned in and asked, "What would happen if I throw it? Will it go all the way to the front of the church?"

"I dare you," he whispered. "Do it!"

I looked around to make sure no one in the balcony was watching, and then I let go of the plane. It sailed silently in slow motion over the congregation. At first, it dipped slightly, and then it started to arch upward, heading straight for the lectern.

Finally, after what seemed like an eternity, the plane struck. It was not a forceful strike, more like a soft bounce. The point had hit Reverend Korselman directly in the center of his forehead just as he finished looking at his notes. A guided missile could not have hit with more precision.

Walter and I quickly slouched in our seats as a few laughs, along with some gasps, erupted from the congregation. Then, the good Reverend spoke. "Walter and Terry, I know it was you. I'll have a talk with both of you after the service but for now, I want you to sit still and behave yourselves."

That was it! No one, including my parents, ever mentioned it. In fact, Mr. Korselman didn't run me down after church. A month or so later, he and his entire family left the church for a new calling in Texas, and I never heard from Walter again.

CHAPTER 13
Cleaning the Coop

Summer of 1955

"I won't be needing your help in the kitchen anymore, Terry," Mom announced at the beginning of summer. "Jean and I can handle the indoor chores. Your dad says he has plenty of work to keep you busy."

As it turned out, Mom was right. Over the course of the summer, my workload increased substantially, and it started in the chicken coop.

"Terry, I'm going to need your help in the coop today," Dad said.

"What do you want me to do?" I asked, somewhat confused.

"We're going to clean it. So, go back to the house and change into your old clothes and put on your winter boots."

"Winter boots?"

"Rubber boots. You know, the ones you wear outside during the winter."

With that, I went to my bedroom and put on my grubs. Then I grabbed my rubber boots from the hall closet and ran downstairs.

"I'll need your help hooking up the manure spreader," Dad said as we walked out the front door.

I walked over to where the spreader sat and waited until he came with the tractor. He backed it up until the bar on the back slid into the hitch on the spreader. I waited until the holes lined up, then I pushed the pin in with the palm of my hand. Without warning, the tractor lurched and the head of the pin suddenly bent forward. Had I been grasping the pin instead of pushing it with the palm of my hand, there's no telling what would have happened.

"I don't want you to put the pin in until I shift the tractor into neutral," Dad shouted in irritation. He obviously knew how close I'd come to an accident.

He shifted the tractor into reverse and eased it back until the head of the pin was upright. Then he put his foot on the brake pedal and shifted the tractor into neutral.

Cautiously, I pushed the pin all the way in.

"Jump aboard," Dad shouted over the noise. I climbed onto the hitch and held onto the seat's bar as he drove to the back of the chicken coop. When he got close to the fence he stopped the tractor. "Do you think you can manage opening the gate without my help?"

"I think so," I shouted as I jumped off.

Unlike the single strands of barbed wire used to keep the cows penned in, the wire surrounding the chicken yard was a galvanized mesh netting that stretched from the ground to the base of the roof. The ends had been secured to a wooden pole. Three wires then held the pole tight against the side of the building.

I walked over to the pole and stared up at the highest wire. Knowing full well I couldn't reach it, I looked around. There, in the grass not far from where I stood, sat a cement block. I placed it next to the pole, hopped up, and untwisted the top wire. I repeated the process with the lower two wires and, holding the pole, I walked the fence in until my father could pass by with the spreader.

Dad made a circle in the yard and pulled up with the tractor facing me and stopped. He got off, reached into the spreader, and took out the manure forks, while I struggled to shut the gate.

"I can't get the gate shut," I shouted, pushing as hard as I could on the pole.

"Here, I'll get that. You take one of the forks and go inside and wait."

I grabbed one, climbed onto the frame of the manure spreader, and jumped the short distance into the chicken coop. With some exceptions, the door to the outside was always open during the summer, so the chickens were scattered everywhere. It took Dad less than a minute to close the gate, and shortly thereafter he joined me.

I must admit that of all the chores I ended up doing on the farm, cleaning the chicken coop was by far the nastiest. I don't have an exact measurement of the building itself, but it had to be close to seventy feet in length and somewhere around thirty feet wide. The feeding zone took up about two-thirds of the space, and the roosts another third.

During the day, the chickens spent most of their time in the nests, in the yard, or on the floor eating. At night, they perched on the one-by-one wooden roosts that ran from one end of the room to the other—it was their bed.

"How many times do we need to clean this?" I asked.

"The feeding area needs to be cleaned twice a year, and under the roosts once a year."

"Are we going to clean under the roosts today?"

"Well, I don't think we'll get to that today, but yes, we have to clean under the roosts."

The waste under the roosts, I would learn the following day, was a good twelve inches deep, if not more, and it consisted of dung and rotten eggs. The depth of waste in the feeding area was the same, but it consisted of chicken droppings, rotten eggs, feed waste, and straw.

We started in the feeding area.

"How do we clean under those?" I asked, pointing at the nearest feeder.

"Easy," Dad replied.

He walked over to it, reached up, grabbed a rope attached to the top of the feeder, and pulled until it was two feet off the floor. Then he reattached the rope and did the same with all the feeders.

I should say at this point that most of the chickens were out in the yard. A few still lay in the nests, and maybe one or two were in the feeding area, but what few there were stayed out of our way.

We started next to the spreader and worked outward. I can still hear the pop of a rotten egg. I'm not sure why a chicken would, every so often, lay an egg on the floor instead of in the nest. Maybe they were seniors who couldn't get to the nest on time. Whatever the cause, when I stepped on one, I would hear a loud pop and, looking down, I would see a yucky green substance oozing from under my boot. This was quickly followed by the fowl odder of rotten eggs.

During breaks, I would walk outside, cough up black gunk that tasted like bitter acid, and then, using my finger, I would close one nostril at a time and blow out more of the gunk. I often tell people that I've never had the flu due to the many times I cleaned the chicken coop.

We finished the feeding area by the end of the first day. Then, on the following morning, Dad answered a question that had been bothering me for some time: How were we going to get at the waste under the roosts?

Taking hold of the first roost, Dad lifted, and a section of roosts went up in the air. He then stuck a long pole under the front to hold it in place. I knew the roosts were divided into three sections, but I didn't know that each section was attached to the back wall with hinges.

As he went about lifting and securing each section, I stuck my fork into the gooey mess and lifted, but instead of a fork full of waste, the dung oozed from the prongs until there was nothing left.

"What! How am I supposed to do this? It won't stay on my fork."

Dad chuckled and said, "We have to use a shovel for this stuff."

He walked over to the front entry and returned with two shovels.

"Here, use this," he said, handing me a shovel.

With that, he pushed his shovel into the gooey mess until it was full. Then he turned, walked across the floor to where the spreader sat, and threw it in.

I did the same, but when I tried to lift the shovel, it wouldn't budge.

"You don't have to fill the shovel. Just take what you can lift," my father said.

After several attempts, I found that I could only lift about a third of a shovel full. But even that turned into a challenge. Not only did I have to walk half bent over, but on many an occasion, when I attempted to throw the manure into the spreader, the gooey mess would hit the side and fell to the ground. Eventually, I lowered it to a fourth full and that worked out.

Anyway, with both of us focusing and not talking, it took two days to clean the chicken coop.

This was also the year I started to help my father clean the cow barn. On average, we cleaned the gutters two or three times a week, and the calf pens maybe twice a year. Cleaning took, at most, an hour and a half. It was dark, dungy, and smelly in the barn but, unlike the chicken coop, it didn't leave an aftertaste.

The first day is memorable for one reason: after letting the cows out, Dad backed the manure spreader into the barn. I remember thinking to myself, Where the heck am I going to work? We can't both be throwing manure into the spreader from the same location. There's not enough space.

When the spreader was in place, Dad got down from the tractor and pointed at a wheelbarrow sitting by the front door.

"Why don't you take the wheelbarrow and fill it. When you're done, I'll bring it to the spreader and unload it. Do you think you can do that?"

"Where do I start?" I asked.

"At the front of the barn. I'll start here by the spreader and work my way toward you."

"OK," I said.

And with that, the space issue was solved.

I started filling the wheelbarrow next to the front door,

while he stood between the spreader and the gutter and cleaned there. When the wheelbarrow was full, he came over, grabbed it, and pushed it over to the back of the spreader. Then, he dumped the manure into the gutter and handed it back to me.

This system worked out great. What normally took an hour and a half, had only taken us an hour and fifteen minutes.

I can honestly say I didn't mind cleaning the cow barn. There were unpleasantries, like when one of the many cobwebs hanging from the ceiling broke loose and slid down the back of my shirt, or when millions of squirmy little white maggots filled the gutter, but none of this came close to the filth in the chicken coop.

I don't recall ever cleaning the pig barn. I helped feed the pigs and I threw fresh straw into the pens but opening a window and throwing pig manure into the spreader doesn't ring a bell. Many people think of pigs as animals who rout in the mud all the time, but that's not true. Pigs are smart. Given a choice, they prefer sleeping on clean straw and not in areas soiled by dung.

Our pig barn was split down the middle. The pigs that were getting close to the right size for shipment to the slaughter house were penned on the right side of the barn. They were free to run outside when it came time for feeding, or if they needed to relieve themselves. At night, however, they always slept indoors on straw. For that reason, the floor stayed relatively clean.

The pens for the sows were on the left side of the barn. Just before it was time for a sow to give birth, Dad would move her into a small fenced-in area on the left. There, the sow would give birth, and she and the baby piglets would stay until the piglets stopped suckling. Then the piglets would be transferred to the right side, while the sow stayed on the left with the others.

Along with the growing work demand, the summer months continued to include church activities, followed by the noon meal at Grandpa and Grandma's. But two new activities did enter my life during the summer of 1955, one of which began my long journey of self-discovery, and eventually, self-worth.

CHAPTER 14
I'll Take Spunk

Summer Sports, 1955

I joined the local 4-H softball team during the summer of 1955. The coach was Mrs. Ruth Lacy—a member of the Lawrence Presbyterian Church and the woman who sold us Blupee.

The name of the team was The Evergreen 4-H Club and the home turf was the baseball field in Wendell. All told, there were seventeen teams in the league, but I don't recall playing on another team's baseball or softball field, and I never bothered to ask why. A past team member, when asked about this, recalled playing one game away from Wendell, but other than that, he couldn't recall playing in another town.

My guess is the hometown fields of the other teams belonged to the school district, whereas the baseball field in Wendell belonged to the town.

One of the things I noticed when I first joined the team was the size and age of the other players. Many were in high school. Jack, one of Mrs. Lacy's sons had to be fourteen or fifteen. I wouldn't be ten until August. As I soon learned, the ages ranged from eight to sixteen, and one team's pitcher was eighteen.

I don't remember if I played the first day, but if I did, I'm sure I was a sub and Ruth most likely stuck me in right field. That's where all the teams put the newbies or the not so good players—a detail I would later take advantage of.

What I do remember is something my mother told me after the game: "I know you're not going to like this, Terry, but I told Mrs. Lacy that your sister could play."

"Really? She doesn't even like softball."

What I meant to say is that my sister had never shown an interest in anything sports-related, let alone a competitive sport, so the thought of her playing seemed out of character. I didn't care if she played, I just couldn't see her standing at the plate with a ball coming at her.

"Well, I was a little reluctant at first, but Mrs. Lacy talked her into it, so we'll see how long it lasts."

What my mother and I didn't knew at the time is that the 4-H league rule stated that a girl had to play for at least three innings. You could play a different girl each inning, but the team had to have a girl on the field and at bat for at least three innings.

Mrs. Lacy was a big woman—both in stature and in heart. I don't know where she got her love or her knowledge of softball but, as I would soon learn, she could see into the heart of her players and she coached to win. She not only accepted and encouraged my intense style of play, but she took advantage of it.

At first, I warmed the bench. Occasionally, Mrs. Lacy would put me in left or right field as a sub, but I wasn't a starter.

The time I spent on the bench gave me time to reflect on

where I wanted to play. I found that I didn't care for the outfield because outfielders didn't seem to get in on the action. I liked first base but someone, probably Mrs. Lacy, told me that size, especially height, was a critical requirement for that position, so I discarded that idea. Shortstop and second base looked like something I might enjoy, but after watching the better pitchers in the league, I chose pitching.

I knew I couldn't be the team's starting pitcher because the one we had was older and, although he didn't use a full windup, he threw a decent fastball—one I couldn't compete with.

"Could I be a pitcher?" I asked Mrs. Lacy during one of our games.

"Well, we don't need a pitcher right now, but if that's what you would like to do, why don't you and Dick go over there and practice," she said, pointing behind the fence.

The "Dick" she was referring to was Dick Enderle, the team's catcher. The only time we could practice was when our team was at bat and he didn't have to go to the plate.

We practiced a few times during games, and I practiced throwing against the side of the granary at home. A few weeks later, Mrs. Lacy came over to me before the start of the game and said, "Terry, you're pitching today." With that, I became the starting pitcher. I didn't ask what had happened to the other pitcher, but I later learned that his father needed him in the fields.

Try as I might, I couldn't master the windmill windup. The ball would hit my hip or slip out of my hand before I could get it into the correct position for release. For this reason, the ball would sail all over the place, often straight into the ground.

After numerous failed attempts, Mrs. Lacy walked out to the mound. "Terry," she said, "don't worry about using the fancy windup, just use an underhand delivery and focus on getting the ball over the plate." And that's what I did for the remainder of the season.

The ball didn't arch like a slow softball pitch. Instead, it sailed straight—right into the bat of opposing hitters, and as they rounded the bases, as they often did, I would watch the player round the bases with a disgusted look on my face.

Toward the end of one game, Mrs. Lacy placed my sister into right field. Standing on the pitcher's mound, I threw the first pitch and the batter immediately hit a grounder that flew past the first baseman and into right field where my sister stood. And, stood she did. She didn't move an inch. Upon seeing this, I ran from the pitcher's mound, past the first baseman and into right field to retrieve the ball, which by this time had come to a stop ten feet behind her.

As I flew by, I yelled, "Why didn't you go after the ball?"

She responded by saying, (very nonchalantly, I might add), "It didn't come to me."

I picked up the ball and threw it to the catcher in time to prevent the batter from going beyond third base. As I started to run back to the infield, I noticed my sister was still standing in the same spot. I loved her, but there were times when I struggled with how she looked at things.

I later learned that my mother told the coach after the game that perhaps I had a little too much spunk. Mrs. Lacy responded by saying, "I'll take spunk any day."

My sister and I also took swimming lessons for the first time. The lessons were held two miles north of Wendell, on the shores of Lightning Lake, and the instructor was Mr. Bruce Wilcox. On Saturday mornings, Mom would drive Jean and me to the lake, then leave to do some shopping in town. Despite having lived three of the first four years of my life a half mile from Lake Vermilion, I didn't know how to swim, but unlike some of the other children my age, I wasn't afraid of putting my head under the water. Noting this, Mr. Wilcox put me with the beginners instead of with the non-swimmers, and before the summer was over, he promoted me to intermediate. I can't say that swimming lessons excited me—not like softball, anyway, but I did take it seriously and gave it my all. Besides, it offered a nice break from farm chores.

Walter, Winifred, and Terry. Photo taken on the side porch of the Ash family farm home.

CHAPTER 15
"A Tail of Two Cities"

Fourth Grade

The school year went by swiftly and with little controversy—well, I must admit I did fall madly in love with the fourth-grade teacher, Miss Hoff. To my dismay, however, about halfway through the school year, she went off and got married. It took me a good week to get over this loss, but, as the saying goes, "All is fair in love and war."

I liked her as a teacher. She kept our attention, she had a sense of humor, and she spoke with confidence. I say this because I would later lean that she was nineteen at the time and not a licensed teacher, which goes to prove that taking and passing a test does not a teacher make.

There was a time in the not-too-distant past when teachers weren't required to have a college education. They were hired because the locals felt they had the right skills to teach. Today, many mothers homeschool their children with amazing results.

Fantasizing about Miss Hoff resulted in my grades slipping—or, did it have more to do with not handing in home-work? Either way, my grades went down in fourth grade.

I suppose I could blame my parents because they didn't stress the importance of homework, but, then again, Mom had tried and my frustration had scared her off. I was consumed with more important things like work, sports, and reading. Work because I had to, sports because I felt a need to prove myself in front of my peers, and reading for the pure enjoyment of it.

It was while I was in fourth grade that I developed the habit of reading my class assigned books within the first month of school. This allowed me to get back to the books I really enjoyed. Besides the Bible, I had taken a liking to reading history books about the Civil War, and, of course, I loved fiction

The school library was next to our classroom and there I found Charles Dickens' novel, *A Tale of Two Cities*. I'm not sure what attracted me to the story, but once I picked it up, I couldn't put it down. I took it home and every night for almost a month, using a flashlight, I would read until I fell asleep. It took that long because I had to continually backtrack when something didn't make sense.

In the closing, the antagonist gave up his life so the protagonist could live and marry his sweetheart. For two years, this act of altruism bugged me to no end. It's incongruent with everything I'd seen or heard in real life. I've read many times where a soldier falls on a grenade to save his buddies or a parent gives up his or her life to save their child, but the idea of a sociopath giving up his life so another man can live with the woman he desires contradicts everything I know.

I went on to read *Oliver Twist*, *Great Expectations*, and *A Christmas Carol*. Focusing exclusively on books written by the same author is a habit I cultivated early in life, and one that I continue to this day.

With the start of school, it was back to softball and for a good month that's all I thought about. Whenever possible, I was the first one on the field and the last one to leave, and if the weather wasn't cooperative, I would mope.

I played shortstop or second base, and by the fourth grade, hitting in the second or third position wasn't out of the question. This wasn't because I got a lot of good hits, but rather, it was due to quickness and speed.

We played through the fall until the first snow fell, and again in the spring as soon as it melted. The athletes who graduated from Elbow Lake and went on to greatness in sports came from Wendell. It might not be the case today, but it was while I lived in the area.

"It's in the water," I remember hearing people joke, but it might've been something more sensible like the fact that Wendell children had to organize their own activities, and that most of us were farm boys. We didn't have a coach, and we had to referee our own games. In Elbow Lake, the boys had organized basketball, wrestling, and baseball at the grade school level, and many were town boys. I don't have a scientific answer, but Wendell athletics— that includes town ball—had a reputation in Grant County for being above average.

CHAPTER 16

A Summer of Drought

Summer 1956

A drought hit during the months of June and July. It wasn't statewide, but it impacted sections of North and South Dakota, as well as midwestern Minnesota. For two months, the wind howled and a fine dust filled the air, often for days at a time. The sand almost buried our fence line. Even today, a small mound runs the full length of the field where the fence line once stood.

Dad did manage to get the planting done in hopes that we would get rain, but it never came and the crops failed—such is the life of a farmer. One bad year could wipe out the savings of many good years. Even the alfalfa crop failed. We cut it twice, instead of the usual three times, and even then large sections didn't flower. To make up for the loss, Dad cut the grass in the ditches alongside the roads, and we baled and fed that to the cows. Because the grass in the pasture didn't get the water it needed, Dad and I extended the pasture to an area just west of the house. For a solid week, I helped him dig holes, put in posts, and string wire.

The water levels in the surrounding lakes also receded, but it didn't stop Jean and me from continuing our swimming lessons. By the end of July, I was doing the breaststroke and starting to master the freestyle.

As for the softball season, the team went through a change of the guard—out with the old, in with the new, so to speak. Except for the coach's son, Jack, most of the older players had departed and a new generation of players now filled the roster.

My sister had decided that she'd had enough of softball, but there were other girls on the team. The only one I really remember is Linnea Hartman, but her older sister, Bonnie, also played, as did Joyce Schuck. They all attended Lawrence Presbyterian Church, but Joyce and Bonnie were older, so I didn't get to know them as well. All three, however, were good players and, according to Neal Jeppson, our third baseman, they contributed to our winning seasons.

My pitching skills saw some improvement. Instead of reverting to the underhand delivery, I used a whirlwind or circular motion. I'd practiced the previous summer and prior to the start of the season by throwing it against the outside wall of the granary. But, I found that after the ball hit the side of the granary, it fell straight to the ground. Thus, making me run all the way to the wall to retrieve it. Then one day, I noticed a crack in the sideboard where the ball had hit. Knowing that I would get in trouble if Dad happened to see it, I switched to the side of the corn crib. It wasn't perfect, but the boards were thicker and the ball bounced back farther.

With practice, I found that the ball sailed a lot faster and it didn't fall out of my hand. But, at the start of the new season—and much to Dick's chagrin—I had some real issues with the strike zone. The ball didn't always hit the spot I aimed for, and, as a natural right hander, Dick had the bad habit of reaching out with his right hand to catch my wild pitches. I remember standing on the mound thinking to myself that I had to be careful and not hit the batter. As most hitters were right hand-ed, many of my wild pitches were high and to Dick's right.

Dick managed to catch most of my wild throws and, from what I remember, he did so without complaint. Mrs. Lacy was another matter. On many occasions, I would hear her yell from the bench, "Dick, catch the ball with your glove, not with your right hand." It wasn't until some thirty years later that I learned why she kept yelling at him.

At an all school reunion, Dick walked up to me and said, "Terry, I've been meaning to thank you for breaking my fin-gertips."

"What? I broke your fingertips?" I said in disbelief. "When?"

"Don't you remember when I used to go after your wild pitches with my right hand instead of with the glove?"

"Yes, but I didn't know you broke your fingertips."

"Yeah, I broke all four of them," he said, holding up his right hand and bending the tip of his index finger a good nine-ty degrees.

"Oh my gosh! I had no idea. Why would you want to thank me?"

He put his fingers down on the table next to where we were standing, and to my astonishment, all four of them shot out at a ninety-degree angle.

"It gave me an edge when I came to the line of scrimmage," he said. "When I put my fingertips on the ground like this, the defensive players would stare in disbelief. Sometimes they even forget to move," and with that, he laughed.

I knew that Dick had played offense guard at the University of Minnesota and in the NFL for the Atlanta Falcons and the New York Giants, but this was news to me.

"Did you get injured when you played professional football?"

With that, the laughter stopped. "Yeah, every time I roll over in bed, a shoulder or a hip gets dislocated."

Shortly after the reunion, they found Dick in his apartment in Manhattan—the newspaper said he died of a heart attack. Thanks, Dick, for putting up with my wild throws, and for the many years we played in sports together.

Softball wasn't the only 4-H activity. Each year, members of the many 4-H clubs in Grant County would showcase a farm animal, or something they made, at the county fair in hopes that they would be chosen to present at the state fair.

I must admit that this wasn't something I took an interest in. For some reason, I've never enjoyed going to noisy spectacles. The carnival atmosphere of the county fair turned me off completely, especially the cons who ran the booths.

Years later, I would read a book called *The Prince* by Niccolo Machiavelli. It's a book I often quote. Machiavelli is known as the founder of political science because he was the first to place politics on a scientific level. He's famous for the saying, "The end justifies the means." He also wrote, "Heads of state should put on grand parades and spectacles to pacify the masses." When I read those words, I was reminded of the feeling I had as a youth about going to the county fair and, of course, the feeling I have today about the many other public exhibitions our tax dollars pay for, and the hours we spend pacifying ourselves.

To pacify me, Dad gave me a pig.

"How would you like to have your very own pig to raise?" he asked one day at the kitchen table. "It won't be big enough this year, but next year you can show it at the county fair."

"How do you raise a pig?" I asked.

"Well, for starters, you can feed him."

"How do I do that? Doesn't he have to be in the pen with his mother?"

"Usually that's the case, but he's the runt of the litter. He'll probably die if someone doesn't feed him. This morning I noticed the other piglets were pushing him out of the way when he tried to suckle."

And that's how he became known as Runt.

Runt slept in a box in the entryway of the house for a good month. I used a baby bottle to feed him until he was big enough for solids. When he reached the proper size, I fixed a place for him in the barn. Unlike the other pigs, he had the run of the farmyard and he followed me everywhere.

In the mornings, Blupee and Blackie would usually be on the front steps to greet me, and often I would hear Runt squealing and, looking up, I would see him rushing toward me, his head shaking with a self-assured, I-am-a-member-of-this-family-too attitude.

Jumping ahead, Runt stayed with us until the end of the following summer. He won a blue ribbon at the county fair, but instead of allowing me to take him to the state fair, Dad told me it was time to sell him.

"Taking him to the Minnesota State Fair is a waste of time and good money," he told me, and that ended the conversation. I didn't put up a fight, but selling him was another matter.

The day we brought Runt to the slaughter house in Fergus Falls is one of those days I don't like to think about, even to this day. I told Dad I didn't want to go along, but in a firm voice, he said, "If you want the money to buy that bike you've been asking for, you'll have to go along."

Reluctantly I gave in, but fortunately, Dad did not force me to watch as Runt was unloaded from the back of the truck. I covered my ears when I heard him squeal and I refused to look. I also refused to go into the office with Dad to pick up the check.

As Dad climbed into the cab of the truck, he said, "Well, he brought in fifty dollars. That should give you a nice bike."

That's how he put it, but he didn't show the check to me and I didn't ask to see it. To this day, I hate to think about what happened to Runt. The bike turned out to be meaningless. It was nice-looking and I rode it a few times, but I was never attached to it, not like I had been to Runt.

In the fall, Dad asked me to do something that, even at the time, caused me to wonder about his motive. The corn yield that year was a real disaster. The cobs were miniature in size and almost bare, so instead of harvesting the corn and then taking it to town, Dad chopped the entire crop and put it into the silo. Because of this, the silo was the fullest it had ever been.

I didn't help with the harvesting, but Dad did ask me to help with the unloading. Getting the silage from the wagon into the silo required the use of a conveyer belt and a high-speed fan. The silage was unloaded onto the belt, which carried the mixture of stocks, leaves, and cobs to the fan, which then blew the concoction through a metal tube to the top of the silo.

When the silo was almost full, Dad pulled me aside and asked, "Would you be willing to climb to the top and tramp down the silage? You don't have to, but it would really help. I would like to get as much of this in as possible."

I had never done anything like that before and it looked scary. Just the thought of climbing the metal ladder on the side gave me the jitters. It had to be at least forty feet high and the ladder wasn't enclosed. One slip and I could end up in the fan. Then, to tramp around while the fan was still blowing silage into the silo made it even scarier, but I couldn't say no.

As I started to walk toward the ladder, Dad grabbed my arm and said, "Wait. Here, when you get on the ladder, I'll hand you this pitchfork. Then, when you get up there, push the silage in the middle to the edges. When it's level, walk around and tramp the silage down."

"Can I climb up from the inside?" I asked, looking at the ladder.

By inside I meant the side of the silo facing the barn. There, another ladder made up of steel bars attached to three-by-three wooden doors also went to the top of the silo. The doors were put into place as the silo filled and taken out as the silo emptied. More importantly, a rounded metal enclosure gave me something to lean against in case I lost my footing.

"No, I already put the last door in place, so you can't get inside from there. You'll have to climb up from this side."

What he meant by this is that the enclosure wasn't open at the very top and with the last door in place there was no way to get into the silo.

"How are you going to feed the cows if you can't get into the silo from the inside?" I asked, dumbfounded by what he had just told me.

"I'll worry about that when the time comes, but right now I need you up in the silo, so let's get going or we won't get done today."

Right, I thought. *That's easy for you to say.*

The climb was exhilarating. First, I had to stand on top of the blower's tire to even reach the bottom rung of the ladder. Then, grabbing with both hands and putting my feet against the silo, I pulled myself up until I could grab the second rung, followed by the third. Once there, I pulled my feet up and placed them on the first rung of the ladder.

"Here's the fork," Dad said, handing it up.

I grabbed it with my right hand while holding onto the ladder with my left. From that point on, I held my body tight against the ladder and continued at a snail's pace until I made it to the top. With my left hand holding onto the top rung, I slung the fork over the lip of the silo. I grabbed the top lip, slid over, and fell onto the waiting silage, which was perhaps three feet from the top.

As things turned out, nothing bad happened. I didn't pass out from the fumes and die—a scenario that had happened to other farmers. I didn't trip and fall, either, but it did get scary when the silage reached the rim of the silo.

Looking back, what saved me was the fact that we didn't have a dome to trap the fumes, and Dad didn't send me up until the silage was close to the top. I also wasn't up there very long, and before I climbed back down, I dropped the pitchfork to the ground. This made descending a lot easier.

To my knowledge, we never filled the silo past the top door again, but I've often asked myself why my father wanted me to do something that dangerous?

He may not have thought of it as dangerous. My adopted

father had grown up at a time when almost everything he did on the farm posed a risk. It wasn't uncommon for a farmer to get kicked by a horse as they put on the harness, or for them to fall off a horse-drawn piece of equipment, as I would later learn my mother did. She fell to the ground in front of the rake the horse was pulling. The blades of the rake turned her over and over, along with the grass, until her uncle ran over to help. Farm accidents were numerous and, all too often, deadly. It came with the territory, and farmers learned to live with it.

CHAPTER 17
An Act of Foolishness

Fifth Grade

Some teachers are naturals at keeping order in a classroom, and then there was Miss Shultz. She was a petite, unattractive spinster with a stern look permanently etched on her face and a shrill, pleading voice that no one took seriously.

By the end of the first month, I found myself feeling sorry for her. It seemed like a day didn't go by without someone acting out. Anything from throwing wads of paper, to sneaking into the clothes closet and staying there until the bell rang, or even gawking and laughing at her odd behavior.

The clothes closet was a long, narrow room at the back of the classroom with open doorways at both ends. One day the class watched as Miss Shultz stopped talking and walked to the back of the classroom. She disappeared into the doorway at one end and Lowell Pargman ran out the other.

The class erupted in laughter and watched as Lowell rushed to his desk and sat down. Shortly thereafter, Miss Shultz appeared in the doorway Lowell had just vacated with a ruler held high over her head.

"Lowell Pargman, you think this is funny, don't you?" She walked over to where Lowell sat and thumped him on the head. Then she looked at the class and shouted, "Stop laughing! This isn't funny. As punishment, I'm going to give all of you another assignment." And with that, the laughter ended.

Her odd behavior didn't stop there. Standing in front of the class or sitting at her desk—and, at times, even in the middle of a sentence—she would stop, stick her finger into her ear, and shake it vigorously. We couldn't help but gawk because she didn't make any effort to hide it.

Chances are it was a form of eczema, or what some people call "swimmers' itch." Miss Shultz lived on a farm with her bachelor brothers, so there's a good chance they bathed with hard water.

When I mentioned Miss Schultz to my sister recently, she reminded me of an incident I'd forgotten about. Miss Shultz loved classical music, and she talked about how some of "today's" songs are adaptations of themes from classical music. To prove her point, she asked the class to bring sheet music of a popular song to class.

"I know that some of you don't have sheet music at home, but you're not going to be graded on this, so don't worry," she said. "Those that do, please bring something to class and I'll show you what I mean."

Our home was one of those that didn't have sheet music. Mom had played violin in high school, but those days were long gone and if sheet music existed, I never saw it. But, as it so happened, I did have a copy of the song "At the Hop" by Danny and the Juniors. I'd seen it in a store in Fergus and begged

Mom to buy it. If you've ever heard the song, it's anything but classical. It's one of those repetitive songs that uses the same lyrics over and over again.

Knowing it wasn't classical but wanting to hear what Miss Shultz would say, I took the sheet music for "At the Hop" to school and gave it to Miss Shultz and did we get an ear full. For a good half-hour, she held it up for everyone to see and lectured us about the rising cultural problems of popular music.

Despite her eccentricities, however, I liked Miss Shultz, and I think she came to like me. It was probably because I never made fun of her. Over the years, she would ask my mother about where I was and what I was doing, so I must've made a good impression.

My interest in music didn't end with a piece of sheet music. With some prodding and encouragement from Mom, I joined the band in fifth grade. I felt I had a talent for music, and the thought of learning to play an instrument excited me.

"Can I play the guitar?" I asked.

"I don't think they offer guitar lessons," she said. "Your father and I thought you'd enjoy the cornet."

"Can I play the drums?" I asked, ignoring her comment.

"You have to learn an instrument first, and then when you get into high school, maybe Mr. Peterson will let you switch to drums. I think it's how he does it. You try the cornet first. OK?"

"What's a cornet?"

"It's like a trumpet. You know what a trumpet is, don't you?"

"Yeah, so why don't they just call it a trumpet?"

"Because a cornet sounds different than a trumpet. I'm not sure I even know the difference."

The Peterson she referred to was Pete Peterson, the band director at Elbow Lake. He was a short, stocky, bowlegged man who walked with a limp. In his youth, he'd come down with polio, which stunted his growth. The limp was probably due to a leg deformity caused by the disease.

Unbeknownst to me, Mom had met with Mr. Peterson and, between them, they had decided I should play the cornet. How much input my mother had is unknown, but I suspect little to none.

I did do something towards the end of the school year that I'm not proud of. It started out as a pretend gesture, but happenstance intervened, and it turned into a potentially harmful situation.

It had rained that morning, so the grass in the outfield was wet when we went outside for recess. Miss Olson, the third-grade teacher, was in charge of outside activities that day. Usually, we never paid attention to the teacher because we were too busy playing but on this overcast and rainy day, Miss Olson stopped us as we were running out to play in the outfield.

"The field is too wet today, so you'll need to find something else to do," she shouted.

"We've played in the rain before and it's not raining now," one boy said, and the rest of us nodded in agreement.

"I don't want you going out there. You're going to come back to class with muddy shoes and wet clothes. No softball today and that's final!"

With nothing to do, some of the boys went back inside while the rest of us goofed off. That's when I came up with the stupid idea of getting down on all fours behind her. I'd seen it in a movie, probably one of the Three Stooges movies, but for it to work, someone had to push her.

Getting onto my hands and knees behind her and with a silly grin on my face, I made a pushing jester to a classmate standing in front of her. That's when she made the mistake of taking one step backwards and with that one step I felt her weight as her body slammed into me and she went crashing to the ground.

Miss Olson was a big, heavyset woman and I swear the earth shook when she landed on the ground. Getting up, I looked down, and what I saw on her face told me everything: I was in trouble.

"Terry, I know you did that...."

Before she could say anything else, I took off running, straight for the schoolhouse and to the principal's office.

His office was on the second floor. When I entered, he looked up from behind his desk and watched as I sat down on the sofa. Not having a clue about what had taken place, he asked, "Terry, what are you doing here?"

I sat there with my hands folded on my lap and my head bowed, and said, "I didn't really mean to do it. Honest!"

"Mean what?" he asked.

"He tripped me," a voice yelled from the top of the stairs.

Miss Olson was stomping toward the office. When she appeared, she leaned over with her hands on her knees, pointed her finger at me, and shouted, "That little shit tripped me!" Then both the principal and I got an earful that anyone in the building could hear.

Maybe it was the "shit" comment, the fact that I came directly to the principal's office, the way I explained my part in the incident, or a combination of all three that kept me out of serious trouble, but I didn't escape altogether. For the rest of that week and the following one, I sat in the principal's office next to a floor vent and listened as Miss Shultz lectured and handed out assignments to the rest of the class.

Despite this very foolish act, my year-end grades didn't turn out so bad, and Miss Shultz, unlike Mrs. Olson, kept me in her thoughts over the years.

CHAPTER 18

Amahl and the Night Visitors

Christmas 1956

Reverend Korselman and his family had moved on to green-er pastures, and after a series of interim pastors, the church set-tled on a new minister by the name of the Reverend Bob Light.

Mr. Light and his wife, Pat, brought a creative spirit that some members of the church, especially the younger adults and those in the choir, took a liking to.

Lawrence Presbyterian Church was well-known in the com-munity for its choir so, as Christmas approached, Reverend Light and his wife came up with the idea of putting on an opera. The name of the opera was *Amahl and the Night Visitors* by Gian Carlo Menotti.

The story is a simple tale of a crippled boy and his mother who live in poverty among the shepherds. The Three Kings, who are on their way to Bethlehem, stay with the family for the night, and the mother steals some of their gold. Caught, she explains that she stole it for her crippled and starving son, and they tell her about the Christ Child. She repents and returns the gold, and her son, Amahl, offers his crutch as a gift for the Child. Miraculously, his act of generosity cures him of his lameness and he follows the kings to Bethlehem.

I had not seen the opera on television, and I didn't hear about the church putting it on until my mother approached me.

"Terry, our church is going to put on an opera and they need a boy about your age to play one of the lead roles. Would you like to try out for the part?"

"What's an opera?" I asked.

"Well, an opera is like a play, but instead of speaking you sing the parts."

I looked up at her with what must have been pure ignorance written all over my face.

"OK, last Christmas you dressed up and played the part of a shepherd, didn't you?"

"Yah," I said, remembering the experience. I didn't do much, but it was fun.

"Well, instead of talking, in an opera, you sing the words. Tryouts are on Sunday night, and I think you might enjoy it."

I shrugged. "Sure, why not. I'll try it."

There were some other boys who tried out for the part of Amahl, but according to what an aunt told me recently, the outcome had been prearranged. Supposedly, Reverend Light had wanted me to play the part of Amahl from the start. I don't know the details of how or who was involved in this decision, but it was a blessing and the experience would influence my life in a positive way.

I learned my part quickly and everything came together with amazing speed. The church was known in the community for having a talented choir with an unusual number of its members having perfect pitch, which was important because we sang our parts a cappella. I can't say I have perfect pitch, but with practice—and the confidence that comes with it—I performed without error.

The only problem I had took place during rehearsals. I may have fallen in love with some of the adults who looked after me in the past, but kissing the minister's wife, Pat, did not appeal to me. Pat was both the director and the mother of Amahl, and in one scene, I had to kiss her. I don't know why, but I couldn't muster up the courage to do it. I'd never kissed anyone before, including my biological mother. I'd hugged my adopted mother for the first time when I ran away after the incident in the haymow, but I hadn't kissed her. It wasn't something I'd grown up with, so I refused to do it during rehearsals, telling her I would do it when we put the show on in front of an audience.

As directors go, Pat seemed to know what she was doing. As I recall, she had a background in theater. She was calm and controlled and totally in charge. At no time did I ever witness frustration or hesitation. When she saw something that didn't work, she would step in and make changes. She also put a lot of emphasis on timing, which I think played a big role in the success of the finished production. In addition to directing, she also edited the opera to make it more suitable for our limited budget and surroundings.

The three men who played the wise men were amazing. Two of them, Henry Reeser and Alan Adams, were blessed with perfect pitch. Show them the sheet music and they could hit the first note without the aid of a piano or a pitch pipe. Roger Kube, the third in the group, may not have been in the perfect pitch crowd, but with practice and a good voice, he blended in well with the other two.

Over the years, I've done some acting and I've worked with professional talent, but these men take the cake. They would spend long hours every day working in the fields or with their livestock, and then show up for a few hours in the evening twice a week and preform with amazing poise.

Rehearsals went on for a little over a month and the result was remarkable. Granted, there were no Enrico Carusos in the group, but if you were to compare the trained voices in the movie version with those in our church adaptation, I think you might consider it a draw—at least I did.

On the night of the performance, the church was packed and everything flowed flawlessly. It was, for me, the proudest moment of my young life. I sang flawlessly and, yes, I kissed the minister's wife. After the opera was over, some of the young girls in the audience embarrassed me with flattering praise. One girl from the Western Presbyterian Church even suggested I could be a professional in the theater. It was an uplifting moment for me, one that gave me a great amount of confidence.

Later, the choir director, Clarice Lacy, asked me to sing with the adult choir. When I showed up for practice the next week, she directed me to sit in the front row with the sopranos. I did as she asked, but I refused to join the choir on Sunday.

"I'm not sitting with the women in the front row," I told my mother, and that promptly put an end to my singing in the church choir, but not an end to singing or to acting.

Singing would later take me halfway around the world and land me on national television, and acting would influence my career choices and introduce me to some interesting, well-known personalities. But before even those things could take place, a role in a high school play would put me in the spotlight of one of the more tragic events of the twentieth century.

This photo was taken during dress rehearsal.

CHAPTER 19

A Mind on the Move

Summer of 1957

Fortunately, the drought of 1956 ended and conditions returned to normal. I was still learning, and this kept my mind occupied. We usually plowed the fields in the fall and disked and dragged just before planting began, which, conditions permitting, took place in late spring. So working in the fields a few hours after school and on the weekends was starting to become a routine.

To help maintain the pheasant population, we left the cornfields for spring plowing. The bent corn stocks served as shelter for the pheasants, and there were always a few cobs laying on the ground for them to feed on.

After plowing the cornfields, Dad would assign me to the task of disking. A disk is made of many circular, concave metal plates with sharp edges. The plates are attached to rotating steel rods shaped in an X, and as the disks are pulled across the ground, they dig into the plowed dirt, loosening and smoothing it.

Dragging came next. A drag is made up of vertical teeth that level and powder the dirt even more. In an effort to further smooth the ground, we chained two-by-six boards to the back of the drag. By the time I had finished both disking and dragging, the ground was as flat as a pancake and ready for planting.

Never once did Dad ask me to do the planting. This, I believe, had more to do with pride than anything else. In a sense, planting is what farming is all about. Farmers take great pride in their ability to drive a straight line. It doesn't matter if it's corn or wheat—if you happen to drift off too much to the left or right, when the seed starts to push out of the ground, the mistakes are very noticeable, and the last thing a farmer would want is a neighbor taking notice of a mistake like that. It also takes patience, and my father knew I didn't have a lot of that.

From the age of eleven on, I did almost all of the cultivating. I spent many hours in the fields digging up the weeds between the rows of corn. It was a repetitious task. I've never enjoyed routine, and cultivating corn was, for me, the king of routine. If Dad had ever bothered to ask me what field job I hated the most, I would've said cultivating. Aside from a willingness to accommodate boredom and the skill to drive in a straight line, the job required very little talent. The only break I got was when Mom would bring lunch to the field. Other than that, I had to keep going until all the weeds were plowed under and, here's the kicker, Dad wanted the corn standing when I was done.

To keep my sanity, I would sing, solve world problems, and dream up stories. As I got better at cultivating, I cranked the tractor up a few notches. Dad didn't like it—and yes, he inspected what he expected—but I never heard him complain. If anything, the speed at which I drove heaped the dirt around the corn stocks and over the weeds that grew between the stocks. As a result, the field looked cleaner. Some weeds managed to wiggle their way out from under the dirt, but the important thing is that I didn't dig up the corn.

I continued to bring the cows in from the pasture, feed them, and more and more I found myself cleaning the barn by myself. Lifting a full milk machine, however, was another matter. I had to carry it with both hands between my legs, which made me look like a penguin waddling across the floor. Every so often, the machine would slip out of my hands and drop to the dirty floor with a thud. Dad's biggest concern was that I might drop it in the gutter, and then we'd have to stop milking and sterilize the suction cups, so we found a middle ground. I would attach the suction cups to the cow's udders and when the milking machines were full, Dad would empty them.

Work took up most of my time, but there was still Bible school, reading, swimming lessons, and softball.

I was now familiar with all of the strokes, so swimming was about getting better and a big part of that was repetition.

I did make one important adjustment in softball. One day, as I stood in the batter's box, I decided to try something new. I turned the front of my left foot toward right field, and then I moved my right foot back farther from the plate. Instead of standing parallel with the plate, I was now standing at a thirty-degree angle. It felt awkward at first, but I started to find myself getting on base more often. This was because the balls were going to right field instead of left, where the better players stood. In fact, my batting average improved substantially.

As for reading, I had moved to John Steinbeck and I continued to read the Bible. At the beginning of the summer, I had moved into the New Testament and shortly thereafter, I came across an enigma in the story of Jesus' birth—one that I'd heard before, but hadn't put into perspective. It didn't fit with reality. At least, not with the world as I knew it at that young age. It was the idea that Mary was a virgin when she gave birth to Jesus. This struck me as odd, if not impossible. I'd read enough books to know what it took to make a child and words like immaculate conception, incarnation, and virgin birth didn't jive.

Confused by this, I asked the Sunday school teacher, "How could Jesus be born if he didn't have a father?"

With that, Mrs. Jandt immediately flew out the door to find the minister or her husband, whichever came first. She most likely wanted an answer fit for a child's ears. It was the second time this had happened. The first time was when I asked her about Adam and Eve's eldest son marrying the daughter of a local chieftain.

I had gained a reputation for asking questions like this in Sunday school, but on this occasion, I knew what they were going to tell her. They would say, "Tell him it's one of those unexplainable miracles,"—or something akin to that, but what she didn't know is that I had something else planned.

This event took place at the end of Bible school. During the week of study, each class had contributed to the making of a large map of Israel on the sandy bottom of a gravel pit, which was just north of the graveyard. Our class had also contributed, but we weren't involved with the finishing touches. During the sermon that morning, the minister had bragged about the map and he encouraged members of the congregation to look at the finished product.

When I heard this, I asked Mom if we could go, but she

said, "We aren't going to have time today, honey, but you can see it some other day."

That's what drove me to ask Mrs. Jandt the question, because as soon as she left the classroom, I got up, walked over to the window, and opened it.

"What are you doing?" my sister asked.

"I'm going to the gravel pit," I said, sticking my head out the window.

"What! Why?"

"You're going to get hurt if you jump from there," Neal Jeppson said, matter-of-factly. "Why don't you just leave by the front door?"

"Because they'll see me," I replied, knowing full well that if Mrs. Jandt or my parents saw me, they would tell me to get back to class.

I stuck my head out the window and looked down. The ground was further away than I had imagined—almost two stories below the ledge. Not wanting to back down, I stuck my feet out the window and wiggled around until I was sitting on the ledge. Instead of jumping, however, I turned and slid onto my stomach. Then, very carefully, I slid down until the only thing stopping me from falling were my hands, which tightly gripped the windowsill.

I stayed suspended like that for a good fifteen seconds, considering my options. Finally, I let go. I landed on the grass with a thud and as I did, I bent my knees and rolled backward, just like parachute jumpers do when they hit the ground.

Smiling proudly, I looked up at my classmates. They were all standing at the window, gawking, but before I could say anything, the door opened and in walked Mrs. Jandt and. with that, I took off running. I ran around the graveyard and shorty after I had cleared the last of the headstones, I came to the edge of the gravel pit. Looking down, I immediately noticed the changes that had been made since my last visit. Next to each of the large stones positioned within the outline of Israel, stones that represented towns, were signs sticking out of the gravel floor, and printed on each were the names of well-known cities or towns. That was it. That was why I'd jumped out the window.

As for the question about Mary being a virgin, I would later learn that the word "young woman" in Aramaic, when translate to Greek, is virgin.

Anyway, getting the answer to what had taken place in the gravel pit didn't prepare me for what would happen that after-noon....

West side of Lawrence Presbyterian church.

CHAPTER 20

A Mother's Son is Born

July 1957

"We're going to Alice and Buds for dinner today," Mom said as we drove away from the church.

"How come?" I asked, grateful that she hadn't brought up the subject of jumping out the church window.

"Well, Grandma isn't getting any younger," Mom replied. "It's a lot of work for her to cook for all of us and the family isn't getting any smaller, so Alice has volunteered to have it at her house."

She was right. The family was getting bigger and I knew it wouldn't work at our place because our kitchen was too small. Besides, we didn't even have a dining room.

Alice and Bud lived about three miles north of church and on the same road that ran past Grandpa and Grandma's, so it only took ten minutes for us to get there. When we arrived, I noticed Bud and Alice's car parked in the driveway.

"Wow. I didn't see them ahead of us. How did they get here

so fast?"

"They left right after the service. Alice told me that she needed to take something out of the oven, and she wanted to do some more work on the meal," Mom replied.

Grandpa and Grandma arrived shortly after us, and then about fifteen minutes later, the Reesers walked in the front door, interrupting the TV sermon the men were watching.

These were the days of black and white television and the picture tube was not only small, but round, making it difficult to see anything other than the face. On top of that, the images were grainy…and they could only get one or two channels. The programs consisted primarily of the news, religion, boxing, baseball, and primetime soaps.

Finally, the food was ready. I filled my plate and adjourned to the living room where Alice had set up some television trays for the children. There were nine, all told and, except for the oldest Resser, Bonnie, we settled on whatever sofa or chair was available. Bonnie, who was two years my senior, never considered herself a child, so she stayed in the dining room with the adults.

The Resser cousins included Carolyn—Jean's age, Kitty—a year younger, and Eileen, who was six at the time. There were three Gehrke cousins. They included Bob—Eileen age, Fay—four, and Danny, who was two at the time. This made me the second oldest of the cousins and the oldest boy.

"Let's go to the haymow and swing on the ropes when we're done eating," Bob said, as he stuffed a bun into his mouth.

I looked at him questioningly. We had ropes in our haymow, but with the open hole in the center, I couldn't swing very far or I'd end up with a broken arm or, much worse, a broken skull, if I fell through the hole and onto the cement below.

"Isn't it dangerous?" one of the girls asked.

"No!" Bob said. "It's really fun. You'll see."

After we had finished eating, we ran to the barn with Bob leading the way. Unlike our farmyard, the Gehrke house sat apart from the rest of the buildings. Their yard was arranged more like the letter J—with the cross on the letter representing the road, and right under that sat the farmhouse. The barn was about fifty yards directly behind the house and, with one exception, the rest of the buildings made up the curve at the bottom of the letter and centering the curve sat the light pole. The one exception was a storage shed. Used for storing machinery, it sat some thirty yards below or under the curve.

When we were all inside the barn, Bob led us to a ladder and each of the children climbed to the haymow. I took up the rear, helping Dan as he frantically tried to make his way up.

"Give me your hand, Dan. I'll help you," I heard Kitty say as we neared the top.

Looking up, I saw her standing at the side of the hole to the haymow, her hands reaching down for Dan. Seeing that she couldn't reach him without falling, I grabbed him by the seat of his pants and pushed him up until she was able to grab his hands and pull him the rest of the way.

As I got to the top, I stretched out my right arm and joking asked, "How about me?"

"I think you can make it yourself," she answered with a laugh.

The adults referred to Kitty as the tomboy of our small clan and she accepted that as her mantle, but I never saw her in that light. To me, she was the most caring and loving of the bunch.

The scene in the haymow looked like the Grand Canyon with a roof overhead. Bales on both ends towered over us, with most stacked at the back. A large mound of loose hay covered the floor in the center but, unlike our haymow, there wasn't an opening, at least none that I could see.

Bob ran over to the bales at the front. He grabbed a rope that hung from the railing on the ceiling and climbed to the top. Then, without waiting for us, he swung out across the bales and when he was above a mound of loose hay in the middle, he let go of the rope and fell into the soft pile. He jumped up and ran back to the edge of the bales and started to climb again, with the rest of us in hot pursuit.

Being the oldest, I reached the top first, but I had to wait for Bob because he had the rope.

"Here, let me try it," I said, taking the rope out of his hands.

I reared back, ran to the edge of the bales, and swung out over the loose hay but instead of dropping, I continued until I touched the wall of bales on the far side. There, I pushed off the bales with my feet and swung back, dropping into the soft hay. It had been an exhilarating ride and I couldn't wait to do it again.

"Let me, let me," I heard some of the cousins shouting as I climbed up toward the top with the rope in hand. Then, I saw Kitty and Dan standing on the bales about a third of the way up.

"Let Dan try it first," Kitty said, reaching out for the rope.

I handed it to her, and then she bent down and placed it in Dan's hands. "Here, do you want to try it?"

Dan took the rope, but I knew he wasn't going to do it. If he let go of the rope before it reached the center of the pile, he would fall onto hay, but it didn't look very deep. On the other hand, we were six bales high—but even a child can sense danger, and I think that's what he was feeling.

"Should we let someone else try it?" Kitty asked.

Dan gave the rope back to her.

"Here, I'll take it to the top so someone else can try it," I said, reaching for the rope.

Kitty handed it to me and I raced to the top and passed it to one of the other cousins.

I found myself running up and down constantly over the next half hour because it would've taken ages for some of the younger children to bring the rope back to the top, so, in a sense, I became the rope bearer.

However, there were times when I would be the last one down and when that happened, I would often find myself back at the top, waiting. At first, I waited for everyone to reach the top before handing the rope over, but then it dawned on me that if I took an extra turn, I could still get the rope back to the top before they were ready. No one seemed to mind—not at first, anyway, but after I had done this about two or three times, Kitty suddenly spoke up.

"That's not fair," she scolded. "You're take extra turns. That's cheating!"

"You're not losing a turn," I said, hurt more by the word "cheat" than anything else. Yes, I'd taken a few extra swings, but I didn't feel like I had cheated her, or any of the other cousins.

"It doesn't matter, it's not fair."

"I didn't take a turn away from anyone," I snapped. "Besides, I ran down to get the rope for everyone else, so there."

"Yes, but you are taking extra turns," she repeated.

Frustrated and hurt, and knowing I couldn't win the argument, I left.

They can run the rope back and forth themselves, I thought.

They'll get tired of it after a while. I'm going to tell on her.

But, after leaving and as I got closer to the house, it dawned on me that I not only didn't know who to tell, but how I would explain what had taken place. *Who the heck was going to listen to my side of the story? Everyone loved Kitty.*

With those thoughts racing through my mind, I walked past the house and down the road toward home. Anyone looking out the window could've seen me, but no one stepped outside to find out what was going on, and not one of the cousins in the haymow had followed me, so it was me against the world, or so I thought.

As I walked, one thing kept racing through my mind: *I wasn't running away from home, I was running to home and I fully expected my parents to pick me up at any moment.* But, as time went by and they didn't show, I started to think about another possibility—the police. *What if they called the police?* I couldn't see them doing that, but I could see Jim Reeser calling them. He wasn't mean, but he was strict. The thought of the police coming after me might seem crazy, but they'd chased me down when I was four years old and it had not been a pleasant experience—I'd ended up in a straightjacket.

An hour passed and still no parents. It was then that I decided I'd show them. I'd walk the rest of the way home even if they came, but to do that, I'd have to stay out of sight—and a cornfield was just the thing.

There hadn't been anything but small grain on either side of the road for the first three miles, but when I reached the crossroad that went by the church, I noticed a cornfield on the west side and, as it was now the latter part of July, the stocks had already begun to tassel and they were a good foot or two over my head.

I entered the field, but instead of walking down one of the rows closest to the road, I chose one farther out. *That way,* I thought, *if they come looking for me, they won't be able to find me. I'll show them!*

However, I quickly realized that I had another problem on my hands—no, it was my arms. The leaves on corn stocks are very sharp and if they brush against the face, they can easily slice into your skin or worse yet, your eyes. To stop this from happening, I held my arms high and out in front. Unfortunately, however, I also happened to be wearing a short-sleeved shirt, so by the time I'd walked an eighth of a mile, I had dozens of little paper-like cuts all over my arms, and I was feeling every one of them.

Suddenly, I heard a car coming to a stop on the gravel road, and then the banging of a car door.

"Terry, we know you're out there!" I heard Jim Reeser shout. "Your mom's very concerned about you, so come out and we'll take you back."

I knew from the sound of his voice that it was Jim, but I didn't know if someone else was with him.

"Come on out, we know you're there!"

Does he really know where I am, or is he just guessing? And, *if Mom's with him, why isn't she saying anything?*

I didn't move for a good thirty seconds. Jim started talking to someone else—another man. *Is my father with him?*

"Terry, if you don't come out, we're going to call the police and they can come and get you. Do you want that?"

There it was, the police. It would take a long time for them to get here and I knew it, but just the threat scared me. Wendell didn't have a policeman, or at least not one I'd ever seen or heard about, and Elbow Lake and Fergus Falls were both a good fifteen miles away. With that threat hanging over my head, I started walking toward the road.

As I neared the edge of the field, I saw that it wasn't just Jim, but Bug and my father. They were all standing on the shoulder next to Bud's car. Dad, as usual, had a blank look on his face, but Bud and Jim appeared angry.

"What did you think you were doing when you ran away?" Jim shouted. "Your mother is worried sick."

With that, he grabbed me by the shoulders, pulled me against his legs, and proceeded to give me a good spanking. He didn't pull my pants down, thank God, but he was a big man and he didn't hold back. He probably struck me ten or twelve times. I felt the full weight of his hand against my butt, but most of the pain came from the squeeze of his left hand on my shoulder, and his fingernails as they dug into my skin.

"Don't you ever do that to your parents again," he said. Then he shoved me into the back seat of the car. My father got in beside me, but I didn't look at him and he didn't say anything. Bud turned the car around and we drove back to his farm.

We entered the house through the back door. As we walked into the dining room, Jim shoved me toward the door that separated the dining room from the living room, and said, "Go in and apologize."

When I entered the living room, I saw Mom sitting on one of the sofa chairs; her eyes were red and tears were streaming down her cheeks.

"I'm sorry," I mumbled. It was an unsettling, awkward moment. I had known from day one that she was a good person, but for the first time since the adoption, I could see that she really cared for me. Tears began to roll down my cheeks. It was the first time that I truly felt love in my heart for her.

With that, I walked over to where she was sitting, put my arms around her, and we hugged. This was, I truly believe, the moment that God entered my life and my soul came alive.

Ironically, no one, including my mother, asked me why I had run away, and if they had, what could I have told them—that Kitty was picking on me? That would've gone over like a lead balloon. To this day, I don't know if any of the cousins told the adults what had taken place in the haymow. As for Kitty, she continues to be my favorite cousin because she has many of the same wonderful traits as my mother.

We didn't stay for the usual snack. Instead, our parents said their goodbyes, we left, and the incident was forgotten. This was the beginning of a lifelong bond between my mother and me. Not the gushy hugging and kissing kind, but a caring and tolerant kind of love. Tolerant in the sense that she accepted me for who I was, rather than for what she wanted me to be.

CHAPTER 21
Some Memorable Moments

Sixth Grade

The sixth-grade teacher, Mrs. Rohm, was a tall, full-bodied woman, and unlike Miss Shultz, the students responded well to her teaching methods. As I saw it, she was a professional. Rather than taking a motherly approach, she was firm and direct. She established rules at the beginning of the school year, and she made it known that we were expected to follow them.

My interest in reading did continue and from out of the pages of the numerous books I read, I'd like to believe came knowledge. How much, I don't know but, as I've mentioned before, I did finish reading the Bible in sixth-grade.

A Sunday school classmate's father introduced to a new genre in literature. The classmate was Linnea Hartman and her parents lived on a farm less than a mile from church. One day, after Sunday school, we drove to the Hartman's for dinner.

When we walked into their small farmhouse, the first thing

I noticed was a bookcase filled with paperbacks. Grandpa Ash had books lying around but I had never seen a bookcase in a private home before.

"You must read a lot of books," I said, addressing the comment to Linnea.

"No, those aren't my books," Linnea said. "They belong to my dad. He reads cowboy books all the time."

"Do you like Westerns?" her father asked, as he walked over to where we were standing.

"I've never read any," I said. "What are they about?"

"They're stories about the Wild West. You know, it wasn't that long ago when cowboys and Indians used to rule the West.

"Really?" I said. I knew what cowboys and Indians were from the history books I'd read, I just hadn't read any novels about them.

"Yes, really. It was less than a hundred years ago when the Indians had the run of the plains. Here, let me show you one of my favorite authors." With that he took one of the books out of the bookcase and handed it to me. "This was written by Louis L'Amour. I love his books."

I don't recall the title but I do remember asking him if I could take it home and read it. "Well," he said scratching his head. "As you can see, I like to keep the books I read but maybe you can ask you parents to buy you one. If you like to read, you'll enjoy a good cowboy and Indian story."

It was an awkward moment for both of us. Me, because I realized I had asked for something I couldn't have and him, because he wasn't about to give up his book.

"I'll buy some Westerns for you the next time we go to town," Mom cut in, recognizing the awkwardness of the moment. That's how I got into Westerns. I stopped reading them while I was in high school but I still have some of the early ones my mother bought for me in one of my many bookcases and yes, it was Linnea's father who got me into the habit of keeping the books I buy. The shelves in my home are filled with all genres and sizes.

Besides school and reading, a few memorable events did take place over the course of the school year, the first of which had to do with the band director. Band was an extracurricular activity and thus, not a part of regular classroom study. Twice a week, Mr. Peterson would drive the eight miles from Elbow Lake to Wendell for music lessons. At the allotted time, the band students would leave class and assemble in the music room. The others stayed in the homeroom to study.

For the first time in my young life, I found myself not only taking a subject home with me, but taking time for both practice and study. In addition, I had taken time off from work to practice during the summer months. Each morning I would go outside and play revelry for our distant neighbors, and in the evening, I would play taps.

Over the course of the summer months, the cornet began to feel comfortable in my hands and I was beginning to feel a certain amount of confidence in my ability to read music. I wasn't fully there yet, but I was getting close. As a reward for my hard work, Mr. Peterson had raised me to the position of second chair. Then, one day toward the end of the year, all of that changed.

"Terry, would you step into the hall? I want to talk to you and bring the cornet with. The rest of you continue practicing," Mr. Peterson, said in a rather serious tone of voice.

Having no clue as to what this was all about, I stood, grabbed my cornet, and followed him into the hall.

When the door closed behind us, he turned to me and said, "Terry, I'm going to have to ask you to leave band."

"What? Why? What did I do? I didn't do anything wrong."

"It's not something you did wrong in band. It's because your grades are not what they should be, so please hand me the cornet," and with that, he stuck out his hand.

"How do you know what my grades are?" I asked, holding the cornet away from his outstretched hand. "I don't even know what they are, and what do they have to do with band?"

"It's my policy that only students with As and Bs can be in band. So, give me the cornet, and then you can go back to your regular classroom. Did you leave the case in the band room?"

"I practice all the time and you just moved me up to second chair," I said angrily, ignoring his question.

"Give me the horn, please."

"Why should I give it to you?" I hissed. "It's not yours." And with that, I threw it as hard as I could on the floor.

Then, without saying another word, I walked away in disgust, my hands clenched. I didn't even bother to look at where the horn had landed, or if it'd been damaged in any way.

A few days after this happened, Mom asked me why I wasn't practicing. When I told her that Mr. Peterson had kicked me out of band, she responded by asking, "Where is the horn now?"

I told her that Mr. Peterson had the horn. It was then that the truth of ownership came to the surface: my parents had rented the Cornet from Mr. Peterson, and since I'd given it back to him, the matter never came up again.

I didn't bother to ask Mom about the rental agreement, but I suspect they had rented it for the school year and not monthly. That's probably why the subject of throwing the horn on the floor never surfaced, and it's also possible the horn wasn't damaged. At least, not in a costly way.

Over the years, I would hear numerous accounts from other students, including relatives, who got kicked out of band for not living up to Mr. Peterson's inflexible standards. In fairness, some or even most of these students may not have had the skill, talent, or desire to play an instrument. Regardless of the whys, Mr. Peterson had, what you might call, a love/hate relationship with the community.

I also got kicked out of Cub Scouts. Unlike band, however, there weren't any long-term effects. But, it does demonstrate a side of me that is, perhaps, overly reactive to situations that most people would walk away from. In this case, it had to do with a fight between two brothers.

Except for some minor scraps on the school bus with the Dohmeyer boys, who grew up in an unstable family, I had managed to stay away from fights during the four years in grade school. In large part, this was due to the community. Unlike the children in the orphanage, the children in my adopted community were well-mannered and family life was, by and large, stable.

The "fight" was more of a squabble. The names of the brothers shall remain unknown because they are both good people, but on the day it happened, I wasn't so sure.

I was new to Cub Scouts—so new that I still didn't own a full uniform. I had a shirt, a neckerchief, and a slide to hold the neckerchief in place, but no hat or pants. I joined Cub Scouts because I was intrigued by the idea of becoming a Boy Scout. I liked the look of their brown uniforms, and going on camping trips sounded fun.

The incident happened on a cold, clear Saturday afternoon. We'd gathered in Wendell at the home of the den mother, and after an informal meeting and a light snack, we ran outside to play in the snow. As I recall, the club had formed that fall, so there were only five of us—two of them were the sons of the den mother.

"Let's play King on the Hill," one of the kids shouted.

Towering in front of the yard and next to the street was a large snow pile, so we all raced to see which one could get to the top first. Pushing and shoving, we struggled to see who would be standing on the hill last, but it quickly got out of hand when the brother in question not only shoved, but man-handled, his younger brother.

"Stop that!" I heard the younger brother cry out. "You're not supposed to be mean."

With that, his brother threw him down the hill.

I had been busy trying to push one of the other boys down the hill, but when I heard the pain in the younger brother's voice, I ran toward the older brother and hit him with all my might. He went down and I got on top of him, pushing his face into the snow. I kept doing this until I heard the den mother shout, "Terry, get off him this minute and come into the house!"

Later, when Mom arrived to pick me up, the den mother told her I'd gotten into a fight with one of the boys. I'm not sure who suggested or made the decision that I could no longer be in Cub Scouts, but that's what happened. It could've been my mother, but she gave me the impression it was the den mother. Either way, I never went to Cub Scouts again. Even now, when I see the younger brother, he thanks me for coming to his rescue.

As the school year was coming to an end, I fell in love again and this time it wasn't an adult. One day, the intercom suddenly blared, "Boys and girls, we're going to be treated to a show today. Some students from Elbow Lake are coming by to put on a dance for us. Teachers, please release your students at three o'clock and have them go directly to the gymnasium. Thank you! I hope you enjoy the show."

At three o'clock, Mrs. Rohm released us and we all hurried to the gymnasium to get a seat. It wasn't really a seat; just a place on the hard floor. I sat down towards the back of the gym and waited for the show to start.

As gyms go, it was miniature. There were two basketball hoops on the side and one at the far end. The stage itself wasn't large. The floor of the stage was, at most, two feet off the gym floor and its width was maybe twenty-five or thirty feet with a height, from floor to ceiling, of around fifteen feet. I remember wondering how many dancers there were and if they could all fit on the stage.

Suddenly, the principle, who had been standing next to the door talking to one of the teachers, walked to the front. "Boys and girls, please quiet down," he shouted.

When the noise had subsided, he continued, "We are being treated to something special today. A girl's dance team from Elbow Lake is going to put on a special show for us. So without further ado, here they are."

And with that, music started playing and out danced the most beautiful girl I had ever seen. She wasn't the only girl, there was a whole line of them, but she was the only one I saw. I couldn't keep my eyes off her. Her long, blonde hair framed a beautiful, smiling face and her graceful flowing moves only added to her attraction. *Is she a sixth grader,* I wondered. And, *will she be in my class next year?* To make the moment even more memorable, *I told myself that someday she would become my wife.*

That thought stayed with me through the summer months. Not only that girl but the thought of going to Elbow Lake for school in the fall. It didn't seem real, I was growing up so fast.

CHAPTER 22

Eight Promises

June 1958

With school out, it was back to farm work, swimming lessons, and softball but, as if by magic, something new entered my life. Out of nowhere my life's mission suddenly appeared.

It happened on a Sunday. It was a beautiful summer day and for some reason, I felt the need to go for a walk. I didn't have a purpose in mind—I just wanted to be alone.

"I'm going for a walk along the creek," I told Mom.

"OK, it's a beautiful day. Don't forget, we're having guests tonight."

"What for?"

"Don't you remember? It's whist night."

"Oh, yeah. I forgot. OK, I'll be back in plenty of time."

The card game of whist was the only social event my parents engaged in outside of family, and it only happened a few times during the year. This was one of those rare occasions when everyone would gather at our place, and by everyone, this meant couples from church.

Grandpa and Grandma never came because their Quaker heritage did not approve of things like cards, but the other couples from church didn't seem to mind. I've always had a difficult time with card games because I need to keep moving, but I did enjoy whist. I especially got a kick out of the awards ceremony at the end of the evening. The winning couple usually scored a new deck of cards, while the couple with the most losses would leave with a broom or a dust pan.

With that in mind, I exited the house and walked across the road to the neighbor's pasture. They had ceased pasturing their horse the summer before, but the path he'd made along the river was still fresh. Before leaving the road, I bent down and tucked my pants inside my socks. The wood ticks were out in full force.

The water level in the creek that year was high, but with no observable downward flow, it didn't generate any noticeable current.

As I walked, my mind began to drift. I thought about my biological mother. *What was she doing? Was she still alive? Would I ever see her again?*

"Haa-taa-jaa," I said out loud.

I hadn't spoken my last name for years, but there it was. I didn't know how to spell it but, in sounding it out, I knew there had to be all kinds of a's in the name. On occasion, Jean and I would talk about our past; not very often, but enough to keep the memories of those years fresh in our minds.

Then, my thoughts started drifting to the more recent past. I thought about the many books I'd read, about softball and pitching, about the opera and the wonderful church community that had become so encouraging and supportive. How different life now seemed from the years I had spent in the orphanage.

"Thank you, God!" I suddenly shouted, my eyes looking up at the sky. "Thank you for looking after me. Thank you for protecting me. Thank You! Thank You! Thank You!"

I don't know what brought that outburst on, but for the first time in my life, I felt completely safe and alive. I had survived. Not only that, I was moving on to school in Elbow Lake in the fall, and everything looked bright.

I was a good three-quarters of a mile from home when I saw a small pond in front of me. It was, at most, fifteen feet wide, and on my side of the creek was a sandy beach.

I quickly walked over and laid down on the soft sand. Then, putting my arms behind my head, I relaxed and stared up at the sky. Two beautiful white clouds were slowly floating in a north easterly direction, but other than that, the sky was clear.

My mind returned to thoughts of God and then, for some reason, I said the Lord's Prayer out loud.

"My Father, who art in heaven, hallowed be thy name.

Thy kingdom come, thy will be done, on earth, as it is in heaven.

Give me this day my daily bread.

And forgive me my trespasses, as I forgive them that trespass against me.

And lead me not into temptation, but deliver me from evil: For thine is the kingdom, and the power, and the glory, for ever and ever, Amen."

Time seemed to stand still as I thought about my life up to that point, not the bad things, but all of the good things that'd happened since the adoption. I thought about how tolerant and caring my adoptive mother had been—how her father, my grandfather, had taken such an interest in me, and about the many skills my father had taught me.

As these thoughts raced through my mind, I gradually began to feel the presence of someone other than myself. Mesmerized by this seemingly real and personal phenomenon, I began to have a conversation with God.

"Thank you, Father," I said. "Thank you for looking after me and for giving me a father and mother who care for me. Please give me the strength and courage to go on and fill me with your love. Give me wisdom to understand the world I live in, and guide me as I continue my journey through life. I love you, Father, and I promise...."

It was at this point that I did something amazingly far-fetched. At least, for me it seemed far-fetched. I promised God that, with His guidance, I would do eight specific things for Him during my lifetime, things that were foreign to me. Some, I understood, even at the time, would not take place until after I had entered my senior years.

After I had made those promises, I returned to the farm and from that day to this, I have devoted my life to fulfilling those eight promises The only person I have ever confided in is Grandpa Ash and I did that shortly after this event took place.

I was cleaning the gutters in the barn one day when Grandpa suddenly opened the barn door and walked in.

"Hi, Grandpa. What are you doing here?"

"Oh, not much. I got bored sitting around, so your grandma has me running some errands."

"I had an interesting conversation with God yesterday," I said. "Do you want to hear about it?"

"Really? Sure, tell me. I'm sure it was interesting."

I told him about the walk along the creek, about my conversation with God, and I closed by telling him the promises I'd made. He looked at me and said, "Well, those are some interesting promises, but you might want to narrow that down to one or two. It seems to me that eight is more than one person can handle in a lifetime."

"Nope," I said, shaking my head and getting back to the job at hand. "I don't know how I'm going to do it, but I made the promises and I'm going to keep them." And with that, I heaved a fork full of manure into the spreader.

To date, I've accomplished most of those promises and as you will later learn, one of the eight was replaced with something more pressing. As my story unfolds, I will disclose the promises I made in the order they happened, but the unfulfilled promises will remain between God and me.

CHAPTER 23

Needles and Salt

Summer of 1958

My adoptive father, like his father and older brother, had Type I Diabetes. How he survived the early years without insulin is unknown. According to my mother, he didn't start taking insulin shots until after they were married. Did the hard work he experienced as a youth prevent the disease, or temporarily push it aside? Physically, Dad looked like he was on steroids. He was short with narrow shoulders and wide hips but, he was all muscle.

Did his medical condition have anything to do with my mother's inability to conceive? I asked Mom why they couldn't have children once and her answer surprised me.

"We were both examined by a doctor and he didn't know who was at fault."

From the way she said it, I got the distinct impression that she blamed herself, but she never explained why.

I would often watch as Mom gave Dad his morning shot. I

can still see her shake the insulin bottle, turn it upside down, and push the tip of the syringe's needle into the bottle's rubber top and fill it up. Then, in that gentle voice of hers, she'd say, "Okay, let's see. Shall we look for a soft spot on the arm or would you rather we do this on the leg?"

"Wherever," Dad would say.

Mom would start poking her finger here and there until she found a spot that felt like it hadn't been hardened by dozens of other piercing's.

Eventually, Mom got around to asking me if I'd be willing to give Dad the shots and, with some reluctance, I agreed. The very thought of sticking a needle into him made me squeamish, but I fully understood her reasoning; she might be gone. So, with that, she showed me how to fill the syringe and handed me an orange to practice on. To my relief, my nursing skills weren't needed and I dodged that bullet.

I write this as a precursor to what happened at the beginning of the summer of 1958. On one sunny afternoon, Dad returned home from the fields but instead of going directly to the barn, as he usually did, he went to the house and took off his boots and socks. I didn't see this because I was busy with chores, but I later learned that Mom found blisters on the bottoms of both of his big toes.

When I asked her how this could've happened, she told me that his boots were getting old and that his big toes had rubbed against the staples holding the soles together. Right or wrong, the blisters later burst, and despite lots of Band-Aids and ointments, they didn't heal.

After a month or so of cleaning up puss, Dad finally agreed to see a doctor. The doctor, after examining his feet and knowing he was a diabetic, prescribed rest. Unfortunately, that was like telling a duck to stay out of the water.

Temporary relief did appear in the form of a grainy powder called Epsom Salt. This prescription, if you can call it that, came from a family member, not the doctor, and it came because she knew he wouldn't listen to reason.

From that day on, every evening after chores, Dad would come into the house, take off his boots, sit in an armchair next to the kitchen table, and stick his feet into a basin of warm water sprinkled with Epsom salt. Healing never took place, but the Epsom salt did keep the puss in check and the sores from spreading.

In my father's defense, he didn't have health insurance and the bills needed paying so he kept doing what had to be done. He could've sold the farm, but it wasn't paid for. Besides, he'd still have to get a job, and where would we live?

Anyway, with no healing in sight and upon my mother's insistence, I began to do more and more of the heavy labor chores by myself—throwing bales and silage, and pitching manure. By insistence, I mean, she told my father to stay away from as much of the heavy lifting as he could—"Terry's big enough to do those chores now."

Dad wasn't the only one in the family who got shots. During the summer of 1958, Mom brought Jean and me to the clinic in Elbow Lake three times to get polio shots and the second shot turned out to be a twosome for me.

"Terry," I heard Mom say from inside the house. "It's time to leave."

I had been sitting on the front steps for a good fifteen minutes dreading the thought of going to the clinic, and when I heard her shout those words, the only thing I could think of was, *How am I going to get out of this*?

"Do I have to?" I yelled. "I hate shots."

"You don't want to get polio, do you?" she replied.

"They hurt," I yelled.

"They may hurt at first, but you'll get over it." There was a pause and then she yelled, "Jean, it's time to go."

"OK, I'm coming," I heard Jean shout from somewhere further back in the house. Shortly thereafter I heard footsteps in the kitchen followed by the opening of the entryway screen door.

"I don't want that stupid shot," I yelled, and with that, I stood and bolted toward the pasture on the west side of the house. I was so out of control that I completely forgot about the barbed wire gate Dad and I had put up during the drought of 1956. Without breaking stride, I hit the wire full force and spun in a circle around the wire before landing on the ground. Or as Mom later reiterated: "It looked like you were doing a backflip."

Usually, a fence consists of three strands of wire spread apart but, at this juncture, there was only one wire. Instead of a gate to the pasture, we had put up a single strand of barbed wire, which we could easily take down whenever we wanted to enter with the tractor.

After Mom bandaged the cuts on my chest, she drove my sister and me to the clinic in Elbow Lake. The doctor gave me two shots instead of one: the polio shot, and a tetanus shot. I still have a small scar across my chest as a reminder.

The rest of the summer passed without incident, but a couple of interesting experiences did take place. Besides softball and swimming lessons, I played baseball for the first time. This took place when I stayed with my Mom's sister, Evelyn, and her family for a week. While out and about the town of Fergus Falls one day, I happened to spot some boys playing baseball, and without thinking, I walked over and asked if I could play. Their coach said yes. So, for the remainder of the week, I practiced with them and played in a game or two.

At the end of my short stay in Fergus, I returned to the farm and found myself learning another skill—driving truck. Not on the road; I was still too young for that. Heck, I couldn't see over the steering wheel. To make this happen, I had to sit on two thick catalogs just to see between the wheel spokes, and reaching the foot pedals was another matter. When it came time to stop the truck, I had to use the steering wheel as a fulcrum to push in the clutch and the brake pedal. When I did this, the only thing visible was the sky or the top half of the combine.

Despite my shortcomings, Dad instructed me to sit in the truck at the end of the field while he combined. When the hopper was filled with grain, he would stand on the tractor and wave. When I got within thirty feet of the combine, he would put up his hand to signal for me to stop. He would then get off the tractor, park the truck next to the combine's hopper, and dump the load of grain into the back of the truck. When the truck box was full, he and I would drive to the elevator in town and unload. Then, back to the field for more sitting, waiting, and thinking—thinking about that girl and the coming school year.

I was now a seventh grader. Instead of getting off the bus in Wendell, I would continue on to Elbow Lake. This meant new teachers, students, and sports. What I didn't think about is what took place during the first hour of class.

CHAPTER 24

"Terrible Terry"

Seventh grade

"Terry? Is there a Terry…." The teacher paused, looked down at his notes, and continued. "Dag-ner? I think that's how you pronounce it. Is Terry Dag-ner here?"

"Deg-ner," I said, raising my hand.

"Deg-ner," he corrected. "Terry, would you please go with Mr. Hoskins." He pointed to a man standing on the other side of the room. He was a stocky, bulldog sort of man with short, cropped hair and, for reasons unknown to me at the time, he was looking at me with what appeared to be a menacing scowl.

I got up from my desk and went to the door. The man opened it and motioned for me to go ahead. As soon as the door closed behind us, he grabbed my elbow and motioned for me to walk down the hall.

"Did you hit Cynthia?" he asked sternly.

"What? What are you talking about? I didn't hit anyone," I said, startled by his question.

"We'll see," he said, now half pushing me.

"I don't know who you're talking about. I didn't hit anyone."

"Shut up and just keep walking. We'll find out soon enough."

We walked down the hall to a set of stairs, one of which went up to the third floor, the other down to the basement. He directed me to the one going down and we descended.

Once we were in the basement, he steered me to the right and we walked down the hallway to what appeared to be a door. He abruptly stopped and pushed me up against the wall.

"Wait here," he growled.

With that, he walked to the door. Looking inside, he motioned to someone and said, "OK, you can come out."

A tall, thin, frail-looking girl—one I had never seen before—emerged from the girls' locker room.

Mr. Hoskins gently grabbed her arm and swung her around until she was facing me. "Is this the boy that hit you in the stomach?"

She glanced up, then looked back down. "No."

"What do you mean? Look at him this time. Is he the boy that hit you?"

Again, she looked at me. "I've never seen him before."

"No! Are you sure?" Mr. Hoskins said, seemingly agitated.

"Yes, I'm sure."

What is this all about, I thought, *and how in the hell did he get my name?* I'd never seen this girl, and I certainly hadn't hit her. I'd never hit any girl.

"All right, you can go back to class," Mr. Hoskins said dismissively. He didn't apologize, but his demeanor had changed from anger to a look of disgust.

I shook my head, turned, and headed back to the classroom.

I don't know if they ever found the person who hit Cynthia

and I never asked. What I did later find out is that Cynthia had a reputation for making up stories to get attention. As for aftermaths, during row call a few days later, Mr. Larson asked the class, "Where's Terrible Terry?"

I didn't respond because I was at home sick but my sister did. According to her, she told Mr. Larson that calling me Terrible Terry wasn't very nice.

Other than that, my connection to the incident with Cynthia ended on the day it began. But, what bothers me to this day is this: Who gave Mr. Hoskins my name and why?

Regardless, I had had more pressing things on my mind— that girl. The one who danced on stage in sixth grade. The one I'd thought about all summer long.

When I'd exited the bus earlier that morning, I looked to where everyone else was headed and I saw her. She was walking up the steps to the schoolhouse. I hurried toward the door. I knew I couldn't catch up to her, but I was hoping I'd be able see the classroom she entered.

Two connecting but separate buildings made up the school complex. The one that girl had entered was for middle and high schoolers. Built around the turn of the twentieth century, it was a three-story, rectangular, brick structure. Another one-story brick structure, which stood to the right of the main building, was the elementary school. It was obviously newer because the tan bricks looked pristine and uncontaminated, while the dark, red bricks on the main structure looked aged and grimy.

It didn't take long to get an answer to that girl's whereabouts. A teacher who was standing in the hallway told me which room to go to, and I spotted her immediately. She was sitting in a desk at the front. The teacher kept shouting, "Come on in and grab a desk, any desk. We'll assign you one later."

I walked over and sat down behind her. My heart was beating rapidly, my stomach tied up in knots, and my brain a muddled mess. I'd never felt this way before. I couldn't keep my eyes off her and the weight of my lovesick fixation must've invaded her senses, because she suddenly turned her head and looked directly at me, and when she did, I almost fainted.

That was what had been going on inside my head when Mr. Larson had asked me to follow Mr. Hoskins.

***

Football practice started at the end of the first day. My failure to find a uniform that fit went beyond frustrating. The shoulder pads fit, but the lower body pads were another thing. My elbows rested on the hip pads, the thigh pads had nothing to cling to, and the knee pads hung halfway between my knees and my ankles.

When fully dressed, I not only didn't look like a football player, but the coach quickly realized that maybe I didn't belong on the football field. The coach's name was Mr. Wilcox. Not my swimming instructor, Bruce, but his brother, Harald. During practice one day, Mr. Wilcox called the ninth graders over to practice with us.

The ninth graders were on the B-squad, but some were at that "in between" stage: too old to practice with us, and not skilled enough to play in any B-squad games.

When we were all gathered together, Mr. Wilcox shouted, "OK, I want the seventh and eighth graders to form a line facing east. Ninth graders, I want you to form a line facing the seventh and eighth graders, and stay about fifteen feet apart from each other. When I give the signal, I want the first player in each line to run at the player across from them. Seventh and eighth graders, you are on the offense." He threw a football to the first player in our line. "Ninth graders, you're on defense. I want you to tackle the ball carrier." Then he brought his whistle up to his mouth.

Before he could blow it, I yelled, "Can we try to get away?"

"No! This is a tackling drill, not a running drill. You can try to fake him, but don't go too far outside the line."

"What line?" I asked, because there were no lines where we were practicing.

"Think of it as an imaginary line between the two of you and try to stay within, let's say, two feet of that line. Do you think you can do that?"

I nodded, but it didn't seem fair because the ninth graders were a lot bigger than we were and my best weapon was quickness.

"Ninth graders," he shouted, changing the subject. "I want you to run straight at the ball carrier and tackle him. Make it clean. Go for the waist, not the legs or the head. When you're done, get up and run to the back of the line and the next person at the front of the line, you do the same thing."

I was somewhere around the middle of the line at the start of the drill. I watched with apprehension as players crashed into each other. When it came my turn, I looked up to see a boy who had a good forty to forty-five pounds on me. His name was Gary Colman. I remember thinking that I must look like an easy target but, putting my fears aside, I ran at him knowing with full certainty that it was not going to be a pleasant experience. In softball, speed and keen hand-eye coordination benefited me, but in this drill, I didn't have a thing to offer, and that's exactly how I felt—like a sacrificial offering.

Gary struck me in the solar plexus and I let out an, "Ooooof!" Then I hit the ground with him on top of me. It took a few seconds for him to get off but, when he did, I immediately realized that I couldn't breathe. I began threshing about on the ground, gasping for air. This went on for what seemed like an eternity until the coach came over and grabbed me by the waist of my pants.

"Don't worry, you just had the wind knocked out of you. You'll be fine in a second," he said, as he pulled me up by the belt several times. Sure enough, within a few seconds, I took in some air and the feeling of helplessness disappeared. When I got to my feet, the coach asked, "Do you feel good enough to go on, or would you prefer to sit down?"

"I'm OK," I said, running to the back of the line.

When it was my turn again, I looked up, and to my chagrin, I saw Gary Colman standing exactly where he had stood when I carried the ball the first time, and the result was the same: he knocked the wind out of me, the coach revived me, and like before, I returned for more. When it happened a third time, however, Mr. Wilcox decided it was time to stop the drill. That was my introduction to football—a sport I would go on to play for another seven years and, with persistence, master.

I went out for basketball after the football season was over, but that was a disaster. I could get the ball to the basket but, other than that, I was a bust: I couldn't dribble worth a damn and hanging onto the ball was an exercise in futility. Knowing the game was not for me, I dropped out after two practices.

In the spring, I went out for baseball. Unlike many school

sports programs today, we didn't have a junior high or B-squad team in baseball. Thus, those who didn't play on game day were practicing for when they would.

When the baseball coach, Mr. Oysted, asked me what position I wanted to play, I said, "Pitcher," and from moment on, the only thing I did during practice was pitch—no batting practice. It seems that Mr. Oysted was a baseball traditionalist. When it came time to penciling in the batting order, the pitchers were automatically at the bottom of the list.

Mr. Oysted taught me two things that first year: how to hold the ball with two fingers and pitching form. For two solid months, that's all I worked on. I would put on my baseball cleats, walk out to the practice field, and throw the ball to a seventh grader who would later became my catcher.

I also went out for track in the spring but unlike the other sports, track didn't have a routine practice schedule. You worked on your chosen event when you could. This meant practicing during recess or Phys Ed, rather than before or after baseball.

One day at the beginning of spring, as I was staring out the classroom window, I saw an older boy running down a short track with a long pole in his hand. When he got to the end, he stuck the pole into a hole in the ground and up he went. Once in the air, he twisted his body and, legs first, he swung over a horizontal shaft that hung from two thin, vertical posts. He cleared the shaft and landed in what looked like wood shavings.

That looks fun, I thought. So, I took up pole vaulting. I don't recall attending any track events in seventh grade, but the following year would prove to be eventful.

As for the educational side of the school year, some interesting changes did take place, the first of which were the teachers. Unlike the teachers in elementary school, who were all female, the teachers in middle school were mostly male. There were a few females, but they tended to teach specialized courses like Spanish and Home Economics.

I've long thought that male energy, both in church and in school, made a positive impact on my life. The female teachers in grade school had been wonderful, especially Mrs. Kavney, but many of the teachers in Elbow Lake would turn out to be good male role models.

During my formative years, I'd lived with men who were drunks, braggarts, and uneducated fools. Now, I was surrounded by educated men. Not all of them were model teachers, but each, in their own way, provided a special insight into the world of masculinity.

My year end grades did prove to be futuristic. I ended up with five Ds and three Cs. It's common knowledge that a student's grades tend to slip when they move from elementary to middle school, and that certainly applied to me. Studies have shown that it's because students seem to place a lower importance on academics as they move up the educational ladder. What they may have found stimulating in elementary school becomes familiar or boring in middle school.

I don't believe that reasoning necessarily applied to me. I continued to read anything and everything I could get my hands on and I performed well on tests, but there's no question: pining for that girl and not handing in homework certainly played a huge role when it came to grades.

Talking about that girl, I ended the school year with nothing to show. I had gone to class every day with longing in my heart, and on those rare occasions when she had stayed home sick, I sat in class, lovesick. For the first time ever, I didn't want the school year to end.

The above photo of the Elbow Lake high school and grade school was scanned from a yearbook. The high school is the three story building to the rear. The student entrance and bus drop-off to both buildings is on the left side of the picture. The playground and sports practice area is on the back side of the high school.

CHAPTER 25

Your Permit is in the Mail

Summer of 1959

"I want you out in the field, Now!" I heard Dad shout, as I bent over in preparation to throw the baseball against the side of the house.

Looking up, I saw him hustling toward me with a serious look on his face.

"I'm going. I just wanted to get in a few practice pitches before I went out, that's all," I replied.

"I want you out in the field now! Not after a little while. I need to get that field planted, so get out there and do your thing."

"You never seem to have time to play ball with me. Why is that?" I asked in defiance.

That stopped him. Not once had he ever offered to play catch with me. Now, he was telling me—no, he was shouting at me, that I needed to get to work.

"Well, someone in this family has to do the work around

here," he finally said. "But, I tell you what. I'll play catch with you if you get out to the fields. Is that a deal?"

"OK. Will you play catch with me now?" I asked, knowing full well that it wasn't going to happen.

And it never did.

If Dad had his say, sports would've been out of the question. If it hadn't been for Mom, he might've even insisted that I drop out of school because that's what he had done. Mom, on the other hand, grew up in a family that believed in education and sports, and she could see what sports was doing for my self-confidence.

As for farm work, when it comes to lifting, size and weight does matter. Our bailor pumped out bales that were around 48" long, 18" wide, and 18" deep. Straw bales were light, but alfalfa bales weighed around 75 to 100 pounds, depending on the moisture content. At my young age, throwing them was out of the question, but I could lift and stack them three high without a problem. The issue arose when I had to stack them six high, which is what it took to fill the wagon. To overcome this, I would stack the bales three high, leave the front row one high, and then use that to get the bales to the fourth level. To stack five and six high, I used a one, two, three stacking arrangement and if I got behind, Dad would stop until I had everything under control. It required a lot of running with an empty wagon, but things slowed down the closer I got to the middle.

When it came time to unload, our positions changed. I would go into the haymow and do the stacking, while Dad unloaded one bale at a time onto the elevator.

I was also doing all the barn cleaning by this time. Dad would stay in the fields or attend to chores that didn't require a lot of walking or heavy lifting. For some unexplained reason, he never did ask me to milk the cows in the morning, but I did find myself doing more of the evening chores by myself.

"OK, it's time to harvest the wheat. I'm going to pull the combine out with the tractor and I want you to follow with the truck," Dad said one morning.

I had driven the truck in the fields the summer before, but never on the road, so I asked, "Is it all right if I drive without a driver's license?" I was happy to do it, of course. What thirteen-year-old wouldn't want to drive on the road?

"Nobody's going to care. Besides, you'll be getting your license soon anyway. It's probably in the mail as we speak."

What he was talking about was a farmer's permit. In those days, a farm boy could get a permit to drive on the road at the age of fourteen. However, I wouldn't turn fourteen until the twenty-fifth of August—that was still a couple weeks away.

Once we were in the field, he said, "OK, we're going to try something new. I'm not sure this will work, but we'll give it a try."

"What's that?" I asked.

"Listen carefully. When the hopper's full, I'll wave for you like I did last year but, when you get here, I want you to pull up alongside the hopper while I continue combining. When the truck's in position, I'll pull the lever and dump the grain. Do you think you can do that?"

Dad had just handed me a challenge, so the only thing racing through my mind at that moment was….

"So, what should I do if the hopper's not empty when we get to the end of the field?"

"I'll signal for you just after I make a turn. That way, the hopper should be empty by the time we get to the other end."

"How will I know when the truck's in the right position?"

"I'll let you know with my hand, but I won't pull the lever to empty the hopper until you're in position, and I'll keep my arm on the lever just in case."

He got onto the tractor and started to combine while I sat in the truck, anxiously waiting for his signal. Then, when it finally came, I drove over to where he was still combining and put Dad's plan into action.

I shifted the truck into first gear, pulled alongside the combine, and lined the bumper of the truck to the tractor's rear tire. I knew from parking the truck that if I could still see about two-thirds of the tire, I was in the right position.

Sounds easy, but I had to be on my toes the entire time. The truck box was only a four-by-eight-foot target, so even a few feet outside the line could cause the grain to miss its target and end up on the ground. When I'd start to get too close to the tire or too far back, Dad would motion with his hand for me to move up or back and I would make the necessary adjustment. I came close to hitting the tire once when Dad suddenly stopped, but I don't recall actually hitting it.

Looking back on those years now, I've come to the realization that Dad did have a lot of faith in me. Either that, or he found that I would stand up to any challenge he threw my way. I did ask Mom if she ever drove alongside the combine as it unloaded, and she said, "No, Dad never asked me to do that."

When the truck box was full, Dad threw another unexpected task my way. He told me to take the truck to the elevator in town. When he said that, my eyes light up. This wasn't a challenge, it was a wow-you've-got-to-be-kidding experience. Wait until I tell my friends that I drove the truck to town.

"But, I'm only thirteen and I don't have a driver's license,"

I said.

"Don't worry, your farmer's permit is in the mail," he reminded me.

And with that, I happily drove into town while Dad continued to combine.

When I arrived at the elevator, I parked at the entrance and went inside to inform the manager. He had one of his employees drive the truck onto the unloading dock. When the truck was empty, the employee parked it outside, and the manager handed me a receipt. With the paper in hand, I got back into the truck and drove to the field for another load.

I do not recall ever getting that farmer's permit. I'm not even sure I had a wallet. I certainly didn't have any money because, as you may recall, I was getting free room and board. By nature, I'm a hoarder of small items. One of those items are the many drivers' licenses I've had over the years. This includes the one I received at the age of sixteen, but for the life of me, I don't recall ever seeing a farmer's permit. Anyway, permit or not, I would continue taking the grain to the elevator the following summer and the next.

I did come up with a couple of other things to do over the summer months. To practice pole vaulting, I made a pole out of a long shaft of wood I found in the junk pile next to the clothesline. Whenever I went out to the pasture to bring in the cows, I would bring it alone and pole vault over the fences. It wasn't very high, but it was fun and it gave my mother something to tell the neighbors.

I also took firearms training for the first and only time. Practically every farm boy hunted in those days, some more than others, and almost every town in Minnesota had a shooting range.

Dad owned four guns: a single shot twenty-two, a single shot twenty-gauge shotgun, a pump action twelve-gauge shotgun, and an antique WWI M1903 Springfield rifle that he kept in the attic. I used Dad's twenty-two for practice sessions. The shooting range was in the basement of the VFW. Yes, the tiny town of Wendell had a VFW. It was not an outdoor range, which makes sense because the land around Wendell was relatively flat in all directions.

After graduating from firearms training, I used Dad's twenty-two around the farm a few times, but I had a tough time finding anything to shoot at. The rodents were in the pig barn, so that was off-limits, and I didn't really want to shoot the birds. I tried a few times and scared them, but I never did hit one. Then one day, I saw a squirrel jumping from branch to branch in one of the trees by the creek. When it finally came to a stop, I got down on one knee, aimed, and fired. I must've hit the poor squirrel right in the heart because he fell to the ground without even a twitch. I felt so bad about what I'd done that I put the twenty-two in the attic and never used it again.

I also recall hearing a rumor about a neighbor boy who used his twenty-two to shoot birds in the haymow. It seems his father found holes in the roof of the barn, and the neighbor boy allegedly got a sound whipping.

By the end of August, we were done with the grain harvesting and when September rolled around, it was back to school and that girl. What I didn't know and couldn't have predicted is that the school year would include another one of those life-changing events—one that would make me even tougher.

CHAPTER 26
Kicked off the Bus

Eighth Grade

Like seventh grade, eighth grade football was all practice and no games. We also practiced a few times with the ninth graders but, fortunately for me, Gary Colman had moved on.

As with football, nothing unusual or special happened with that girl. During the summer months, I'd thought of her off and on, but once I saw her at school, it was back to the previous year's routine. I didn't follow her or go out of my way to look for her, but I certainly enjoyed seeing her and if she happened to be absent, I felt an ache in my gut. I did get the impression that she might've felt my attentiveness, or maybe fondness is a more accurate description, but it never amounted to anything.

Not long after the start of the school year, Dad invited me to go pheasant hunting with him and his brother, Harry. I'd walked the cornfields to scare up birds for Dad in past years, but this time he allowed me to carry a weapon.

I can still remember that early fall Saturday when Harry

came to hunt with us. He drove into the yard just as we were finishing the noon meal. Dad offered to feed him but, as I recall, he told us that he had stopped in Wendell to eat at one of the two restaurants.

It was a perfect day for hunting. There wasn't a cloud in the sky and the temperature was in the mid-seventies, quite a drop from the middle of August when the temperatures were in the nineties. The corn stocks were starting to dry out and turn brown, but the corn was still on the stock. This translated into easy walking because there weren't any bent stocks to stumble over, and the pheasants hadn't been disturbed from their summer home.

The cornfield abutted the east side of the river with the rows running north to south. Dad was on my left and Harry on my right as we started our first southward journey through the corn. The gap between us was, at most, ten rows. Fifty feet later, the first of many birds flew up and one was directly in front of me. As soon as it cleared the top of the corn tassels, it turned and flew to the west in front of Harry, but before Harry could get his gun into the firing position, I pulled the trigger and the bird fell to the ground a few rows from him. That's how it went for the rest of the afternoon. I shot every bird, and many fell directly in front of Harry.

I later learned that Harry told Dad I was too young to be shooting a gun. More likely, he was mad because I shot all the birds and he didn't even get in a shot. Dad had instructed me to wait until the pheasant had cleared the tassels of the corn and I did, but he didn't tell me to wait until Harry could get in a shot.

That was the last time Harry went hunting with us. Had I taken the fun out of it? Probably, but I'm not certain if it applied to my father. We would go pheasant hunting together a few times over the next two or three years, but I went by myself a good share of the time—usually after school.

Pheasants were plentiful in western Minnesota during the 1950s and the early 1960s. Many farmers back in those days didn't bother to plow their cornfields until spring. Waiting gave the pheasants droppings to eat, and the corn stocks gave them shelter from the cold winter winds. Farmers understood this relationship, but somehow it got lost as tractors got bigger. By the end of the '60s, many farmers plowed all their fields before winter set in, leaving nothing for the pheasants to survive on, and their population decreased substantially. Today, their numbers are on the increase due to modern farming methods and conservation, but it's still not back to where it had been when I was in my teens.

***

Starting with seventh grade, the bus trip to and from Elbow Lake had become somewhat unruly. On many occasions, I would return home with buttons missing or a torn shirt. Two brothers by the name of Brian and Bradley Dohmeyer were the culprits. We didn't get into fights because they were older and bigger, but I did my best to stick up for myself.

Brian was the older of the two, and during my years in grade school, he had been a constant thorn in my side. Bradley took over after Brian graduated, and it was he who became my tormentor on the bus in eighth grade. He was a senior at the time, and what we used to call a greaser. He had thick, black hair that was slicked back with gobs of oil, and every other word that came out of his mouth was a swear word.

As I recall, I was the only one who stood up to him. It wasn't unusual for me to end up under the seat of the bus. Usually it was over something like the possession of a seat, or the snatching of a book or an article of clothing, like a winter hat. Refusing to let him push me around, I fought back. It wasn't about winning, because I knew I couldn't win, it was about letting him know he couldn't bully me.

It finally came to a head after the football season ended. It had been a cold, wet fall that year. The ground was saturated, and the ditches were full of cold water. The scuffle I had with Bradley that day was over a seat. We didn't have seating assignments. It was common courtesy to let the older students sit in the rear of the bus, so I chose a seat about two-thirds of the way back. The ride from Elbow to Wendell went without incident but as we left Wendell, Bradley decided he wanted my seat. Plopping down beside me, he said, "You're in my seat, shithead."

"This isn't your seat. I was here first," I replied.

"No, I sit here all the time."

"You do not!"

"I do, so get the f**k out."

"I'm not going to go, you go," I shouted.

And with that, he started to pull me out of the seat. Bradley was stronger, so eventually he got me out, but not without pulling the shirttail out of my pants and ripping off a button. When he had me in the center aisle, he pushed me forward. I stumbled and fell to the floor.

Looking up, I said, "I hate you, you creep."

He made a move toward me, so I quickly got up and found an empty seat on the passenger side, near the center.

You might wonder why the bus driver, Morris Bossen, didn't

intervene. I've wondered the same thing. Today, a bus driver will call their supervisors and request an intervention from a teacher or principal. If it's a serious fight, the transportation department might even ask the police to intervene, but in those days—at least in rural Minnesota—the bus driver ruled.

On the day in question, Morris didn't intervene when Bradley pushed me but something else happened that was just as good: he overran Bradley's driveway. I don't know if it was intentional or if he was paying attention to the scuffle and overran it by mistake, but he stopped a good fifteen feet from his driveway.

As Bradley walked by me, he snarled, "I'll see you tomorrow, you little creep," and with that he gave me another shove.

I watched as he walked toward the front of the bus and then I slid over to the window with the intent of giving him a dirty look as he walked by. Looking out, I immediately came to the realization that Bradley not only had to walk back to his driveway, but he would have to do it on a narrow path next to the bus because the ditch was full of water.

Seizing the opportunity, I ran to the front of the bus, grabbed the vertical pole that held the front seat in place, and with my feet, I pushed Bradley with all my strength toward the ditch just as he was about to step off the bus. Not able to stop his forward momentum, Bradley walked into the water. He didn't fall, but with the steep slant of the ditch, he couldn't stop himself. He kept walking forward until the water was waist-high.

I didn't see Morris because he was behind me, but he must've been just as captivated by what had happened as I was because he didn't react, not at first anyway. Bradley turned and started to walk back toward the open door, anger written all over his face. Morris didn't act until Bradley was maybe two feet from the door.

"Bradley," he shouted, "I'll handle this. You go home," and with that, he grabbed the handle and closed the door in Bradley's face.

Then, I heard Morris pull on the emergency brake. He stood and without saying a word, he grabbed me by the shirt, lifted me off the ground, and carried me to an empty seat. Then, he slammed me hard against the window. I can still feel the levers of the window digging into my back.

"Terry, you have two choices. You can either go out for wrestling, or you can find a new way to school. I don't want to see you on the bus next week. Is that understood?" With that, he dropped me onto the empty seat and returned to driving.

The scuffle with Bradley happened on a Friday, and on Monday of the following week, I went out for wrestling. According to what Mom later told me, Morris had suggested wrestling as a diversion, some time prior to the incident so it didn't come out of thin air. Besides, Morris's son was a wrestler, so there was a history behind his recommendation.

CHAPTER 27

First to Letter

Eighth Grade Continued....

I made varsity before the end of the first week. The wrestling coach was my football coach, Herald Wilcox. It wasn't the first week of practice, as that had started prior to the incident on the school bus, but I do know that the first match of the year took place at the end of my first week. To make varsity, I had to wrestle three other boys, and to my knowledge, each had been in wrestling in seventh grade, and at least one was older.

Wrestling was not an easy chore—both physically and emotionally. I was five pounds under the lowest weight class. Not only that, I'd never seen a wrestling match.

Despite this, or maybe I should say because of this, after three days of training, the wrestle-offs took place, and I ended up on top. Then on Friday of that same week, I surprised both the coach and the team when I pinned my opponent in under a minute.

The following Friday, however, turned into a lesson in humility when my opponent pinned me in ninety seconds. He was a senior from Wheaton, Minnesota, and the humility, or more precisely the instruction he physically forced upon me, began before the match even started. Instead of walking out to the mat when called, he waited until I had reached the side of the referee. Then, he ran toward us, and to my astonishment, he did a complete forward summersault, landing next to the referee, his hands shaking, and his body moving rhythmically.

Then, as if on cue, the referee said, "OK, shake hands, do a hundred and eighty, and come out wrestling."

My opponent grabbed my hand firmly and then used his grip to propel himself forward, but instead of just walking in a straight line to the other side of the circle in the center of the mat and then turning, he did a backward, one-hundred-and-eighty-degree turn, letting go of my hand as he did. Then, he fell to the mat on all fours with a loud and deliberate thud before I was even completely turned around. Still on his knees, his hands gyrating, he slapped the mat with resounding force, and then, while I was still disorientated, he came at me with the speed of a grizzly. He didn't have to use any fancy moves because I was still mesmerized by all the flair. He put his arms around my chest and, using his forward momentum, he had me on my back before I knew what was going on. I managed to hang on by keeping one shoulder and then the other off the mat, but within ninety seconds, I heard the referee slap the mat with his hand and the match was over.

For the first time in my short wrestling career, I had been completely humiliated. Seeing the confused look on my face, the coach took me aside, put his arm around me, and said, "Terry, don't get down on yourself. He's one of the best in our division and he's headed for college next year."

I would not go on to use the lessons the Wheaton wrestler taught me until the following year, and the reason, as silly as this may sound, is because I didn't want to be accused of stealing his moves.

However, this wouldn't stop me from using them the following year. I did make one minor change. Instead of the forward summersault, I did a backflip out to the mat. I didn't do it all the time, but my sister reminded me not long ago that it became my signature move. They say ninety percent of any sport is mental, and that certainly applies to wrestling—maybe even more so.

I ended the season with a five and ten record and, according to Mr. Wilcox, it was a school record in the ninety-five-pound weight class. I think what he meant to say is that it was a record year for an eighth grader—or for a first timer—but I have no proof one way or the other.

Besides football and wrestling, I went out for baseball and track again. Baseball practice began right after school was out and it took place in the large field on the east side of the school building. The game field itself took up part of the football field on the southwest side of town.

Baseball turned out to be pretty much a continuation of the first year. The coach continued to stress the delivery motion but, unlike the year before, he felt that I was ready to learn a variety of new pitches. He showed me how to grip the ball for a curveball, a screwball, and a changeup. I would later add a sinker.

My routine consisted of warming up with twenty fastballs. Then I would mix in the other pitches for a maximum count of seventy-five. That was the extent of practice for me. I didn't throw batting practice—that would come later, and I seldom took batting practice. I had told the coach I wanted to be a pitcher, so he treated me like one—a regrettable decision considering my high on-base percentage in fast pitch softball, and my team leading average when I later played town ball in my thirties and forties.

After practice, I would shower and dress and then get on the activity bus for the trip home. Our farm was twelve miles from Elbow, but with a stop in Wendell and detours to drop other athletes off at their farms, the trip usually took over an hour. As I was the last one off, I would arrive home around seven o'clock. I would grab a bite to eat, attend to a few chores, and head off to my bedroom to read.

As for attending varsity baseball games, I never watched a game from the stands. We didn't have a game bus to take students home. This meant Mom either had to attend the game with me, or come later to pick me up. Had I asked her, she most likely would've agreed to pick me up, but I never bothered to ask.

Eighth grade track and field turned out to be rather interesting. I took first place in pole vaulting and, better yet, the coach told me I had almost broken the state record.

"How close was I?" I asked.

"I think you came within a few inches," he answered. "I believe the record is ten feet. It's too bad they didn't let you make another attempt."

Ten feet today doesn't seem very high, but those were the days of aluminum poles. I also don't know if it was a varsity or junior high record, and I don't recall the level of the meet. It was out of town and there were lots of competitors. Regardless,

I would wear this achievement with pride and I looked forward to another year of pole vaulting.

***

One day toward the end of the school year, I walked into the house to find Mom sitting at the kitchen table reading a letter.

"Congratulations," she said, "I see you earned a letter in wrestling."

"Yeah, I guess so. Did they send it?"

"No, according to this, you'll have to go to the sports banquet to receive it," she said, holding up the letter.

"What do they do at a sports banquet?" I had never heard of a sports banquet before, let alone seen one.

"I don't know, I've never been to one, but I suppose you get to eat with the other letter winners and their fathers. Then, at some point, they hand out the awards. That would be my best guess, anyway."

"Will Dad go?" I asked, knowing full well that he wouldn't.

"No, you know your dad. That's not something he would do."

"Who's going to go with me then? Will you?

"No, I don't think it's for mothers. I'll ask your grandfather. Maybe he can go with you. I don't know if he ever won a letter, but he did play basketball when he was in high school."

"Grandpa went to school in Elbow Lake? I didn't know that. I always thought he went to the country school."

The country school I was referring to was the one-room schoolhouse that stood by the Adams' farm, which was across the field and about a mile from Grandpa and Grandma's farm.

"Yes, of course. He started out in the one-room school, but

in senior high he attended school in Elbow Lake. In fact, he was in the first graduating class at Elbow."

"Really?" I said. "I didn't know that and I wouldn't have guessed he played basketball."

I didn't say it, but he stood five-foot-four, so I had a tough time imagining him out on the basketball floor. Years later, I would see a picture of him in his basketball uniform standing next to his teammates and, sure enough, he was the shortest player on the team, by far.

"Well, I think things were different in those days," Mom said, as if reading my mind. "Anyway, I'll ask Grandpa if he can take you, but if he can't, I don't know what to tell you. You might not be able to go."

As it turned out, Grandpa did take me and we had a good time. In many ways, he was the only person who had shown a real interest in me, and I had become his confidential sounding board. He's the only person in the world who knows all eight of the promises I made to God, and I'm probably the only person who knows that he wasn't happy about having to take over the family farm. He told me privately once that he was envious of his two older brothers—one went on to be a professor, the other a missionary and world explorer.

"I know it's a sin to be envious of your brothers," he said thoughtfully one day, "but there are moments when I get downright depressed. I've always wished that I'd gone to college. Don't let someone else dictate your future. Follow your dreams."

The banquet turned out to be a blast. I saw many of the older boys proudly displaying the medals they'd won on their blue and gold letter jackets, so the thought of being the first in my class to wear a letter excited me.

The award ceremony turned out to be a first for both of us. Grandpa had not won a letter in school—I'm not even sure they had letters in those days—and with five daughters, he had never been to an athletic banquet. I, of course, was in total awe of the company we were keeping. I watched as athletes like Butch Beckman and Richard Larson, both from Wendell, strode to the front to get their awards. Butch was Mister Everything in sports, and he went on to be a standout running back for St. John's University, and the MVP when they won the national championship in 1962.

So, there I sat, the smallest boy at the banquet, and I was about to join that elite crowd to receive my first letter. It happened about two-thirds of the way into the program when the announcer said, "Terry Degner, would you please come to receive your letter?"

Grandpa gave me a reassuring shove and I stood and started walking toward the front.

"This is Terry's first year in wrestling," the announcer said, "and his record was five and ten."

My head was spinning when I reached the front. Someone handed me a varsity letter along with two medals, and then shook my hand. I had a big grin on my face. It was one of the most important moments in my young life. I get goose bumps just thinking about it.

When I returned home that night, I showed Mom my letter and the medals. One was of a wrestler and the other a bar, which represented the number of times I lettered. The next thing to come out of my mouth was, "Mom, can I get a letter jacket?"

"We'll see," she said. "Not right now, but maybe we can get you one by the time school starts next year."

I had to wait until fall, but eventually I got my blue and gold letter jacket. I put the wrestling medal and bar on the big letter "E" for Elbow Lake, and Mom sewed it onto the jacket.

I wore it proudly for the next two or three years. I stopped wearing the jacket when it got too small and I never bought another one. I still have all the letters I won.

Everything else during the school year moved along pretty much as it had in previous years. I still couldn't keep my thoughts off that girl and I didn't take any school work home, so the Ds kept showing up on my report card. I was probably the only student on the school bus who didn't carry books or paperwork back and forth. I continued to read. I was into, of all things, German philosophy by this time—Goethe, as I recall. The reading made an impact on my grades in social studies and history, and especially in English, but it didn't help me with math.

CHAPTER 28
Out of Body

Summer of 1960

I was awarded an advanced swimmer's certificate during the summer of 1960, and I went on to complete my junior course in lifesaving and water safety. This concluded my swimming lessons. Had I taken the senior course, this would have allowed me to get a summer job as a lifeguard, but that would've required travel and time away from farm work. The closest lake with a lifeguard in attendance was Pomme De Terre, which was sixteen miles from our farm, and even Mom wouldn't have agreed to let me take that much time off.

4-H softball had become routine. I took my pitching and hitting skills for granted, and I seldom thought about the game during the week. It's ironic because I believe this was the year we took first place.

By this time, I had taught myself a variety of ways to hold and throw the softball. It wasn't easy because a softball is almost twice the size of a baseball But, with practice, I had learned to throw three different pitches with efficiency.

My underhand fastball was better than my overhand in baseball, and I added a screwball by snapping my hand at the last moment to allow the ball to slide over my index finger. In a way, it behaved like a curveball. It didn't curve down near as much, but it would sink at the last moment and move into a right-handed batter, or away from a lefty. In addition, I added a changeup. A changeup is, in appearance, a fastball minus the velocity. To throw a fastball, I would hold the ball with my fingertips. To throw the changeup, I would hold the ball with more palm grip. To the batters, it would look like I was throwing a fastball, but the velocity was much slower, which kept them off balance. This pitch was only effective if you had a good fastball, and by this time, mine had a decent amount of speed on it.

I asked Mrs. Lacy about my batting average once, and she told me she didn't know, but according to her, I got on base eight out of every ten times I came to the plate. She probably kept track of how often I came to the plate and how often I got on base, but she didn't keep track of how I got there. In other words, did I get on base because of a solid hit, a walk, or was it due to an error on the part of the opponents?

A stay at Uncle Herb's farm and the beginning of some out-of-body experiences were the most memorable summer events in 1960.

At a family gathering one day, Herb mentioned that it was getting close to time for him to shear his sheep. As no farmers in our area raised sheep, I asked, "How do you shear sheep?"

"Well, you'll have to come and watch, won't you?"

And that's how it started.

My guess is that Herb's wife, Gertrude, discussed this with my parents over the phone and then a few days later, Mom asked me if I'd like to spend a week with them to help Herb with the shearing.

Uncle Herb's farm was northeast of Pelican Rapids, Minnesota. As it turned out, he didn't ask me to help, but I did watch as he held the ewe between his legs and slowly shaved the fur off its back. When done, he would flip the ewe onto her back, and do the same with her belly. The process took a long time because he used a mechanical device that looked like a pair of large scissors, rather than an electric shaver.

Herb was my dad's older brother. In many ways, he was like my father—both in stature and in personality. He was stunted and short on words, but with one major difference: Herb showed genuine interest in me. Nothing specific, but he had a tenderness in his voice and a warm, friendly face, as opposed to Dad's more sober nature. Herb didn't take life as seriously as Dad but, then again, he didn't have to put the long hours into fieldwork, and he didn't have late evening chores. He wasn't lazy, but he could afford to be more laid-back. At least, that's how I saw it. He was also the first adult to tell me a dirty joke. I remember the joke but, unfortunately, it's too dirty for this book.

His wife, Gertrude, who had been a grade school teacher before marriage, not only towered over Herb, but she also had a lively, affable, and communicative personality—everyone in the community, including my mother, loved her. Kathy, who was a year or two older than me, looked and acted much like her mother. She was tall for her age and she, too, had a gregarious personality.

The stay turned out to be shorter than planned. It ended on

the fourth day when Frank Degner, my grandfather and the patriarch of the Degner family, burnt his hands on the kitchen stove.

It was a black, wood burning stove. Instead of turning it on or off, like an electric or gas stoves, they had to keep wood burning in the stove all day, which also meant that the top of the stove was always hot.

I had just come down from upstairs and walked into the living room when I saw Grandpa walking toward the kitchen window that overlooked the farmyard. I stopped and watched as he walked over to the stove. Then, to my horror, he rested both of his hands squarely on the top surface of the stove and casually leaned forward to look out the window. My first thought was that someone had failed to throw wood into the stove to keep it going.

I continued to watch as Frank stood in that position, moving his head back and forth, like he was trying to find Herb. It wasn't until I smelled burning flesh and saw smoke rising from Frank's hand that I realized what was actually taking place.

"Grandpa," I yelled, moving toward him. "Take your hands off the stove!"

That's when Gertrude suddenly appeared out of nowhere. She either had just walked into the house or she had been working in the far corner of the kitchen—an area out of sight from where I stood. I stopped and watched as she ran over and pulled his hands off the stove.

"Frank," she yelled. "Couldn't you feel your hand burning?"

Looking at Gertrude, then at his hand, he mumbled, "No, I didn't feel a thing."

I never had an opportunity to look at his hands because Gertrude hurriedly guided him out of the house to the car.

She brought him to the hospital and he survived, but it was the beginning of the end for Frank. Like my father, Frank had diabetes, and he'd lost all feeling in his hands.

Frank was born on a farm outside of Ragensberg, Germany in 1874. He died on July 31, 1961. His wife, Caroline, nicknamed "Lena," died on May 1,1954. Someone once said, "Getting old is not for sissies," and I believe it. How Frank survived all those years without insulin is a tribute to something we don't understand today—hard work.

It was around this time that I started to have out-of-body experiences. The first night it happened, I was tense and lying in bed after a long day in the fields. I had read in a magazine about a way to relax the body and I thought, *why not try it?*

"Start at the toes and work your way up. As you do, tell each part of the body to relax. For instance, tell the big toe on your right foot to relax and when you feel it go numb, go to the left toe. Do the rest of the toes on each foot and then go up to the ankles, then the calf on each leg, and continue until you reach the very top of your head—the more specific you are with body parts, the greater the chance of success. Once you're completely relaxed, feel your body sink into the mattress."

I did everything the article suggested, and as I started to sink into the mattress, I felt my soul begin to float out of my body. I did not see my body, only the ceiling, but I did feel separated or suspended. It scared the daylights out of me, and just as suddenly as it had happened, I was back in my body.

The next evening, I repeated the process, but this time instead of staring up at the ceiling, I intentionally turned and looked down at my body. I wasn't as scared as the night before, but I do recall wondering how long I could do it and what would happen if I couldn't get back into my body. *Will I stop breathing?* I wondered. Then I heard a door slam downstairs, and I was suddenly back.

With practice, I found that I could shorten the relaxation process, extend my time away from the body, sink into a cloud instead of the mattress, and travel great distances. I floated over Wendell, Elbow Lake, and even as far as Minneapolis, or what I thought was Minneapolis. All I saw were lights, but having never flown before, how could I have known what city lights looked like from the sky? I even made several attempts at going as far as Washington, D.C., but the distance kept scaring me, so I finally gave up. It had been an interesting adventure while it lasted, but before I graduated from high school, I made a conscience decision to stop. I'd come to the realization that it wasn't going anywhere. Attempts to go in for a closer view of people and scenery had failed, so I didn't see any purpose in continuing. Recent attempts have been unsuccessful.

According to the science community, one in ten people have at least one out-of-body experience during their lifetime, but scientists know little about the phenomenon. How I could replicate it so easily at such a young age might be one for the record books, because I could turn it on and off with ease.

It was also around this time that I came up with one of my favorite sayings, one that I still say to friends. I'm not certain, but it most likely came from reading magazines in the barbershop as I waited to get my hair cut. They weren't dirty as magazines go, but they targeted men. I was into cars, and while I was surfing the pages, I came across one that caught my eye. It was a small convertible, sleek and manly. The ad called it a Mercedes-Benz, and I wanted one when I grew up.

"Where do they make these cars?" I asked, showing the barber a picture of one as I settled into his chair.

"Those are German-made cars," he replied. "They're probably the best ever made. Wish I could afford one."

"I'm going to get one when I grow up," I said, and that birthed the saying: "I'll know I've made it when I have my very own Mercedes-Benz." Later I added, "and a diamond-studded jockstrap."

As for farm work, I don't recall learning anything new that year. By this time, I had learned and done just about everything.

CHAPTER 29
Grades and Sports!

Freshman Year

As had been the case for the past two years, I was excited about seeing that girl and when I did, I got the butterflies again, but we didn't engage in any conversations. Football practice started at the end of class that first day and I found myself on the B-squad.

The coach was the head basketball coach, Mr. Jacobson, and the ninth-grade players, with the coach's help, began the process of discovering their natural position. Some players simply didn't have a choice. The coach put them where he thought their size or speed fit, and they complied without a fuss.

I got the distinct impression that, like Mr. Wilcox, Mr. Jacobson didn't know what to do with me. The bench was probably his first choice and as I recall, that's where I spent most of my time. I do recall practicing with the seventh and eighth graders at least once, but I didn't knock the wind out of any of them.

In a small school like Elbow Lake, just getting enough players on the field had an impact on who stayed and who didn't, so I continued to practice my chosen position—quarterback.

On the first day of practice, Mr. Jacobson gave each offensive player a playbook to take home to memorize. I remember thinking on the bus that, besides the cornet, this was the first time I'd ever taken any homework home. And, I must admit, I did study the plays. At first, they seemed complicated, but after going through the playbook a few times, a big picture emerged and from that point on, everything fell into place.

Knowing the plays was not the same as calling plays. When it came to this, Mr. Jacobson pulled me aside and stressed the importance of looking for ways to set up the defense. For this to happen, I needed to look for weaknesses in the defense, and he went on to give me examples of what to look for. He stressed the importance of always having a series of at least three plays in mind at the beginning of each down to fool the defense into thinking we were going to do one thing, but instead do another.

The B-squad did play against other teams, but to my recollection, I didn't attend the games or, more likely, I wasn't invited. With a growing realization that my likelihood of playing football didn't look promising, I started to look for a way to improve my chances. The answer came during practice one day when the team's punter blew a kick. Instead of the ball heading in a straight line downfield, it flew off to the right and landed on the sidelines.

"That is not the way to kick the ball," the coach yelled. "You didn't move your body into the ball, and you need to strike it directly with the instep of your foot. Not with the side of your foot. Now, try it again!"

As I watched, it hit me that the size of the punter was not the main factor, it was how the ball and the foot came together. So, I started to practice punting. It didn't pay off in ninth grade, but it did get me some playing time over the next two seasons—one of which turned out to be rather electrifying.

As for wrestling, I led the team in wins with a fourteen and five record. I had grown both in height and weight during the summer, so I wrestled at the one hundred and three-pound weight class. The only losses I sustained were in the Heart-O-Lakes Conference, and in the District.

I took pride in this accomplishment. It certainly helped my self-esteem and, of all the sports I've ever been in, wrestling was the most physically demanding. However, as a crowd pleaser, it was at the bottom; basketball drew the largest crowds. During wrestling matches, the janitors didn't even bother to open the sliding doors to expose the larger bleachers in the auditorium because the only enthusiasts who showed up were a few parents. I seldom saw a student in the stands. The high school cheerleaders would occasionally show up, but they'd leave as soon as the match started.

My mother turned into an avid fan. In the eighth grade, Mom had picked me up after a match, but with the wins piling up, she started to come early to watch. She quickly learned how the scoring went, and by the end of the season, I would look into the bleachers and see her teaching the other parents.

Going into the baseball season, I knew I didn't have a chance to get playing time because I was a freshman and there were too many good pitchers ahead of me. Over the summer months, I had found time to throw against the side of the front porch, and the assortment of pitches the coach had taught me were beginning to drop in for strikes.

Shortly after the season started, the coach pulled me aside and said, "Terry, I'm going to let you throw batting practice this year because I can see you've got your pitches under control, but don't attempt to strike the hitters out. Let them hit. OK?"

Yeah, right, I thought. *I'm supposed to practice letting them get hits off me? Nope! Not going to happen.*

Every pitch I threw in batting practice was thrown to strike the batter out. Not once did I throw the ball over the plate for the explicit purpose of letting the batter get a hit, and when they did make contact, I kept track of how and where it was hit. I also kept track of how often they swung and missed. I especially loved it when they bitched to the coach about what I was doing. He would reiterate, "Terry, just throw it over the plate so they can hit the ball," but there wasn't a lot of enthusiasm in his voice, so I kept at it. In the end, it would pay off.

***

Grades are on everyone's mind these days. I heard a politician recently shout, "We won't stop until every student gets good grades, until every student graduates from high school, until every student…."

He made many promises about what his party was going to do with the tax increases they were asking for. My own experience has shown that pouring money into education can't overcome the emotional or domestic circumstances of every student.

I had a love of learning, and I continued to read everything I could get my hands on, but grades, as I've said before, did not concern me. If I couldn't get an assignment done during the school day, it didn't get done. I had too many other things going on after school and I wasn't going to give up my reading time in the evening.

It wasn't unusual for me to bring my report card home and throw it into the waste basket without even looking at it, and with one exception, I don't remember my mother ever asking to see it. As I recall, the exception occurred in ninth grade.

"Is that your report card?" she asked, as I walked into the kitchen after school.

"Yes," I said, looking down at the paper in my hand.

"Would you mind if I looked at it?"

"Sure, I don't mind. I haven't even looked at it," I said, tossing the report card onto the kitchen table. "Let me know what you find."

I walked over to the refrigerator and opened the door to see if there was anything to eat. Not seeing much, I walked into the bathroom and shut the door.

When I returned to the kitchen, Mom was still at the table with my report card in her hands.

"So, what kind of grades did I get?" I asked.

"Oh, Terry, I really think you could do much better than this," Mom replied.

I shrugged and asked, "So, what did I get?"

"You don't know?" she asked in astonishment.

"No. Like I said, I didn't look at it."

"Well, you got a couple of Cs, but the rest are all Ds."

"That's because I didn't hand in any homework."

"Well, Jean has homework and she gets it done. Why can't you?"

"Because I don't have the time," I answered, raising my hands in frustration. "Jean gets home at five o'clock, and I get home at seven and Dad usually has something he wants me to do. Heck, I do fine on tests. I wish they would grade me on those, instead of that dumb homework stuff."

I started to leave, but then thought of something else. "The only thing I don't want is an F and I didn't get that, did I?" And with that, I turned and left.

Grades had never been a hindrance to playing in sports. Not once had the football, wrestling, or baseball coach seemed concerned about grades, but track turned out to be different.

Because of my accomplishments the previous year, I was excited—not only about the real possibility of becoming a four-sport letter winner, but maybe even going on to break the state record in pole vaulting. I had taken first place when I almost cleared ten feet in a track meet the previous year, and from what the coach had told me, it was close to a state record.

The first day of track practice was held indoors. Not only was it cold, but snow still covered parts of the playground. So, instead of canceling practice, Mr. Gordon, the new track coach, instructed us to gather in the gymnasium for introductions and a light workout. I had seen Mr. Gordon in the hallways over the course of the school year, but I didn't know him by name because I hadn't had him for any of my classes. I didn't even know he was going to be the new track coach until that first day.

"Are you Terry Degner?" he asked.

"Yes," I responded, with a little pride. I couldn't help but think that maybe someone had told him about my accomplishments.

"What do you do in track?" he asked.

"I pole vault, but I've also done some high jumping and the broad jump."

"Terry, I know you're not going to like this, but I'm going to have to ask you to leave."

"What? What have I done? I didn't do anything wrong."

"It has nothing to do with doing something wrong," he said. "I just don't think track is something you should be doing."

"Why? I took first place in a meet last year and you haven't even seen me pole vault."

He considered my comment for a few seconds, and then he said, "I tell you what. I'll reconsider this if you can climb this rope." He pointed at one of two ropes hanging from the gymnasium ceiling.

I'd climbed the rope many times in gym class, so when he said that, a grin spread across my face.

"OK," I said, walking toward the rope.

"Wait," he said. "You not only have to climb to the top and touch the ceiling, but I want you to do it without using your legs."

"Do I have to come back down without using my legs?" I asked, wanting to make sure we were on the same page.

He hesitated for a few seconds, looked at me oddly, then he said, "Yes, you have to come down the same way."

I put some talcum powder on my hands, grabbed the rope, and up I went—my legs pointed out at a ninety-degree angle for balance. Touching the ceiling was the tough part. Holding the rope tightly with my left hand resting against my body for support, I quickly reached out with my right hand and touched the ceiling.

Coming down was a little trickier because my arms were tired, but I made it without using my legs. "There," I said, jumping to the floor and turning to face him.

Mr. Gordon appeared mortified. "I…" he stammered.

We stood there staring at each other for a few seconds, and then he said, "I'm sorry, Terry, but I still have to ask you to leave. I know it's not fair, but I can't let you be in track with your grades."

There it was. How did he know anything about my grades? I had never had him as a teacher, so someone must've intentionally pointed me out. I couldn't image any coach, let alone a new one, taking the time before the start of the season to look at each student's grades.

I should've asked if Mr. Peterson was involved, but I didn't. It could've been the principal or almost any one of my teachers, but only Mr. Peterson had shown a proclivity for doing something like this.

Ironically, this was the year schools switched from aluminum to fiberglass poles. It was also the year a student in Glenwood, Minnesota impaled himself on a pole. When I read about this, the first thing that ran through my mind was: Someone was looking out for me.

As for that girl, I finally got up the courage to ask her to the freshman dance, and to my surprise, she accepted. How I got up the courage is beyond me, and as it turned out, I was a lousy date. I played ping-pong for most of the evening while the others danced. The ping-pong table was in the upper gymnasium and the dance floor was on the main floor. At one point, she approached and said, "Aren't you ever going to dance?"

"I don't know how to," I replied. "Besides, I'm having fun."

She grabbed the paddle out of my hands and ran. I chased her around the table, and then it happened. She went flying. I hadn't pushed or touched her, but for some reason, she lost her balance and down she went, her dress flying above her waist, exposing her underwear. I quickly looked away, but it was too late; the damage had been done. Embarrassed, she got up, threw the paddle at me, and walked away.

I felt sorry for what had happened, so when the person running the show announced, "This is the last song of the evening," I walked over to where she was standing and asked her to dance. I wanted to make up for it. I'll never forget the last song. It was a popular one called "A White Sports Coat."

I had to ask her how to dance, and after stumbling a few times, I quickly adjusted and we got through it without any major incident.

Afterwards, we ate together in the lunchroom, I became aware of something I hadn't noticed before—she didn't stop talking, she repeated herself, and it was all small talk. Not only that, I couldn't get a word in edgewise. This is when I began to feel uncomfortable about my feelings for her. I would continue to have a fondness for her, but it gradually diminished over time.

CHAPTER 30

The Green Hornet

Summer of 1961

The days of Saturday morning swimming lessons were over, but there was still 4-H softball. We had won the championship in 1960, but from the start, things didn't feel the same. This was due in part to the loss of some key players. As I understood it, the high school baseball coach had invited them to play American Legion baseball in Elbow Lake during the summer.

The coach never got around to inviting me, but I understood why: the American Legion team had two strong pitchers, and they were both one year ahead of me. They also were from the Elbow Lake area.

Despite this, we won our share of games during the season, but I don't believe we came in first. I do remember one game, but only because of a batter. I can still see the ball sailing in and hitting the catcher's mitt as the referee shouted, "Strike three!"

I struck him out two times in a row. For me, this was the highlight of the season because the batter was the number one pitcher on both the high school and the American Legion base-ball teams—the same one who was one year ahead of me in school.

This would end up being my last year in 4-H softball. Ironically, this would also be the last summer that I worked for my father. As I look back on the years spent on the farm, and at our relationship, my greatest regret is that we never bonded as father and son. My father had a good heart; his morals were implacable, but we were opposites in so many ways.

Let it just be said that my father enjoyed farming. To him, the world revolved around his three hundred acres. My head was in the world of books. By this time, I was into philosophy, world history, religion, and fiction. When I was in the field or the barn, my mind was on anything but farming, and it was racing a million miles a minute. My father wanted to work, I wanted to get the work done.

The summer of 1961 brought our differences to the surface in ways that would eventually lead to our parting. It began with a radio, and would end the following year with a trip to the Twin Cities.

The radio I'm referring to belonged to Uncle Jim Reeser. During a short visit to the Reeser home in Fergus Falls, I walked down to their basement with Jim to help him find something that the women wanted. While there, I saw a radio sitting on a table among a bunch of old tools and, out of curiosity, I asked Jim if it worked.

"I haven't used it for a long time, but I think it still works," Jim replied. And then, without any prodding on my part, he asked, "Would you like to take it home with you? It's not doing me any good."

"Yeah, I'd love it," I said without hesitation. "I'd like to put it in the barn so I can listen to it while I'm cleaning."

I brought the radio home and without Dad's permission, or knowledge for that matter, I nailed a wooden orange crate to the wall in front of where the cows stood with the open side facing toward the front of the cows. Then I placed the radio inside. The box not only served as a shelf, but it protected the radio from falling debris.

As there were no AC outlets on that side of the barn, I drilled a hole in the wall and plugged it into an outlet in the adjoining room—an extension of the barn used for storing ground-up feed and machinery, along with a larger pen used for housing the older calves.

That done, I turned the radio on, but I could only tune in two stations—a Country Western station out of Nashville, and WCCO, a station broadcasting out of the Twin Cities. I was disappointed, but—what the heck, it gives me something to do while I cleaned the barn.

Dad didn't put up a fuss at first because he wasn't spending much time in the barn and if, weather permitting, there was pressing fieldwork to get done, especially during the planting season, he would allow me to do the evening milking by myself.

On one such evening, I happened to have the radio tuned to the Nashville station when Dad walked in. The first words to come out of his mouth were, "That noise is going to frighten the cows. Turn it off. It'll reduce their output. You can use it while you're cleaning, but I don't want you playing it at milk time."

"I heard someplace that music soothes the cows," I countered. "And if they're soothed, it should increase the milk output."

He would have nothing to do with it, so I turned the radio off and let it go. Then about a week later, I came up with a new idea.

While we were finishing the milking one evening, I said, "Dad, I can do all the milking in the evening if you want to stay in the fields. That way, you'll be able to stay off your feet."

It was one of my more brilliant moves. From that time to the end of summer, Dad stayed away from the barn in the evenings, and I had the radio all to myself.

At least, that's what I thought. But I had one more problem: I could barely hear the radio above the noise of the milk machines. I didn't mind this inconvenience when I listened to music, but it was another thing when it came time for The Green Hornet.

WCCO's signal did not come in as loud as the Country Western station, and even with the volume knob turned up as far as it would go, I could barely hear a thing over the noise of the machines. Music is background fill, but missing a key moment in a suspense-filled drama can drive you nuts. In those days, I couldn't record the program or, like a book, return to a previous page to reread a section that hadn't registered the first go-around.

The solution I came up with was the same one I'd used while cultivating—I went into fourth gear. I would hook a machine up to a cow's udder, and then run to stand by the radio. When it was time to unhook and empty the second machine, I would run and unhook it, empty its contents into a milk pail in the center of the barn, hook it back up to the next cow, and then run back to the radio. It took me less than two minutes to accomplish this, and the speed at which I worked didn't seem to bother the cows. I did miss bits and pieces of the program, but I was usually able to keep tabs on what was happening. Unless, of course, I missed the ending—an all too common occurrence.

All in all, the new arrangement worked out great, and on those rare occasions when he returned from the field while I was still milking, I would hear the tractor turn into the yard and immediately turn the radio off.

CHAPTER 31

Corruption Begins at the Top

Summer of 1961 continued....

I was disconnecting the suction cups from the udder of a cow and listening to the radio when I suddenly heard the door to the barn slam shut. Looking under the belly of the cow, I saw Grandpa Ash walking over to where the milk pail stood.

Picking up the now full machine, I stepped from between the cows and out into the alley, being careful not to step into the gutter. "Hi, Grandpa, I didn't know you were here. "I'll be right with you."

I dropped the machine onto the straw-filled floor in the center of the alley and ran to turn the radio off. Over the noise, I heard him say, "Your grandma asked me to drop something off for your mother, and I just thought I'd stop in and say hi."

That's like him, I thought. *Anything to get out of the house.*

Do to having a number of strokes over the course of the past twelve months, he'd sold all his animals. He hadn't lost any of his mental sharpness, but serious farm work was out of the question.

I picked up the milk machine again and lugged it toward where he was standing, and as I did, he asked, "How long before you're finished?"

"Oh, maybe another hour or so," I answered. "Usually it takes about two hours and I've been at it for close to an hour."

When I reached the milk pail that stood at Grandpa's feet, I dropped the machine onto the floor and straightened, pulling my shoulders back to work out the kinks.

"I hate this job. Maybe I should go back to the fields and let Dad do the milking."

"I think you're doing the right thing. Your dad needs to keep off his feet and milking isn't the best for doing that," he replied.

"You know what I hate the most?" I said, without acknowledging his comment. "I hate the cobwebs. It's got to be the dirtiest barn in the world. Why can't my dad whitewash it?"

It wasn't really a question because I knew the answer: we sold Grade B milk. Only farmers who sold Grade A milk had to whitewash their barns. They also had clean rooms where they stored and cooled the milk in large, stainless steel vats. Some systems even had pipelines that moved the milk directly from the cow to the storage vat. The requirements for Grade B milk were not as stringent because companies like General Mills turned the milk into powder for commercial processing. That's why Dad hadn't bothered to whitewash our barn and why long cobwebs hanging from our barn's ceiling rafters: cobwebs that when weighted down with enough grime and dust would break loose and fall to the floor or down the back of my shirt. Particles from the ceiling were always floating in the air.

"Why don't you whitewash the barn?" Grandpa asked in a, if you don't like it, do it yourself, tone.

"Because it's too big a job for me to do by myself," I answered, and then I said, "I'll do it if you'll help me."

"Well, maybe that can be arranged," Grandpa replied.

With that, I twisted the lid on the milking machine and lifted it off, exposing the fresh milk inside. Without being asked, Grandpa lifted the lid from the pail as I struggled to lift the heavy milking machine bucket off the floor. When it was high enough, I rested the lip of the bucket on the rim of the pail and slowly poured the contents inside, which was already two-thirds full. When the bucket was empty, I returned it to the floor and twisted the lid back into place. That's when I noticed that six flecks of dirt had settled onto the top of the milk.

"Oh, yuck, I hate that," I said in disgust. "This barn is so dirty."

Without hesitating, Grandpa reached down and with the tip of his finger he carefully lifted each of the specs from the milk, wiping the mixture of dirt and milk on his clean blue shirt.

"Don't get upset. The milk won't spoil. Not unless the specks settle to the bottom," Grandpa said, and with that as his lead in, he proceeded to tell me something I've never forget. "You know, the same thing happens in the real world. Corruption begins at the top, and if we don't put a stop to it before it works its way down to the common people, it will eventually destroy the collective soul of the nation."

I have never forgotten those words of wisdom. I would later learn that President Lincoln not only felt the same, but he offered a solution. In his opinion, every one hundred years or so, a nation must go through a civil war to rid itself of corruption at the top.

Of course, Mr. Lincoln assumed that the common people

would always have the same weapons as the government, but those times have changed. Today, the weapons gap between those who rule and the ruled is like it had been in the Middle Ages. That was a time when kings and lords had complete control over the peasants. The lords had knights and the only weapons the peasants had were pitchforks.

That's why our forefathers, many of whom had fled Europe to escape these conditions, insisted that we have the right to bear arms.

Today, our government not only has superior weapon power, but they know where we live, what we do, how much we make, who we talk to, and what we say on the phone. They know more about us than the kings and lords of the Middle Ages knew about their subjects.

CHAPTER 32

No Swearing Allowed

Summer of 1961 continued....

"Get off my farm right now," my father yelled, his face beet red, his hand shaking as he pointed his index fingers at me. "I will not have someone talking like that on my farm."

"What did I say that was so bad?" I asked, in shock. It was the first time he'd ever yelled at me.

"I'm not going to repeat what you said. You swore and I won't have swearing on my farm, so leave this instant."

"Where am I going to go?"

"Go over there," he said, pointing in the direction of the road. "And sit in the ditch until I say you can return."

This incident took place around the first part of July. I know that because the corn was knee-high and it was time to cultivate for a second time. After the first go around, I had unhooked the cultivator from the tractor and left it sitting in the grass next to the light pole in the center of the yard.

To hook it back up, all I had to do was aim the front tires

between the two halves and stop when the frame of the cultivator was in position. After that, it was just a matter of putting in the screws that held it to the side of tractor. To do that, however, I had to crawl under the steel frame of the cultivator, and that's where it happened.

With a wrench in my left hand, I pushed the large screw into the hole but, to my dismay, I found that the screw didn't match up with the hole in the tractor frame. Dropping the wrench to the ground, I pushed up on the frame of the cultivator in a failed attempt to match the holes up,

Realizing that I would need to get up to reposition the frame, I started to stand and, in doing so, I hit the top of my head on the frame. I crawled out, stood, kicked at the frame as hard as I could, and instead of yelling, "You son of a Siberian sheep shearer" like Grandpa had taught me, I had shouted the naughty version.

Was I wrong? Perhaps, but I had no idea that Dad was in the vicinity. He had been in the barn when I parked the tractor next to the cultivator. Maybe I shouldn't have used the naughty words, but it had hurt like the dickens, and getting a concussion from hitting your head on a solid metal object like that isn't unheard of.

Anyway, I did as I was told. Stunned and somewhat baffled, I walked across the road and sat down in the tall grass on the embankment of the ditch. A half hour later, I heard the screen door on the house slam. Turning, I saw Dad walk to where the tractor and the cultivator sat. He finished putting the cultivator on, and when he was done, he walked to the road and shouted, "OK, you can return, but I do not want to ever hear you swear again, is that understood?"

I nodded. "I'm sorry! I didn't realize you were standing there. I won't do it again."

"It doesn't matter if I was standing here or not. I will not have swearing on my land."

"Alright," I said, baffled by what had taken place and knowing full well what his next words would be.

"I finished hooking up the cultivator, so now it's time for you to get to work." And, with that, he walked back to the house, and I drove out to the fields.

A genuine father/daughter relationship with my sister, Jean, had existed from day one, but unfortunately our relationship never ascended to the same level. It leaned more toward what I would consider to be an employer/employee relationship, and now even that seemed to be deteriorating.

As I was doing the research for my first book, *My Brave Little Man*, I learned that my adoptive parents had put in a request at the adoption agency in St. Paul for a baby boy. When told they were too old to adopt a baby, they had switched their preference to a girl. It wasn't until the social worker in Duluth contacted them that I came into the picture.

As I would learn, the social worker called to tell them about the availability of a young girl. During their conversation, she told them that the girl had an older brother and she asked if they would be interested in adopting me. Well Mom immediately jumped at the idea, Dad, caught in the middle, went along with her…but not enthusiastically. Add to that the attachment Dad had with the hired man, and you have a picture of someone pushed into agreeing to something he might not have wanted. Then, of course, there were our physical and intellectual differences, plus our character traits, which didn't help.

I must stress at this point that despite the absence of a father/son relationship, Walter Degner was a good man. In the long run, working for him did wonders for me. In fact, the long hours, especially the physical labor, turned out to be a valuable growth tool—one that would benefit all young boys. As for the swearing, if I hit my head on the cultivator today, I'd do the same thing. Dad never heard me swear again, but his reaction to the swearing was unlike him and from that time on, our relationship began to unravel at a quicker pace.

Then, something new entered our home that summer, and with it, the gap widened even further.

CHAPTER 33
The Lawrence Welk Show

Summer 1961 continued....

The Radio Corporation of America (RCA) appeared without warning during the summer of '61 and parked itself in our living room. There were no family discussions prior to its arrival. There was no nagging: "How come everyone else has TV and not us?" It just showed up.

I think it might have had something to do with our neighbors, Nels and Olga Berg. Their farmhouse bordered on the eastern edge of Hereford, and their comparatively sparse farmyard was an eighth of a mile south of the Hereford church. Unlike the many two-story homes in the area, their house was a small, single-story building.

The Bergs had a television set and, at some point, Jean and I started going to their place to watch television. The invitation had come at the conclusion of a whist party at the Bergs.

While the adults played cards, Jean and I parked ourselves in front of the television set. One of the programs we watched was a show called *The Adventures of Rin Tin Tin*. I immediately fell in love with the show and it must have registered, because as we were starting to walk out the door, Olga asked Mom if Jean and I could come over after school on Friday afternoons to watch it.

Olga, who was in her forties and childless, most likely saw this as an opportunity to be around children. It would've worked if not for two things: First, like all children, once we started to watch the show, we made for poor company. Second, Mom made it a habit to pick us up just as the show came to an end. This gave Olga little, if any, time to engage in conversation or play with us. In that sense, I've always felt bad that we didn't spend more time with her.

Our trips to the Bergs came to an end when the show went off the air. This, and the fact that we were the only farm family in the neighborhood who didn't have a television set, is probably why Mom and Dad finally broke down and bought one.

In truth, I was not privy to the how or the why and, in fact, I wasn't even there when it arrived. I had been working in the fields all day and as I drove into the yard that evening, I figured something was up when I spotted an antenna sticking out of the roof of the house.

I parked the tractor and ran to the house. "Did we get a television set?" I asked the second I stepped into the kitchen.

"Yes," Mom said. "It's in the living room. You can go in and see it, but don't turn it on until Dad has had a chance to talk to you and Jean about what you can and can't watch."

I walked into the living room, and there on the floor sat an RCA television set. It was encased in a metal cabinet, which had been painted to look like woodgrain.

It wasn't until after super that Dad asked us to go to the living room. With great anticipation, Jean and I sat down on the couch and listened as he explained the rules.

"I don't want you children watching television all the time, so here are the restrictions," he said. "You can watch your *Rin Tin Tin* and *The Lawrence Welk Show*. That's it."

"*Rin Tin Tin* isn't on TV anymore," I said, interrupting him.

"Well, then it's *The Lawrence Welk Show*. You can watch the news at suppertime if you want, but that's it."

I thought it was restrictive at the time, but I didn't try to talk him into letting us watch another show, because I didn't know what shows were on TV.

I did end up watching parts of maybe two or three episodes of The Lawrence Welk Show over the course of the summer, but that was the extent of it. Instead, I would go to my bedroom to read. That changed, one rainy Saturday morning, when I walked downstairs and, knowing that no one was around, I turned on the television.

It took a few seconds for the set to come on, but when it did, rock and roll music emanated from the speaker and dancers filled the screen. *What is this?* I thought, sitting down on the couch.

I watched as the camera cut to close-ups of young couples; the boys in suit coats with well-groomed hair, the girls in Poddle skirts with tight belts around their waists. One had a streak of white running through her dark hair.

The music stopped and the camera cut to a commercial. When the show reappeared, an announcer's voice said, "Welcome back to *Dick Clark's American Bandstand*." I was captivated, not only with the music, but with the dancing.

The program went on for about fifteen more minutes. I had tuned in late, but I now knew what I wanted to watch—and it wasn't *The Lawrence Welk Show*.

I ended up missing a few episodes, but not many. Occasionally Mom would come in and tell me that Dad wanted me in the fields, but I'm not sure if he knew that I was watching television. I was in the fields at least six days a week and I milked the cows every evenings, so how much gripping could he do?

Even Dad found a show he enjoyed. After the evening meal, he would sit on the sofa chair in the kitchen and soak his feet in Epsom salt. After I had gone upstairs to read, he would turn on the television, crank the volume up, and watch professional wrestling. I loathed professional wrestling. This so-called sport is an insult to real wrestlers.

To deal with the annoyance, I would put the covers over my head and read with a flashlight. I could still hear it but after a few minutes I would lose myself in a story. Thank goodness for selective hearing. Next to a dog, it's man's best friend.

It wasn't until after the start of school that the television set disappeared from the living room Its departure had nothing to do with school or *American Bandstand*, and everything to do with the *Minnesota Vikings* and a quarterback by the name of Fran Tarkenton.

When the 1961 season started, I began to turn the football games on after we returned from church. Thankfully, Dad didn't object. That is, until Fran Tarkenton threw a pass that an opponent intercepted and ran in for a touchdown.

One Sunday afternoon, while Dad was in the barn, Mr. and Mrs. Brutlag stopped by for a visit. I first realized it when I head the screen door slam. Looking out the window, I saw Mom walking to their car. Then I saw Dad walking toward the car from the barn.

Returning my attention to the game, I watched as the Vikings moved the ball down the field. As each successful play unfolded, I would throw my football against the back of the couch and wait for it to bounce back. I was psyched for the big moment when Tarkenton would throw for a touchdown… and then it happened. Tarkenton fell back to pass. He started to run to his right, and just as he was about to run out of space, he planted his right leg and threw the ball across the field. It seemed to sail forever, and just as it appeared to be in the receiver's grasp, a defensive player stepped in front and intercepted the ball. To make matters worse, I could see there were no players between the opponent and the goal line.

I didn't bother to watch the rest of the play. I turned and, in frustration, threw the football at the back of the sofa with more force than anticipated. But instead of hitting the sofa, it sailed right through the living room window. The glass shattered, and the ball landed in the yard about ten feet from the Brutlag car.

An eerie silence followed, and then I heard Mr. Brutlag say, "Well, honey, I think we better get back on the road." With that, they got into their car and left.

Dad stormed into the house and turned off the television. He then proceeded to tell me in no uncertain terms that my television watching days were over, and that I would have the pleasure of replacing the pane of glass. Then, unhooking the TV, he moved it to a corner in the porch. While he was doing this, I kept my mouth shut. I knew that I had done something stupid, and nothing I said could make a difference. I also knew that the television set wouldn't be coming back anytime soon.

After he left, I walked into the porch and looked at where Dad had put TV and my brain went into action. I knew exactly what I had to do, but I also knew that I'd have to wait until everyone was out of the house.

The wait didn't last long. On the morning of the following Saturday, I put my idea into action. During the week, I had found a long AC cord, cut off the male and female parts, and stripped off an inch of plastic at both ends. Taking this down to the basement along with a mechanical drill, I proceeded to drill a hole into the floor leading to the porch. I had measured the distance from the outside wall to where the television stood, so I knew exactly where I had to drill to make it work. This done, I stripped a half inch of plastic off the television antenna cord that ran from the roof into the basement, and from there, into the living room. I attached the ends of the electrical cord to the exposed antenna wire, ran the other end of the AC cord up through the hole in the porch, ran upstairs and hooked the wire up to the television, plugged the television into the AC outlet, and voilà! I had achieved my goal just in time for *American Bandstand*. Not wanting to get caught, I would keep my eye on the window and when I saw Mom returning to the house, I would quickly turn the television off.

Over the course of the school year, I was able to watch parts of both *American Bandstand* and the *Minnesota Vikings* and, to the best of my knowledge, no one in the family ever found out about my scheme.

CHAPTER 34

Classes Taken—Lessons Learned

Sophomore Year

I read somewhere that the sophomore year is considered the forgotten year, because it's hidden between the preppy freshmen and the college prep, junior years. For some that might be true, but for me the sophomore year turned out to be a year during which two lessons would aid me greatly in years to come.

It began with the classes the administrators or the teachers allowed me to take. I don't know who made the decisions, but I do know that someone or a group of someones had placed restrictions on the classes I could take. For instance, when I asked Mrs. Stensland if I could take her class she said, "I don't believe Spanish is in your future. I think it's a little over your head."

Mrs. Stensland taught Sr. High English, Spanish, and Speech. I had seen her in the hallways and I knew her by name, but I never had her as a teacher. Was she convinced I would never make it into college and for that reason, I didn't need to take a foreign language? Was my grade-point average a topic of conversation in the teacher's lounge? And finally, what role, if any, did Mr. Peterson play?

I don't have answers, but during my sophomore year, they did offer me one class that would later prove to be a priceless tool—typing.

That's right, typing. In those days, real men didn't type. Girls were the future secretaries of the world, not men, and sure enough, I ended up being the only boy in class.

Mr. Swanson, the typing teacher, had at one time been a boy, but this didn't seem to stop him from teasing me from the start about being the only boy in class. Indeed, he was tough on me, and by the time the year ended I was typing sixty word per minute—not bad for a farm boy.

I stress the importance of this because as you might imagine, with the age of the computer just around the corner, knowing how to type with all ten fingers would turn into a real blessing. You might say that story-telling and finger dexterity go hand-in-hand.

Playing quarterback in football also proved to be of significant value. I remember very little about the games—how many we played, who we played, or what the scores were—but I do have some memories. The one that stands out the most is a feeling of being rushed. After taking the snap of the ball, the opponents were on top of me in seconds.

Due to this, many of my calls were either up the middle or quick underhanded throws to our running back Jim Melvel, who would then run toward the sideline and around the defensive back. Jim wasn't a big player. He was close to me in size, but he had one big advantage: he had breakaway speed and knowing this, I tried my best to use it to the team's advantage.

I do recall throwing a few short passes to the tight-end and to Jim, but long passes were out of the question. I would've had to move back a good ten yards to give the receivers time to get in the open, and without blockers that would have been impossible.

As for play calling, I did as the coach had instructed during my freshman year. I went into the huddle with a sequence of three plays in mind. For instance, on the first play, I might hand the ball to the fullback going between the right guard and tackle with the right halfback leading the way and then fake tossing the ball to the left halfback who would run as if going to the far right. On the next play, I might again have all the running backs going to the right but instead of handing the ball off, throw the ball to the tight end running to the sidelines on the right side. With the defensive now mentally engaged in that direction; on the third play I might again fake handing the ball off to running back moving to the right but instead toss the ball underhanded to a halfback running to the left.

The idea is to get the defensive players into thinking one thing, but in reality another would take its place—a mind game.

I did not call audibles at the line of scrimmage and there were limits to the number of plays I could call but, all told, I learned some valuable lessons in play calling. Besides calling plays, I also learned the value of getting rid of the ball as quickly as I could—let the talented players do their thing. As a future coach would say, "You have a quick release of the ball." Our porous offensive line taught me that lesson.

Mom would always drive me to the games and let me drive home. I had turned sixteen in August and I had my driver's license, but driving me to the games either gave her an excuse to get out of the house or she enjoyed watching her son play football. After all, she had been coming to home wrestling matches and picking me up from "away matches" for the past two years and that continued. There is one other possibility: had Mom not taken me to the games, would Dad have allowed me to take the truck? As he never attended any of my sporting events, I believe the answer is no, and Mom knew it.

CHAPTER 35

The Heart-O-Lakes Conference

Sophomore Year continued....

The wrestling season proved to be especially eventful. As I've often pointed out, there are events in my life that stand out and one of those took place in wrestling during my sophomore year and it would affect me physically for years to come. It happened at the Heart-O-Lakes Wrestling Conference in 1962. My win/loss record was 11-0 going into the conference.

The Heart-O-Lakes Conference was an annual event held in the small town of Frazee, Minnesota, which was approximately seventy miles north of Elbow Lake. As a team we seldom if ever won. But there were individuals on our team who had a chance at placing, and with my win/loss record I was perhaps on the top of the list.

The team took a school bus to the tournament, arriving somewhere around nine o'clock in the morning. We went straight to the boys' locker room and changed into our blue and gold wrestling uniforms. Before we could leave the locker room, each wrestler had to weight in.

A man standing next to a scale and holding a clipboard asked for my name and the weight class I was wrestling. I told him the 112-lb. class. I had been wrestling at a higher weight prior to the tournament but at the coach's suggestion, or maybe I should say, with his permission, I dropped down in weight for the tournament, a decision that would repeat itself over the years - one that I would come to regret.

The person responsible for weigh-in, slid the weight balance across a horizontal rod and stopped at the 112-lb. mark. "Ok, you can get on," the man said, pointing at the platform.

I stepped onto the scale, and to my relief the horizontal rod stayed in the down position. It wasn't unusual to see one or two boys fail and then leave for the bathroom in an attempt to make weight.

With that out of the way, I waited for the team to weigh in and then we all headed out to the gymnasium to await our first match.

As I was in one of the lower weight classes, it didn't take long before my name was called. My first opponent was one of the Johnson boys from Pelican Rapids. I say Johnson boys because wrestling was their family tradition. I didn't know about the family at the time, but when I did some digging for the writing of this book, I learned that their father was the wrestling coach at Pelican Rapids and his sons made quite a reputation for themselves in the wrestling community. The first I knew anything about them was when Mr. Wilcox approached me during my warmup and whispered, "This is not going to be an easy match, Terry, so be on your guard."

"What do you mean?" I asked.

"Someone told me he won the state last year, that's all I'm

saying. Just be on your guard."

When it was time, I ran out to the center of the mat. The coach had frowned when I suggested a backflip, so I did my usual hand and head gyrations. I even skipped the sudden drop to my knees followed by a loud hand slap on the mat. Under these circumstances, it didn't seem appropriate.

From the first, I could tell that it wasn't going to be easy. Instead of locking heads, as wrestlers often do, we both went for the legs, which resulted in a stalemate. Then the real wrestling started. I don't remember who got the first takedown and it doesn't matter because the entire match was one move after another. Neither one of us could hang on for more than a few seconds. A sit-out was quickly followed by another sit-out, a takedown by an escape, and another takedown. We could not hang onto each other. We were like two greased pigs. At the end of regulation, the score was an unheard of, twenty-four to twenty-four and the crowd was into the match.

Usually at events like this, the crowd, made up mostly of parents or grandparents, didn't get into a match until their progeny was involved, and even then it was rather subdued. Getting into a match that involved someone else's son was unusual. I hadn't noticed the crowd or the noise until the coach said. "You're doing well, Terry. Keep up the good work. Look, the crowd's even into the match." With that, I looked at the bleachers and instead of small groups of people scattered here and there, many of the onlookers were sitting together in front of our mat and from the noise I heard, they appeared to be into what was taking place.

With the score tied, we went into overtime. In 1962, up to three one-minute overtimes was unusual, but allowed. If a wrestler scored during overtime, the match continued until the minute was up. If there was not a clear winner at the end of three overtimes, the referee was instructed to decide the outcome of the match based on who he felt worked the hardest during the last overtime.

The moves slowed to a crawl, and by at the end of our second overtime, the score remained the same. I'm not sure what happened—if I actually passed out or if Mr. Wilcox just felt that a jolt of smelling salts would help, but that's what he did. He broke a package and swiped it under my nose. I remember the jolt of ammonia invading my nostrils and I remember shaking my head to get away from it. "What happened," I asked as I pushed myself up to a sitting position.

"You're doing great," he whispered in my ear. "You still have a shot at winning, so give it your all, and don't worry about anything else." With those words, he helped me to the standing position and the match resumed.

The third overtime was just as blurred as the other two had been and, at the end, the score remained tied. Mr. Wilcox came out to the mat and stood next to me as we waited for a decision. Because it was a conference match, someone had to be the winner. It was up to the referee. He left the mat and conferred with several of the men who had been keeping score. Then he walked back out to the mat and said, "This decision was difficult. Both of you worked hard but in my opinion the wrestler from Elbow Lake gave it more of an effort in the final overtime, so I'm declaring him the winner," and with that he grabbed my arm and raised it in the air.

That's how I won. The match should have gone to both of us, but because it was a tournament, someone had to win and that someone turned out to be me.

My legs felt wobbly as Mr. Wilcox walked with me off the

mat.

"I need to sit down," I said.

"Do you want to sit on the bleachers?" Mr. Wilcox asked, pointing in their direction.

"No, I need something more comfortable."

The very thought of sitting on a hard bench did not appeal to me. What I really needed was a bed.

"I saw a wicker chair on the stage when we came in. Why don't you go up there and rest." With that he turned and shouted, "Steve, come over here! Help Terry to the stage and see that he gets comfortable."

Steve, a natural 112 pounder, was not in the tournament. I had replaced him when I went down in weight.

Walking over to my side, he asked, "Do you need my help?"

It was a good question. Not only were my legs wobbly, but I was starting to have equilibrium problems and my eyesight was fuzzy.

"Here, let me help you," he said, and with that he put my arm around his shoulders and half carried me to the edge of the stage and up a set of steps. Then, I felt (rather than saw) the curtain brush against me as we entered what must have been the school's theater.

"There's a wicker chair over there," Steve said, as he continued to assist me.

"I can't see a thing," I said, squinting my eyes.

"Yeah, it's kind of dark back here."

Dark? It was pitch black, and why couldn't I see the chair? I wondered.

"We're here," Steve said. "Turn around," and with that he grabbed my shoulders and twisted me in a half circle. "Ok, now you can sit down."

Gently pushing me, I half fell, landing with a thud on a soft cushion. Then I leaned back onto what must have been the back of the wicker chair Mr. Wilcox had mentioned.

"This is crazy," I said, "I still can't see anything."

"Well, like I said, it's dark, but you should be able to see something. Look over to your right. Can you see the edge of the curtain?"

"No," I said, turning my head. "I can't see a thing."

"Wow, that's strange. Where's your water? Maybe if you have something to drink that'll help."

"I left it by my chair in the gym."

"I'll get it. Will you be OK?"

"Yeah. I just need to sit here for a while."

A while, turned into at least four hours, during which time I barely moved. An hour, or so, after Steve had helped me into the wicker chair, I began to see shades of gray around the bottom edge of the stage curtain. Gradually the light brightened and my eye sight returned to normal. At noon, Steve brought me water and something to eat but, other than that, I continued to sit without moving, listening to the noises coming from the auditorium.

Then, somewhere around two o'clock, Steve again returned. "Hey, Terry, you're in the championship round."

"What? You're kidding," I said. "How the heck did that happen?"

"The guy you were supposed to wrestle next injured his eye and had to drop out, so you got a buy into the championship."

Luck was on my side, but could I take advantage of it; that was the question.

"How long before I have to wrestle again? I asked.

"I'm not sure, but the coach didn't think it would start until after three."

Why the coach never came to check on me is a question I've wrestled with, but one that will forever go unanswered. Obviously, he had other wrestlers to take care of, but you'd think he might have been somewhat concerned about my health. On the other hand, I don't know what Steve told him.

"Did you tell him where I'm at?"

"Yeah, he knows you're up here. He said, just stay where you're at until your name is called."

So, he had known where I was all along, I thought. I guess that made sense. Steve wouldn't have waited on me without the coach's instructions.

"I've got to go. Do you need anything else?" Steve asked.

"No, let me know when it's time."

I could hear noises coming from the gymnasium, but the curtain made it impossible for me to understand even the announcements over the intercom.

It was after three when Steve returned. "You're up next. Can you make it, or should I tell the coach you're done for the day?"

It was decision time and I still didn't know the answer. I dreaded the thought of wrestling again. What if I ran into another tough match. What would I do? I'd give up, that's what I'd do, but I also knew that I had to give it a shot. I slowly stood and without saying a word, I walked with Steve back to the gymnasium.

The match, it turned out, was a breeze. I pinned my opponent in forty-eight seconds and took first place. It was surreal compared to the first match Winning the championship was a first for me, and I was proud of what I had accomplished. But was it worth the price I would later pay?

I went on to win the next two matches of the regular season, but as the weeks passed my energy level continued to go downhill.

Then, on Friday of the third week, the symptoms returned with a vengeance. I lost a match, the first of the season, and I missed school for a week. I couldn't move and I did not get out of bed until Thursday or Friday of the following week. In some ways, it was like the time I came down with Scarlet Fever, I kept seeing stars floating at me from out of the darkness. I didn't feel nauseous or sick, just frozen to my bed. I have no knowledge of going to the doctor and my mother can't remember taking me. She brought food and water and I eventually started sitting up in bed, but I didn't go downstairs to eat until the end of the week. I returned to wrestling just in time for the regional tournament, but I lost and ended the season with a fifteen and four record.

The effects I experienced in 1962 would become a cyclical occurrence, happening every ten years. I explained this to my doctor once, and his first thought was that I may have damaged my autoimmune system.

CHAPTER 36
Shamed

Sophomore Year Continued....

I only heard Mom raise her voice once during the eleven years I lived with my parents, and it wasn't directed at me. It happened on the afternoon of April 22, 1962. It was Easter Sunday and instead of going to church, the four of us climbed into the truck and drove to the Twin Cities to celebrate the occasion with Mom's sister, Edna, and her family.

The drive was uncomfortable and unnerving. Jean and I weren't children anymore. We were crammed like sardines into the front seat of our small quarter ton pickup and to make matters worse, the trip took almost five hours.

This was the first time I had seen my father drive on the highway for any long stretch of time, and it was scary. Instead of driving in the right lane, he centered the truck on the line in the middle of the highway. He would move to the right when meeting oncoming traffic, but only slightly, forcing them to swerve to avoid hitting us. We were on pins and needles the entire trip.

When we finally reached the outskirts of the Twin Cities, Dad pulled into a truck stop for gas and directions. While he filled up the gas tank, Mom went inside to buy a map, and Jean and I used the restrooms. Once back in the truck, Mom unfolded the map and spread it across her lap, the edges resting on both my sister's and my lap.

"I think we're right here," she said, pointing to a spot on the map.

"I can't see that from here," Dad said in frustration. "Just tell me where to turn."

For someone not used to driving in traffic, getting verbal directions proved to be horrifying for all of us. On more than one occasion, I slid down in the seat to avoid what I thought was going to be an accident, and as I did, I would hear Mom shouting at him to turn this way or that.

Despite these hair-raising moments, we finally arrived at our destination: sore, stiff, and somewhat late, but at least we were in one piece.

As we entered the house, Edna said, "You're late. I thought you'd be here a lot sooner."

"I'm sorry," Mom said. "We're not used to this heavy traffic."

"Well, we're glad you made it, but I do have to tell you that the food has been sitting on the table for a while. I hope you don't mind if it's not hot."

Lukewarm is probably the best word to describe the meal. As I recall, we had ham with mashed potatoes, gravy, carrots, and, best of all, an apple pie.

Afterwards, the adults continued to sit at the table while Jean and I visited with our cousins. Edna and her husband, Herald, had three children—two girls and a boy. The oldest girl was my age, but because we seldom saw them, we never bonded to any extent.

Two hours later, the adults were still sitting around the dining room table talking when Dad suddenly announced, "Well, it's time for us to leave. We need to get back for the evening chores."

After a hug from Edna and some goodbyes from Herald and our cousins, we squeezed back into the pickup and off we went.

With Mom giving directions again, Dad managed to get onto highway 169, but when we came up to Highway 55, instead of taking the west off-ramp, he took the ramp going east.

"I'm afraid you're going in the wrong direction Wally," Mom said, rather sternly. "Turn around at the next off-ramp."

Despite Mom's repeated instructions, Dad kept driving past the off-ramps until there were no more in sight, only cars flying by and cars behind honking at the slow moving truck traveling in the left lane of a busy four-lane highway.

In hindsight, I think Dad was in a total state of confusion—his mind frozen. He had not said one word during the entire time. Both hands were tightly clutching the steering wheel, he was leaning forward in the seat, and his face had fright written all over it.

"Look," I said pointing at what I would later learn was the VA Hospital. We were still perhaps a good mile from the building, but it looked like the highway ran past it. "Maybe, you can go there and turn around."

Suddenly, without turning on his blinkers, Dad put on the brakes and made a U-turn into oncoming traffic. Why we weren't hit is a miracle. I recall seeing at least two cars fly by, their horns blasting. It wasn't until we were heading in the opposite direction that I saw the carnage. To our immediate left,

I saw that at least five cars had plowed into each other. The drivers were blowing their horns and many of them were giving Dad the finger as we drove by.

"Walter, I want you to pull over to the side of the road right now! I mean it!" Mom shouted.

Ignoring her, Dad kept driving. It wasn't until the carnage was out of sight and Mom yelled again that he finally pulled off the road and parked.

"OK, Walter, you come over and sit where Terry's sitting. Terry, you drive," Mom said in a demanding voice. Dad obeyed without saying a word.

"Do you want me to drive all the way home?" I asked, as I climbed into the driver's seat.

"Yes. Please take us home."

During the trip back, not one word was spoken by anyone and four hours later, we arrived safely home.

That ended the one and only vacation our family ever took. It had lasted eleven hours—nine on the road, two in the home of family members. I don't know if my mother later brought up the subject to Dad about what had taken place, but I do believe I would later pay a price for the humiliation he went through.

As for the remainder of the school year, there were some changes, but they weren't significant. I went out for baseball for the fourth year in a row and, as before, I didn't get to play in any games. However, I did get my picture into the yearbook. Also, my GPA improved. I'd averaged a D during the middle school years. In ninth grade, it had shot up to a D+. Did my fading thoughts about that girl play a role, and would this up-hill climb continue?

CHAPTER 37

Income + Room and Board

Summer of 1962

It was mid-morning on a Monday when Dad drove into the yard in an older model, light brown car. I had just finished gassing up the tractor and was walking toward the barn when he pulled in. I walked over to where he had parked and asked, "Where did you get that from, and where's Mom?"

"I bought it and she's right behind me," he said, getting out and slamming door.

"Why did you buy a car?" I asked.

"We're going to strip it down and make a hay wagon out of it."

By "we're" I assumed he meant "us," and the thought of stripping a car immediately intrigued me, but *why would he tear apart a car that still worked*, I wondered.

"What did you pay for it?" I asked.

"Twenty-five dollars."

"Twenty-five dollars," I said in astonishment. "And it actually runs?!"

"Yeah, it's old, but it seems to run fine."

"Well, if it still works and it only cost twenty-five dollars, instead of tearing it apart and turning it into a wagon, I'd like to have it," I said.

"Well, I have to be honest with you. The real reason I bought the car is because you're going to need it to get back and forth to a job I've arranged for you."

"A job? What job? What are you talking about?"

"I've made arrangements for you to work for Arnold Stock this summer," he said. "They live by the Western Presbyterian Church, so you'll need a car to get around."

I was at a loss for words. There had been no discussion, no opportunity to express my feelings, just this statement of fact: I would be working for the Arnold Stock family, effective immediately.

"Are they going to pay me?"

"Yes, they'll pay you fifty cents an hour."

"When do I start?"

"Now," Dad said. "They need you today."

Mom, who had returned with the pickup and was now standing close by, said, "You'll need to pack some clothes, Terry." And that was the end of the discussion.

I packed the few things I needed while Mom made me dinner, and after eating, I drove my used, twenty-five-dollar car to the Stock farm.

It was a 1950 Chevrolet, the interior smelled like sweat, the front bumper was ready to fall off, it took a quart of oil every time I filled the gas tank, and the steering column was about ready to fall off. Aside from that, it would get me where I needed to go.

Many years later, I would ask Mom if she knew why Dad had farmed me out, and she responded by saying, "I think he felt it was time for you to experience what it's like to be on your own."

Was it an act of altruism, or did it have something to do with the humiliation he had gone through at Easter time? It certainly wasn't in his best interest. Without my help, he would have to do the heavy-lifting chores by himself, and with the sores on his feet, his health would continue to decline.

Whatever the reason, at the age of sixteen, I left home to become an adult. For the first time since my orphan days, I would have spending money. Not much, but enough to pay for expenses and a few simple pleasures.

With only directions and the keys to my new car, I drove the fifteen miles to the farm of Arnold and Florence Stock. I'd met and played with some Stock children in Bible school and I knew there were numerous Stock families in the area. However, I had never met any of the parents, so I was totally in the dark about who they were and their relationship to the children.

Arnold and his wife Florence owned a large spread south of Fergus Falls. They had four children—two sons and two daughters. Denny, their eldest son, was seven years older than me. Bob, their youngest son and my boss-to-be, was twenty-one. Judy, their oldest daughter and the one I knew from Bible School, was two years older than me, and Elizabeth, a change of life baby, was still in her pre-school years.

After introductions and a light snack, Arnold sat me down for a heart to heart talk. He told me he would be leaving the next day to join his oldest son in Oklahoma for the annual custom combining tour. Denny had departed Minnesota with their combines and a crew of men during the middle of the week.

I would later learn that Arnold and some of his brothers were part of what had been called the Combine Brigade. As I understand it, during WWII, a farmer could not get a loan for a new combine unless they joined the Brigade. In the spring, these farmers would load their combines onto trucks and take them to one of the southern states. Once there, they would hire out their services to local farmers, and then start working their way north, arriving back at their own farms just in time for the fall harvest.

When he told me about leaving the next day to join his son, I immediately assumed I would be handling all the farm duties on the home place.

"Who's going to be in charge when you're gone?" I asked.

"My son, Bob, knows what needs to be done and, of course, you can always see Florence if you have any questions."

He then went on to tell me about the farm and the duties. As I recall, they had around fifteen hundred acres of farmland, which in those days was considered a large farm. They had lots of corn to cultivate, alfalfa fields that needed cutting and bailing, and they had beef cattle to feed.

In addition, he said, "Bob might call on you to help with some of the chores around Hermon's place, and maybe even at Henry's, and Addison's." Hermon was his father, and Henry and Addison were his two brothers.

Without my asking, he finally got around to income. "Did your dad tell you about what we're going to pay you?"

"Yes. He told me I'd get fifty cents an hour."

"That's right. Fifty cents an hour. We'll also provide room and board, or you can drive back and forth to your farm. It's up to you."

As there was no mention of an increase in pay to drive back and forth, I chose room and board and that ended our discussion.

As for the pay, I'm not sure what the going rate for a hired man was in 1962, but even I knew that fifty cents an hour wouldn't go very far. With gas at twenty-five cents a gallon and the Chevy averaging something like ten miles per gallon, I would have to work over an hour just to drive home.

The meals turned out to be great. They had a television set and the bed didn't squeak. Better yet, they didn't have milk cows, pigs, or chickens. This would mean time off, if it rained. I wouldn't get paid, but I could enjoy an occasional respite from the boredom of fieldwork.

I slept at their place that first night, and before Arnold left for Oklahoma, I was already in the field cultivating. Unlike the ten-to-twelve-hour days I'd become accustomed to, I would put in eight hours a day and then, at Florence's insistence, call it quits. I would also work Saturday mornings, then take the afternoon off.

There was one painful twist—the one behind my hiring. In the spring of '62, Bob had lost three middle fingers on his left hand in an auger accident, leaving only his thumb and little finger. The doctors had reattached the index finger, but it never became fully useful. In the past, Bob had been the son who had stayed home to take care of the farm work. Due to the injury, however, there were limits to what he could do. That's why they had hired me. In a very real and sad way, this relationship was like the one I had with my father. And, like with my father, I found myself doing all the heavy lifting. Besides alfalfa, we cut and baled roadside grass, which is twice the weight of alfalfa.

With Bob's hand on the mend, he would drive, and I would

do the stacking on the wagon and in the haymow. Working with the cattle, however, turned out to be a breeze. Beef cows don't require near the attention as milk cows. Almost all the work I did that summer took place in the fields, and a lot of that consisted of cultivating corn. I'm not sure how many acres of corn they had, but the numbers kept me busy.

I ended up doing some work for Hermon, but very little for Henry and Addison. Hermon was the patriarch of the family. The matriarch, Clara, who had given birth to nine children, had died some years before. Hermon was getting up there in age. He still owned the land around the home place but his children did all the work.

I didn't meet Hermon on my first visit to his farm because he was in town, but I did get an impression of what he might be like. As I waited for Bob to get whatever it was he had dropped in for, I got out of the car and looked around. I didn't see anything of interest until my eyes suddenly focused on the garage. Inside, car parts hung from the ceiling and the walls—they were everywhere.

When Bob returned, I asked, "Why does he have all those car parts hanging in the garage?"

Bob laughed. "We hung them there to remind Grandpa of all the car accidents he's had."

That was my introduction to Grandpa Stock, and a week later, the introduction became a reality.

The day started out innocently enough. While sitting at the breakfast table on morning, Bob said, "I need you to take the cultivator over to Grandpa's farm this morning and cultivate the cornfield across from his place."

"You mean the one right across the road from his driveway?"

I asked.

"Yeah, that's the one. It will probably take you most of the day, so I'll call Grandpa and have him drive you back to our place for the noon meal. That way, you won't have to come back with the tractor."

"Is he going to pick me up, or should I walk over to his house?"

"When it's close to noon, park the tractor across from his driveway and knock on his door. He'll be waiting."

At eleven thirty, I parked the tractor and walked over to the farmhouse. I knocked on his door, and after a few attempts to get his attention, he came out and shouted, "You must be Arnold's hired man. My grandson called and said I should drive you to their place for dinner."

I nodded, and without another word, we both climbed into his car.

Hermon was a short, stern-looking man, and I assumed from the way he shouted everything that he probably couldn't hear well. He fumbled around with the car keys, and he hit the steering column a few times until finally he found the ignition. "OK, here we go."

He took a left out of his driveway onto the dirt road. Then, bringing the car up to a top speed of ten miles per hour and using the middle of the dirt road as his guide, we headed for Arnold's place. *It's a good thing I quit at eleven thirty*, I thought. *At this rate....*

Little did I know.

The highway that ran past the church to Arnold's farm was only a mile from Hermon's place, but at ten miles per hour, it seemed to take forever to get there. As soon as we did, I knew we were in trouble. Instead of stopping to look for oncoming traffic, he kept on driving. From what I could tell, he didn't even attempt to make a left-hand turn. Instead, he drove across the road and into the ditch. When that happened, I slid down in the seat; my left hand gripping the cushion, my right on the door's armrest, my feet pressing hard against the floorboards. I thought the car was going to flip over because the sides of the ditch were steep, but by some miracle, he managed to get the car turned. Shortly after that I head a loud bang and looking up, I watched as a sign disappeared under the front of the car. At no time did Hermon say anything. He just kept driving up the steep embankment as if he had no concerns and then, we were back on the highway.

Later, I told Bob and his mother about what had happened, and we all had a good laugh. After the meal, Bob took me back to the field and they never asked me to ride with Grandpa Stock again.

A day or two after the driving incident, while sitting at the breakfast table, Bob said, "I need to go over to Addison's to pick something up. Why don't you come along. I'll introduce you to his family and if I'm not mistaken, I think Byron's around your age."

Addison's farmyard was located about a mile east of Hermon's. As it turned out, he wasn't home, but his wife, Joyce was. They had five kids—three sons and two daughters. The oldest boy was Wayne, followed by Byron, then Mark. Carol and MaBeth were the two girls.

I knew Byron. Like Arnold's daughter, Judy, I had met him in Bible school. We hadn't connected in any meaningful way, so when Bob mentioned his name, I didn't associate it with a face. Not only did I know him from Bible school, but when I saw him, I realized that we had wrestled each other in eighth grade.

Bob and I didn't stay long, but before we left, Byron asked me if I'd like to get together some evening. I said fine. With that, we made plans to drive into Fergus Falls after work on Saturday, and that was when I ventured into the wild side of life.

CHAPTER 38

The Wild Side

Summer of 1962 continued....

As arranged, I picked Byron up on Saturday afternoon.

"Let's go to Richard Kanton's place," he said as I drove out of their yard.

"Who?"

"Richard Kanton. He's a good friend and a classmate of mine, and his mom always has beer in her refrigerator."

"Does she let you drink it?"

"Yeah, that's what it's there for. She knows we're going to drink anyway, so she feels it would be better if we did it at her place. That way, she can keep an eye on us and we won't get into any trouble."

"Did she tell you that?"

"Yeah, and the beer is free."

"I'd tried beer once and I didn't like it," I said, wrinkling up my nose in disgust.

"How long ago?" Byron asked.

When Florence asked me to get something from the basement for her last week, I saw some open cases of beer sitting on the floor. I opened one, took a swig. and almost gagged.

Byron laughed and said, "Trust me, beer tastes a lot better when it's cold."

We arrived at the Kanton's around five in the afternoon. Their home, a small, two-story structure, was the last house on a dead-end dirt street on the east side of Fergus. To the south and east, there was nothing but open fields.

"I know it's a little early for partying, but it'll give you more time to meet my friend Richard and his mother," Byron said as we got out of the car.

We didn't have to wait long. Before we reached the house, Richard stepped outside to greet us. "Hi, Byron," he said. "You're a little early."

"Yeah, we got done with work early today, so we thought we'd come by to say hi. I wanted you to meet Bob's new hired man, Terry."

Bob's new hired man? What's that all about? I though. *Why not simply introduce me as a friend?*

It wouldn't be the last time Byron introduced me in that manner, but I never bothered to correct him. Besides, everyone knew Bob, and in a way, that's who I was—Bob's new hired man.

Richard was an interesting character. Like me, he was short in stature, but unlike Byron, he was serious by nature. He acted and carried himself like a professional, but he wasn't overly confident. Another thing that stood out from the start was the difference between him and the people who came to their place to party. Where Byron fit right in, Richard was aloof. He was cordial and inviting, but I never saw him as part of the crowd, and I would seldom see him drink.

Richard led us into the house and introduced me to his mother, Evelyn. She was a widow and mother of three—two boys and a girl. Over time, I would come to know her as both pleasing and inviting but not particularly chummy or jovial.

"If my sons are going to drink, I'd rather have them do it in my house than at a bar or in some farmer's field," she told me.

I would later learn that her oldest son had gotten into trouble with the law and it was because of this that she started inviting his friends to her house. I don't know the details, but as I understand it, Richard's older brother invited his friends, and his friends invited their friends. Before she knew it, a small gathering had turned into a large crowd. It wasn't unusual for Byron and me to drop in and find the house packed with teenagers, along with a few twenty-somethings, and it was normal to see the kitchen table filled with bottles of scotch and whiskey, along with a case or two of beer.

Byron and I would spend some, but not all, of our Saturday evenings at the Kanton's, but there were no free drinks. Not for us, anyway. Every so often I would see Byron with a drink in his hand, but only when he stayed outside with some of his buddies. As an underage outsider; who looked to be in his early teens, no one at Richard's ever offered me a drink.

.

"Hey, let's go to the Balmoral Pavilion tonight," Byron announced the following Saturday.

"What's that?"

"It's a big dance hall and it's easy to get drinks there."

"Aren't we going to Richard's?"

"Yeah, we'll go there first and ask Richard if he wants to go."

"Where is this Pal, what did you call it?"

"Balmoral Pavilion. It's on Otter Tail Lake."

"Where's that?"

"You don't know where Otter Tail Lake is?" he asked in surprise. "I thought everyone knew that."

"Well, I don't know. I'm not from around here."

"It's about fifteen or twenty miles north of Fergus. I'll show you how to get there after we've seen Richard."

Richard, it turned out, did not go with us. I think it had something to do with his mother's wish to keep him at home.

After filling up at the M&H in Fergus, Byron and I headed for the lake.

It's funny, but we always used my old jalopy and as I think back on those times, I don't recall Byron ever offering to help pay for gas. He had access to a white Tempest, but he had to share it with his older brother, Wayne, who seldom relinquished title to it.

It was dark by the time we arrived. The parking lot was full, so I made a U-turn and parked on the side of the road bordering the lake. As we made our way toward the music, I noticed small groups of people standing next to a car. They all had drinks in their hands. Some looked to be of drinking age, but many, especially some of the girls, looked underage.

The pavilion was a large wooden structure with a wide staircase leading up to a set of double doors—one of which I could see was open. We walked up to the door and made our way inside. The dance hall was noisy and packed. Many of the people looked to be teenagers and young twenty-somethings, but some were middle-aged adults, and a few were even seniors.

On the far side of the dance hall, a live rock 'n' roll band stood on a stage, playing "At the Hop"—made famous by Danny & the Juniors. Young and old alike danced in front of the stage, their arms and legs swaying to the beat of the music.

"Can anyone just go over there and get a drink?" I shouted over the noise, pointing at a bar to the right of the dance floor.

"No," Byron shouted back. "I think you have to be twenty-one. We'll have to go outside for that."

Suddenly, the band stopped playing. The lead singer plucked a microphone off its stand. "Ladies and gentlemen, we're going to take a short break. Visit with your friends and have a few drinks. We'll return shortly."

"Do you know who that is?" I asked, motioning across the dance floor at a girl.

"Yeah. That's LeAnn, she's a good friend of Mark's."

I didn't know if he was talking about his brother, or some other Mark.

LeAnn was good looking, but that wasn't the selling point. It was the way she'd been swaying to the music. I was intrigued. With the band still doing their off-stage thing, I walked over to where she was standing.

"Would you like to dance when they start up again?"

"Sure," she answered.

For the next five minutes, we stood next to each other in total silence. It was embarrassing, but when the music finally started up again, I motioned for her to join me on the dance floor. Our embarrassment faded as we worked up a sweat, dancing without interruption. She was indescribable. I still remember the energy and the rhythm we generated together.

Despite my overly youthful looks, I didn't have a problem finding a partner for the rest of the night, and I didn't stop until the music was over. I fell in love with dancing that night. It came naturally—thank you, American Bandstand.

I went outside between one of the sets to find Byron and

sure enough, he was talking and drinking with some people I had never seen before.

"You want a beer?" he asked, bending down and pulling one out of a cooler.

"No," I said, "I'm having fun dancing and it doesn't appeal to me right now."

I would, on occasion, have a beer and I found that dancing and drinking went well together…as long as I didn't go overboard. One or two would make me tipsy, but if I kept dancing, the effects wore off by the end of the evening. Because I was the duty driver, I made a point of never having a drink after the last set.

I can't say never. I did end up getting drunk after one of our evenings at the pavilion. Instead of going straight home after the dance, I drove us to the home of a friend of Byron's. His friend was one of the better wrestlers on the Fergus Falls squad, but as I would learn, wrestling wasn't his only skill—he was a ladies' man. He was one of those guys who could walk into a room, and fifteen minutes later, walk out with a girl on his arm.

I remember sitting in a room drinking with a bunch of other males, but I don't remember what I drank, the time we left, or the drive home. I do, however, remember waking up the following morning. I not only had a throbbing headache, I'd wet the bed. I hadn't had an accident in years.

It was Sunday and fortunately the Stocks had gone to church. This gave me time to wash and dry the sheets, but I'd learned a valuable lesson: don't drink to excess or you'll wake up to find yourself in hot water—literally.

It was around this time, that I started having problems with the car. One Saturday evening, as I drove out of Arnold's yard on the way to pick up Byron for our evening out, I turned the steering wheel to the right, but the car didn't respond as quickly as it should have. Instead of turning, I kept going straight. I slowed to avoid going into the ditch, but after turning the steering wheel a few more degrees, I made the turn. I probably should've canceled our outing that evening, but I didn't.

Instead of going straight to Richard's house, as we usually did, Byron suggested that we drop by the Skagmo Café to meet up with some of his other friends. The café was downtown, on the corner of Lincoln and Mill Street.

I parked, and for the next hour, we ate and visited with his friends, some of whom I had seen at Richard's. When it came time to leave, two girls asked if they could come with us to Richard's, and we said yes. One of the girls got into the front seat with me, and the other one climbed into the back with Byron.

As I pulled away from the curb and headed down main street, I thought I'd have a little fun with the girl sitting next to me. As I neared an intersection, I turned on the blinker to make a right-hand turn. Then, just as I entered the intersection, I very nonchalantly turned the steering wheel as if to make the turn, but, to the girl's surprise, the car kept going through the intersection. I must admit that I exaggerated my action, but I'll never forget the look on her face.

As I look back on it now, it's amazing that I made it home, but I did and knowing that I had to fix what ailed my beloved car, I parked directly in front of the machine shed. On Sunday morning, I lifted the hood with the full expectation of finding the problem, but nothing. Everything looked normal. Then, I did something unplanned: I grabbed the steering column and when I did, the entire column moved away from the frame of the car, exposing a rather large hole where a bolt had at one time kept the column securely attached to the frame.

Oh no, I thought. *The hole had to be at least an inch in diameter, and the length of the bolt must be at least five inches or more. Where am I going to find a replacement for something that size?*

I looked through boxes of bolts in the machine shed, but after an hour of finding nothing, I gave up. That's when I spotted the welding torch. Why not? I reasoned. If one bolt could hold the steering column in place, why not just weld it to the frame? And that's what I did. It wasn't pretty, but it worked—problem solved.

CHAPTER 39

My Summer of '62

Summer of 1962 continued….

When I first watched the movie, *The Summer of '62*, I couldn't help but think about the older girl I met during my summer of '62. In so many ways, it paralleled that of the main character in the movie. I met her at the pavilion in July. She was twenty-one and her name was Nancy. She had come with some friends, one of whom was Ann, a girl who I had often run into at Roger's. Ann was attractive, but at five-foot-eight and four years my senior, she didn't see me as a potential suitor, and I didn't consider her to be anything other than a casual acquaintance.

It was Ann who introduced me to Nancy and it was Ann who did most of the, let's call it, sexual foreplay. Upon spotting Byron and me standing by the dance floor in August, Ann walked over and casually asked Byron what we were up to.

"Oh, we just thought we'd see what's going on," Byron said.

"Yeah, right! You wanted to find something to drink. I know

you, Byron."

"Yah," he said, shrugging.

"Who's that?" I asked, pointing in the direction of the slim, beautiful girl she had left standing on the far side of the floor.

"Oh, that's Nancy. We came here with Jimmy and Robbie."

I knew of the men. Jimmy was twenty-one, and I had always assumed Robbie was the same age because they hung out together. I'd seen them at Roger's, but I'd never seen Nancy. She wore tight clothes that highlighted a curvy figure. Her face was dainty and perfectly symmetrical, and she had straight, light-brown hair that hung down past her shoulders.

"Why don't you guys ask someone to dance?" Ann asked, taking my attention away from her attractive friend. Before either Byron or I could respond, she said, "I forgot, you don't dance do you, Byron?"

"No! I'd make a fool of myself," he mumbled under his breath.

"I like to dance," I said, thinking maybe she had offered to dance with me.

"Well, go and ask someone. There's lots of girls here. I've got to get back to my friends."

With that, she walked across the dance floor to where Nancy was standing.

Byron muttered something about going outside to get a drink as the music started up again, and off he went, leaving me standing by myself.

I continued to watch Ann and Nancy as they huddled and, on occasion, I found them looking in my direction. Were they talking about me? I wondered.

It wasn't until the following Saturday that I met Nancy. Byron and I stopped at Roger's, and when I walked into the living room to see who had shown up, I saw Nancy and Ann sitting on the sofa. Having nothing else to do, I settled into the armchair across from them. Upon seeing me, Nancy smiled and then, without warning, she stood and walked over.

"Hi, Terry. How are you?"

"Great."

"I don't know if Ann told you or not, but I'm Nancy."

"Yeah, she told me who you were last week. So, what are you two up to?"

"Oh, nothing. I was just wanted to introduce myself. Would you like some company?"

"Sure, that would be great. Here I'll...." Before I could finish standing, she pushed me back into the chair.

"Don't move," she said, bending over and putting her hands onto the armrest. "I'll just sit here." She slid her left arm around my neck, sat on the arm of the chair, crossed her legs, and moved in close.

"Ann tells me your parents own a farm by Wendell. Is that true?"

"Yes. It's about four miles out of Wendell," I replied.

"I grew up in Campbell."

"You're kidding. Campbell's not far from our farm," I said, and that's how the conversation went. It was all small talk and mostly questions. Did I have any siblings, what were my parents like, what kind of farm did we have, what sports did I like—questions of that nature. She didn't tell me her age, and we didn't discuss anything of a sexual nature, but her actions, the heat she generated, and the excitement I felt was enough to scare the crap out of me. I didn't have a clue about what to do.

Ten minutes later, Ann walked over to where we were sitting and said. "Nancy, it's time to go."

"See you around," Nancy said, and with that, she got up and left, leaving me confused and excited at the same time.

On the following Saturday, Byron and I were again at the pavilion. I had half expected to see Ann and Nancy, but I didn't see them once...not until it was time to leave. Then, out of nowhere, Ann appeared.

"Terry, are you going home, or are you going to Roger's?" she asked.

"I didn't see you. Were you here all night?"

"Nancy and I have been sitting in the back with some friends."

"Does Nancy ever dance?" I asked. "I don't think I've ever seen her on the dance floor."

"Yeah, she dances, but not very often. Anyway, that's not what I came to see you about. We were wondering if you planned on going to the Kanton's afterwards."

"No. It's too late."

"It's never too late. There's usually a group of people there all night." She was right on that score and I knew it.

"Well, I suppose we can. I'll ask Byron."

Byron agreed and when we arrived he stayed outside to talk with several friends who were standing by a car drinking. I walked into the house and found Ann and Nancy in the kitchen. Upon seeing me, Nancy asked, "Do you want something to drink?"

"Sure," I said. It was the first time anyone had offered me a drink at the Kanton's,

"Where's Roger?" I asked as Nancy handed me a beer.

"I think he's already in bed," Ann cut in. "Let's go into the living room and talk."

The three of us walked into the living room and I found

myself completely alone with these two older women. It was almost as if they had planned it that way, and in a way I believe they did.

"Let's sit together on the sofa," Ann suggested.

She sat down and patted the seat next to her. I sat down, and Nancy sat on the other side of me.

"Terry, have you ever done a threesome?" Ann asked.

I'd like to say I remember every word spoken, but I don't. I do remember standing and walking around as they made suggestive comments. I remember sitting back down, and I remember Nancy putting her hand on my leg, but that was it. I was an ignorant sixteen-year-old. I'd never heard of a threesome, let alone participate in one. Heck, I'd never come close to experiencing a twosome and here they were; two older women hinting at having sex with me.

At some point during this unexpected and bizarre game Ann told me to kiss Nancy and that's when my summer of '62 came to an abrupt halt. For when I attempted to kiss her, she suddenly stood and said, "That's not how you kiss a woman," and with that, they both flashed a "gotcha" smile and left. A few seconds later I heard them laughing and giggling in the kitchen. Dumbfounded by what had taken place, I got up, and left by the side door—the one seldom used.

A week later, I learned that Nancy had left Minnesota to marry an older man from North Dakota. Not just any older man, but a senior. Was she pregnant and, if so, who was the father? As for Ann, we would run into each other again, but we never spoke.

Things moved quickly after that. This event had taken place on a Friday evening. On the following morning, while sitting at the breakfast table, Florence informed me that Arnold and the crew would be home on Sunday. Bob and I had finished swathing the grain fields on the home place, so I knew exactly what this meant—it was time for harvesting. What I didn't see coming took place that very Saturday afternoon. That's when Bob decided it was time to show me how tough he really was.

At the beginning of the summer, Florence had questioned me in front of family members about my sports activities. During the conversation, I had talked about my sophomore year in wrestling, but I didn't expect Bob, who was a good six inches taller and fifty pounds heavier, to be envious of this. Over the two-plus months I had worked with him, he'd said things like, "So you think you're tough?" or "I think I could show you a thing or two," but I had never taken him seriously.

I was stacking bales in the haymow when Bob suddenly appeared and without warning, he wrapped his arms tightly around my neck.

"Let's see how tough you really are," he said into my ear.

Instinctively, I pushed his elbow away from my neck and effortlessly slid my head out of his grasp. The move to free myself took less than two seconds and I ended up behind him. I then bent down, wrapped my arms around his legs, and with my shoulder, I drove him forward. Had he been my weight, he would have gone down immediately, but with the extra fifty pounds, it took some shoving to topple him.

From that point on, I kept him under control. When he attempted to strike me or to get onto his knees, I would push him back onto his belly; his face rubbing against the coarse straw in the bales. This continued unabated until finally, he mumbled something about his "hand hurting" so I released him, and he left without saying another word.

On Sunday afternoon, my services were terminated. Did the fight have anything to do with this? Probably not. My work was done: the cultivating and baling seasons were over, and I wasn't needed for harvesting. So, I packed my things, jumped into my car, and drove to my parents' farm.

On the trip home, a new problem surfaced. I had first noticed a faint knocking sound coming from the car's engine after my last outing with Byron. I didn't give it much thought but during the drive back to my parents' farm it suddenly turned into a loud banging.

When I got home, I asked Dad to listen and without hesitation he said, "I think you've thrown a rod."

"What's a rod?" I asked.

"Rods are connected to the crankshaft," he answered. "Put your car in the garage and I'll show you."

I parked in the garage and with some timely instruction, I unbolted the engine from the frame, lifted it out with a pulley, and took the oil pan off.

"That's the crankshaft," Dad said, pointing at an oil infiltrated shaft that ran the full length of the engine's belly.

"So, where's the rod?"

"This is a six-cylinder engine, so it has six rods. Each rod is connected to the crankshaft and at the other end there's a piston that goes up into the motor. When gas enters the engine, it explodes and pushes the piston down. This turns the crankshaft, which then turns the wheels of the car."

"So, which one is broken?" I asked.

"Well, it looks like I was wrong. None of the rods are broken so most likely it's one of the bearings that connects the rod to the crankshaft," and with that, he started rocking each of the rods back and forth.

"This is most likely the bad one," he finally said, pointing at the second one from the end.

"So, what do I have to do to fix it?"

"Well, you'll have to take the crankshaft off and have it ground down and then replace the bearing."

I had it back in running order before the start of football practice and while doing this, I helped Dad with combining and bailing. I also cleaned both the cow barn and the chicken coop. If he had farmed me out to teach me to work, he was sorely mistaken. Working for the Stock's had been a vacation.

CHAPTER 40
Third Down

Junior Year

Once football players reached their junior year, they were automatically placed on the varsity squad and, unlike previous seasons, practice began one week before the start of school, not on the first day of school.

I didn't show up for practice with expectations of playing in a varsity game, but I did hope that the coach would call on me if an injury occurred to the backup quarterback. Of course, I was also a punter. I can't say with any certainty that I was a good punter, but I had continued practicing in hopes that this would lead to my getting into a varsity game.

Interestingly, it was my punting skill that turned into some unforgettable moments at quarterback, but not at the varsity level.

Not long after the start of the season, the head football coach, Mr. Hoskins, pulled me aside and said, "Terry, Mr. Jacobson was wondering if you would be willing to play in a

B-squad game on Friday. You don't have to, but their punter is injured, and he doesn't have a backup."

"Can I do that?" I asked.

"Yeah, I don't think anyone will care. Besides, it's only for one game. Give it some thought and get back to me."

I wasn't excited about the idea. For me, it was a demotion, not a promotion, but I didn't know how to say no, so after practice I told Mr. Hoskins I'd do it.

I don't remember the name of the opponent and I must admit that I didn't keep track of what was taking place on the field. Instead, I sat on the bench my head resting on my hands, my elbows on my legs waiting for someone to let me know when it was time to punt.

Unexpectedly, Mr. Jacobson appeared in front of me. "Terry, weren't you a quarterback when you played for us last year?"

"Yes."

"OK, we need a quarterback. Chuck turned his ankle on that last play. Are you up for it?"

"Sure," I said. What's the down?"

"It's third and ten, so get out there and get us a first down."

I ran onto the field and called the team into a huddle. "All right," I said. "Square out to the right."

Pulling the receiver to the side, I said, "Make sure you go down exactly ten yards, and when you make the turn, look for the ball because it's going to be there."

And that's what happened. I hit the receiver as soon as he turned, and we made a first down.

Again, I called the players into a huddle, but before I could call the play, the first-string quarterback tapped me on the shoulder, and said, "I'm back."

"Good job, Terry!" the coach yelled as I passed him on the

way back to where I had been sitting.

I didn't bother to respond. Instead, I took my helmet off and threw it on the ground. They're beating the pants off us, the quarterback isn't doing a thing, and the coach benches me after I get them a first down.

Time passed and again my mind drifted away from what was taking place on the field.

"Terry, get out there!" I suddenly head the coach yell.

What the heck, I though. I've only been sitting here for a few minutes and now he wants me to replace the quarterback again.

Not knowing or bothering to ask what the down was, I ran back onto the field and called the players into a huddle. "Quarterback sneak to the left," I said. Then, on the way to the line of scrimmage, I grabbed the center. "Pinch to your right and take the middle linebacker out." And that's what he did as I ran through the middle of the line for another first down.

I called for another huddle but, again, the first-string quarterback came out and tapped me on the shoulder.

"I'm back."

As I ran past the coach this time, I noticed that he had a dirty look on his face. What's that all about? I thought and with that, I took my helmet off, threw it on the ground.

Five or ten minutes later, I again heard my name called. "Terry, you're in."

When I ran onto the field, I noticed that we were a good ten yards back from where we had been when I had left the field before. Suspecting that we had to make some good yardage this time, I huddled the team up and said, "OK, here's what we're going to do. I want the receiver on the right side to go down ten yards, make a turn to the right to do a square out, but when the defensive player makes his move, turn back to your left and go straight downfield. I'm going to arch the ball high over your left shoulder. Got it?" I shouted.

He nodded in agreement and a minute later we had another first down.

As I called the team to huddle up again, I heard some yelling on the sidelines. Not only did I see the quarterback running toward me, but I also saw the coach waving his arms and stomping his feet. *What the heck did I do now?* I thought.

This time, as I ran past the coach, he yelled, "That's the second time I've sent you out to punt on fourth down, and what do you do, you call a stupid play. You're damn lucky you got a first down both times, but when I want you to punt, you punt, is that understood?"

I shook my head in disgust and gave him my best don't-bother-to-put-me-in-there-again look and he never called my name again. Our team lost by a large margin and the coach never called on me again.

As things turned out, I did get to play in a varsity game. It was against the town of Alexandria. The town had a population of around twenty-three thousand in 1962, while Elbow Lake maxed out at thirty-five hundred. In those days, schools weren't divided into sections determined by enrollment. This made for some exciting moments in Minnesota sports, especially whenever a small town would go on to win a state championship.

On average, the Alexandria players were noticeably bigger. Someone sitting on the bench next to me mentioned the word cyclops, and it fit. Their size advantage also had a direct bearing on the score: Cyclops 24–David (as in David and Goliath) 0. I don't recall the actual score, but they were beating us by a large margin and they were marching in for another touchdown when Coach Hoskins stopped in front of where I was sitting.

"Degner," he shouted. "Get in there for Ron."

He was talking about Ron Ehlers. Not only was he our middle linebacker, but he was almost twice my size.

Startled by the idea of playing defense but in compliance, I stood and started to move toward the field. Before I took one step, however, Mr. Oysted, the assistant football coach, put a hand on my shoulder.

"Sit down, Terry," he said in a quiet but commanding voice. "You're not going anywhere."

Breathing a sigh of relief, I sat back down.

After the next play, Mr. Hoskins again approached me. "Terry, I thought I told you to go in there for Ron. Now, get out there!"

Unfortunately, Mr. Oysted wasn't in the vicinity to stop me this time so I got up and ran out to where the team had gathered in the end zone. Walking up to Ron, I yelled, "The coach told me to come in for you!"

Ron and the rest of the team looked at me in disbelief. Hell, I couldn't believe it myself. What was I doing out here? I was a midget compared to the rest of the players. But, without saying anything Ron ran off the field, leaving me to again wonder— *What the hell was the coach thinking and what was I doing out here?*

My thoughts were interrupted when I heard the "Cyclops" clap their hands. Then I watched as they came up to the line of scrimmage. *What am I supposed to do? And where do I stand?*

Heck, I'd never practiced playing defense and here I was, playing middle linebacker at the varsity level against some giants who were on the five-yard line moving in for a touchdown.

In total ignorance, I positioned myself in the center of the field behind the defensive line and watched as the offense positioned themselves at the line of scrimmage. As they did, I couldn't help but notice that the entire line, the quarterback, and even the running backs, were looking directly at me.

"Ready, set," the quarterback shouted.

The linemen went down on all fours.

"Hut one, hut two," the quarterback yelled, and then everything became a blur.

I don't know who hit me first. All I remember is being knocked flat on my back, then I heard the whistle signaling a touchdown. I got up, checked to see if all my limbs were still intact, and walked off the field.

As it turned out, it was the only varsity game I played in during my junior year and, for this, I should have been awarded a varsity letter. I'm still waiting Mr. Hoskins.

CHAPTER 41
Goodbye Coach!

Junior Year continued....

Mark Neilson took over as the head wrestling coach in 1963 and the change didn't help my situation. By situation, I mean the lack of a male guiding hand when it came to weight loss. I didn't have an ounce of fat on my body to lose and deep-down, I knew it. Despite this, I couldn't stop myself. Whenever a tournament was drawing near, I would feel a calling to go down in weight because that's what other wrestlers did. I needed a male father figure in my life; one who would stand firm and say, "No! Stay at your normal weight. Losing weight can only hurt you!" Unfortunately, Mr. Neilson didn't fit that calling.

So, with the Heart O' Lakes Conference just around the corner and my win-loss record at 9-0, I made the stupid decision of going down in weight and it cost me dearly.

My co-conspirator was Mr. Van Swol, the chemistry teacher. When I told him about my wish to lose weight, he said, "Instead of going to lunch, why don't you stay here in class and eat with me."

"What do you eat?" I asked.

"I eat from the caskets of grain meal I have in the back room of the lab."

"Really? I won't get sick?"

"No. I do it all the time, but I'll warn you, it isn't tasty. You'll have to drink lots of water to wash it down, but you'll definitely lose weight."

For the next week and a half, I ate dried wheat germ, flax, oats, and chopped-up corn. It was dry and tasteless, but within a short time frame, I lost ten pounds. Then, a few days before we took on the Fergus Falls wrestling team, the effects of starving myself hit...and hit hard.

Wrestle-offs took place on Thursday, with matches taking place on Friday. The coach would call out the weight class, and the wrestlers who fell into that class would wrestle each other to see who would represent the team on Friday. Usually, the coach would say, "Terry, what weight class do you want to wrestle on Friday?"

I would tell him, and then he'd half-heartedly ask the other wrestlers, "Anyone feel up to challenging Terry?"

With maybe a few exceptions, there hadn't been any takers since the eighth grade. But on the day before the match with Fergus, a senior on the team held up his hand.

"I will," he said.

I'm not sure what the score was when the match came to a stop, or how long we wrestled, for that matter. What I do remember is the total fatigue I felt. I simply could not get my body to respond to what my mind told it to do. It was, in every respect, the return of what I had gone through the year before.

It wasn't until the senior shoved me off the mat and against a scalding hot radiator that the coach called an end to the match. Again, I don't remember the score, but the coach called the match in favor of the senior. It was the first and only time that I would lose a wrestle-off.

"It looks like you've got some burns on your back," the coach said, after inspecting the back of my right shoulder—the burns later turned into large blisters.

After practice, I told the coach about the fatigue, but instead of mentoring me to gain the weight back, he said, "Take it easy for a couple of days. I'm sure you'll feel better."

I thought about staying home from school that Friday, but after eating a big supper and getting a good night's sleep, I felt better, so I changed my mind and drove to school. I also hadn't planned on traveling with the team to the wrestling match that evening but when I told the coach this, he responded by saying, "If you don't go, you're off the team."

I should have taken him up on the offer. I say that because during the bus trip to Fergus, he badgered me continually about filling in for an open weight class. The class he was referring to was two weights above my own. On top of that, the Fergus wrestler at that weight was the captain and the top wrestler on their team. I knew this because I had gone up against him during the holiday season. Instead of practicing with the Elbow Lake team, I'd practiced with the Fergus Falls team.

"Terry, we don't have anyone wrestling in the one forty-five class. Do you think you could fill in?"

"I have blisters on my back," I said.

"Well, we need someone to fill that spot, and a few blisters shouldn't stop you."

"I didn't bring any clothes."

"What size shoe do you wear?"

"Eight and a half," I said.

"Does anyone here wear eight and a half shoes?" he shouted above the roar of the bus engine.

"I do," one of the wrestlers said.

"Will you let Terry wear them after you're done wrestling?"

"Sure, I guess."

"What about a jockstrap and socks?" I asked.

"I'm sure he'll let you wear his jockstrap and socks, too," he said.

"What about a uniform?"

"I have the uniform."

Had he thought about this ahead of time? Of course. Did he believe me—did he believe what I had told him about being fatigued? No. He had not been with the team the year before—he had no idea about what weight loss had done to my body.

I did not want to wrestle, and it disgusted me to think about wearing someone else's sweaty clothes, but the coach wouldn't let up. He kept badgering me until I finally gave in.

Except for the blisters on my back, I did feel better. I wasn't back to normal, but with four square meals behind me and lots of water, I was not nearly as fatigued as I had been during the wrestle-off.

As for the match, my opponent won by a few points. Later, on the trip home, I decided I'd had enough. On Monday, I deserted the team. Some questioning disapprovals did take place, but not from the coach. Apparently both my mother and sister had enjoyed watching me wrestle so, in unison, they reprimanded me. Dad, on the other hand, saw the benefits—he put me to work.

CHAPTER 42

Him Again!

Junior Year continued….

With one exception, the academics want as they always had—test scores high, homework zero, grades poor. Besides English and Social Studies, I took basic physics and math, and I continued to read everything I could get my hands on.

The exception was choir. I hadn't looked at a single musical note since the day Mr. Peterson kicked me out of band, but I still had an inner desire to be able to read music. I knew the rudimentary principles, but I wanted to be able to pick up a sheet of music and know instantly what each note meant.

An opening occurred at the beginning of the year when I ran into Mr. Brown. Mr. Brown was our new choir director. He had an inviting persona, and this, more than anything, is what gave me reason to hope that I could get into his class.

Due to the relationship I'd had with Mr. Peterson, I cautiously approached Mr. Brown at the beginning of the school year.

"Mr. Brown, could I be in choir?"

"I'd love to have you. Are you first or second tenor?"

"I'm first tenor," I responded hesitantly. I had been a sopra-no when I played the lead in *Amahl and the Night Visitors,* but my voice had changed—I just didn't know what it had changed to, but I knew that I didn't have a deep voice.

"OK. Well, you can certainly join us in class."

"What room do I go to?" I asked.

"We practice in the band room, so I'll see you there tomor-row, and if you have any questions or you need help, don't hesitate to ask. Can you read music?"

"A little," I said, hesitantly. It wasn't his question that caused the uncertainty, it was his reference to the band room. What if Mr. Peterson sees me there?

"That's OK. I'm sure you'll do just fine" Mr. Brown said, and that's how I got into choir.

On the following day, I took a seat in a packed band room. Upon seeing me, Mr. Brown said, "Terry, please come down. Let's do a test to see where you belong."

I walked to where he sat at the piano and, after singing the notes he played, he said, "I think we'll put you with the first tenor's and with that he seated me behind the sopranos with the other first tenors.

I enjoyed singing with the other students, but regrettably, the welcome mat was pulled out from under me before the end of the first week.

"Terry, would you please come to the front of the room after class," Mr. Brown announced unexpectedly.

I made my way to the front of the class as the other students were in the process of leaving and stopped as I neared him.

"You wanted to see me, Mr. Brown?"

"Yes. Terry, I'm not sure how to tell you this, so I'll come right out and say it. Mr. Peterson told me you can't be in choir."

"What? What does Mr. Peterson have to do with it?"

"He's the head of music and I have to follow his orders.

That was the end of my music career at Elbow Lake but, ironically, Mr. Brown gave me a B in choir at the end of the year, despite the fact that I had only attended choir for one week.

I never confronted Mr. Peterson about the numerous times he had interfered in my life. I'm not even sure I could have if I'd tried for whenever I passed him in the hallway, he would make a point of staying as far away from me as possible and from the look on his face, it was deliberate.

Except for two other occurrences, the rest of the school year was relatively uneventful. One had to do with a fight. I hadn't gotten into fights since my days on the school bus with the Dohmeyer brothers, but they hadn't really been fights, they had been more like scuffles.

The incident I'm referring to took place on the schoolyard. The boy in question was the son of a local bar owner, and it started after I made an inquiring comment about something he had told another boy.

"I understand you've been watching girls go to the bathroom in your dad's bar. Is that right?" I asked.

"What the f****'s it to you?" he growled.

"I was just asking. I'm not going to play pool there anymore. Hell, you'll probably be watching me when I go to the bathroom."

The fight itself was short-lived. It lasted five seconds at most. The boy took a wild swing at me with his right hand, but instead of stepping back or ducking, I moved in closer, which affectively negated his punch—it landed on my back and not my head. I grabbed his upper arm with my left hand and, bending over, I pulled his torso downward. Then, I shoved my right forearm between his legs and hoisted him over my shoulders. Once there, I threw him over my head and he landed with a thud on the ground at my feet. Before he could get up, I grabbed him from behind in a wrestler's hold and held him in place.

As this was taking place, some students had gathered around to watch and shortly thereafter, Mr. Wilcox, the English teacher, dropped in for a visit. He was on his way home for dinner and we were directly in his path.

"What's going on here?" he said, shoving a student aside to get a better view. "Oh, it's just you, Terry. Well, don't hurt him and make sure you get back to school before the bell rings." And with that, he walked off.

I often think about that incident when I hear stories about bullies and the actions teachers are forced to take today. Was I the bully or was I the one who put an end to the acts of a bully? Or, in this case, the act of a sexual predator? What I do know is had I done today what I did in 1963, I'd be in trouble.

Mr. Wilcox couldn't have known who had started the fight, but he knew the boy was bigger, and he may have known about his reputation. He could also see that I had things under control and that I wasn't hurting him.

The second incident wasn't as dramatic, but it holds a special significance for me. As the school year was coming to an end, Mr. Reeves, the school counselor, called me into his office for a one on one.

"The purpose of this session," he said as I sat down in a chair across from his desk, "is to help you plan for the future."

Mr. Reeves was a likeable person. Physically, he reminded me of Bob Stock with his dark hair and good looks, but unlike Bob, he came across as a serious academic.

"Terry, have you given any thought to what you want to do after you leave school?" Before I could answer he continued, "I suppose you plan on taking over your father's farm someday?"

"No, I'm going to college."

He paused, looked down at the papers on his desk, and said, "Well, I'm looking at your grades, Terry, and I think you'll have a tough time getting into college. If you don't want to farm, you might want to consider the military or a trade school, but I think college is probably out of the question."

"No" I said, decisively, "I'm going to college,"

I didn't know how to tell him about the promises I had made to God; the first of which was college, but as I look back on it now, even that wouldn't have changed his mind. I was learning, and I knew it, but I also knew that I wasn't playing their game—my grades were terrible.

"Do you know where you'll go to college?" Mr. Reeves asked.

"Yes."

"Where?"

"The University of Minnesota," I replied.

I'd attended a football game there at the beginning of the school year, and I fell in love with the campus. There was something about the old buildings that made me feel at home, and seeing the students walking around gave me a sense of belonging.

"Well, good luck with that, and if I can be of any help,

please let me know," and that ended his consulting session. I never asked him for help, and we never talked again.

During the school year I did read one fictional story that has had special meaning in my life, and in the lives of my children. The name of the book is *Forever Amber* by Kathleen Winsor. It isn't a classic, as books go, but it was popular for a time and a movie sprang from it.

What intrigued me was the heroine's character. Simply put, she did what she had to in order to survive. In the end, she allowed the father of her son, a son she loved dearly, to take him to the new world without her. It was an act of altruism. At the time, I associated this with my own birth mother's actions. She, too, had given up her children so they could have a better life.

I was so overwhelmed with the heroine's actions that I promised myself if I ever had daughters, I would name them after the main character. Thus, all three of my daughters have Amber in their name. A name that has now been passed down to my granddaughters. It is my hope that they, too, will do whatever it takes to care of their children, and that they would always be there for each other.

Before I knew it, the baseball season came to an end. I didn't pitch or play in any games, but I did get a varsity letter—not in wrestling, in baseball.

CHAPTER 43

The Chicago Cab Driver & Family

Summer of 1963

Dad shipped me off to Underwood, Minnesota, at the end of the school year. How he found the job and why, is again, unknown. For eleven solid weeks, I milked cows and worked in the fields for the Green family. For this, I received seventy-five-cents an hour—a twenty-five-cent raise over the previous year.

Ray and Eileen Green had an unusual story. Eileen had grown up in the Fergus Falls area. In 1943, she moved to Chicago to work for the US Treasury Department. Ray had grown up in a lumber community in Wisconsin. After his school days, he moved to Chicago and took up taxi driving.

In 1949, Ray and Eileen met during a New Year's Eve church service. They later married, and not wanting to raise their children in Chicago, they moved to Minnesota. In 1952, with the help of Eileen's uncle, they rented and then bought a dairy farm. The taxi had moved with them. It sat rusting on tireless rims in the mud to the left of the barn.

By the time I arrived, Mrs. Green had given birth to four children: three boys and one girl. (They later added another girl.) Randy, the oldest, was big enough to help around the farm. Except for meal times, I seldom saw or interacted with the other children.

The Greens had forty-one milk cows and they sold Grade A milk. This meant early morning and late evening chores, white-washed interior walls, and no heavy lifting as the milk went directly from the cow through a sterile pipeline into a bulk tank.

I cleaned the barn a few times over the summer months, but Mr. Green did most of the cleaning, while I attended to the fieldwork. They had more cows, but cleaning the gutters was easier. Instead of a single row of stanchions, they had four. The two gutters behind the stanchions in the center of the barn were cleaned at the turn of a switch. When the switch was turned on, a metal bar would pull the straw-less manure across holes built into the gutter. The manure would fall into the holes and be swept away by currents of water that flowed into a giant tank. The holes were like the street drain vents you see in towns. Once a week, a company in town would send out a truck to empty the tank. They then sold the manure to local farmers for fertilizer.

The gutters behind the other two rows of stanchions did have to be cleaned by hand. This waste, unlike the watered-down variety, was used to fertilize the Green's land. Using a shovel instead of a fork, Mr. Green would throw the manure into a wheelbarrow and dump it into a spreader that sat below floor level at the far end of the barn. As he didn't mix in straw and he did this on a daily basis, the process didn't take long.

The Green's farmed approximately one hundred acres, and like the previous summer, I did most of the cultivating and the bailing. Bailing was easier. Instead of using a wagon, they used a skid. It was like the skid we had used for picking up rock, but with one exception: the center had a three-inch gap that ran from front to back.

The Green's oldest son would drive while I piled the bales. When the skid was full, which amounted to about fifteen bales, I would slam a six-foot steel rod into the ground through the opening in the center of the skid. Holding firmly onto the rod while the tractor continued moving, the bales would slide off the skid onto the ground where they would stay until need-ed—like the large round bales you see in fields today.

Mrs. Green was an excellent cook and while we ate, both she and Ray showed a genuine interest in me. They asked ques-tions about my social life, about sports, and about my dreams for the future. I remember coming to the sad realization that, except for Grandpa Ash, they knew more about my ambitions than my parents.

Because of the cows, I worked longer hours. For that reason, my social life wasn't as active as it had been when I worked for Arnold Stock. The Greens took every other Saturday off to socialize with family and friends. On those Saturdays I worked from sunup to sundown. I did have every Sunday and every other Saturdays off. On the off days, Byron and I would meet in Fergus and find something to do, or I would just stay in my room and read. The *Summer of '62* days were behind me.

I did go home twice. On one Saturday evening, I told By-ron that I needed to go home "the next day" to pick up some extra clothes. As he had never been to our farm, he volunteered to go with me, so I picked him up on Sunday morning and off we went.

I didn't expect to find anyone at home in the early afternoon. Usually, Mom, Dad, and Jean went to the Gehrkes' after church. But, to my surprise, Mom walked out of the house as Byron and I were getting out of the car.

"Hi!" I said, "I didn't expect to see you. Are Dad and Jean here?"

"No. I'm the only one here today, Terry. Dad's helping Harry, and Jean's baby sitting. What are you doing home?"

"I just stopped by to get some extra clothes. This is Byron Stock, Mom. I don't know if you ever saw him at Bible school or not, but he wanted to see where I lived."

"Hi, Byron. No, I don't think we've met before, but thank you for coming."

Instead of inviting us into the house, as she normally would have done, Mom looked at me, and said, "I'm glad you stopped by, Terry, but I'm afraid you're not going to like what I have to say."

"What do you mean" I asked. "Did I do someone wrong?"

"Oh no, I didn't mean to put it that way. It's not you. Your grandpa stopped by to feed the cows, and he forgot to turn off the water. I'm afraid the barn is completely flooded."

Flooded was an understatement. When I opened the door and looked inside, I saw brown watery waste everywhere and from what I could tell, it had to be above my ankles

"What do you want me to do?" I asked.

"I'm sorry. I'm sure you have plans for the afternoon, but someone has to clean the barn and you're the only one here. I'd do it, but I don't think I can."

Looking at Byron, I shook my head in disgust. "I'm sorry, but I guess I'll have to stay and take care of this mess. You can take the car into town and come back for me later if you want."

"No, no, I'll help you," he said, shrugging. "If we both do

it, we can still get to Skogmo's in time to meet Richard and the other guys."

"Are you sure?" I asked. "You don't have to."

"Yeah, what the heck. This won't take long."

With that, we both rolled up our sleeves and went to work. We couldn't use the manure spreader because the gook was too watery, so I opened several windows on the west side of the barn and, using shovels instead of pitchforks, we started flinging the brown watery mess through the open 2 1/2' X 2 1/2' windows and into the barnyard, which was half-mud, half-manure anyway.

The shovels weren't funnels and the small windows didn't make good targets. Our engineer boots kept our feet dry but some of the watery waste would miss a window and hit the wall, which caused a splash back and with that, brown spots began to appear on our clothes and body parts.

"This is going to take forever," I finally said. "Let's try something else."

With that I walked over and picked up a five-gallon pail. Swinging it into the watery mess, I fill it about half full and threw it out the window.

"That'll make things go faster," I said, and sure enough it did. But, we quickly found that more of the watery waste hit the wall instead of the opening, and the splash back was worse than it had been with the shovels. By the time we finished we were drenched from head to toe in smelly shit—our hair was drenched, brown blotches covered our face and hands, and our clothes were dripping wet.

When we were finally done, we walked outside to the well next to the water tank. I picked up a hose and sprayed Byron from head to foot and he did the same to me. Then, we went to the house to take a bath. Mom thought we were both nuts when we walked in the door, but when we told her what had happened, she let out a giggle and we all had a good laugh.

After the bath, I changed into some of the clothes I had come to pick up and I gave Byron a clean set of clothes to wear. Then, after saying our goodbyes, we headed for Fergus and the Skogmo Café.

The first thing Richard said when we sat down in the booth next to him was, "What's that smell? What have you guys been doing all afternoon?"

"Oh, pitching shit," I said, and for the next six months, whenever one of our friends would run into us, they would say, "Been pitching any shit lately?"

I did go home a second time, but not to get clothes. I went because someone had told me about an upcoming party that would take place on Saturday evening—not just any party, a kegger; as in beer keg. I'd never been to a kegger, but I'd heard plenty of stories about them.

The party's host lived on a farm north of Wendell. I didn't know the host very well, but I went to school with one of his younger brothers. Knowing that Byron had to work late, I decided that I'd drop in and say hi to my parents and then stop at the kegger on the way back to Fergus.

Nothing special took place at home. At lease, nothing that sticks out. I do remember leaving our farm around six and arriving at the kegger somewhere around six-twenty. Pulling into their long driveway, I found the fields on both sides filled with cars. In each field, a person was directing traffic. I drove into the field on the left and, following instructions, parked at the end of a second row of cars.

I had to walk about fifty yards from my car to a wooded area that surrounded the farmyard. When I cleared the woods, I came face to face with dozens of teens and twenty-somethings. They were talking and laughing and milling around a large keg of beer that sat atop a pile of bales. I approached the throng to not only see if I knew any of them but to get a better feel for acceptance—would I be a welcomed visitor or out of my element?

However, before I got to the edge of the crowd, someone shouted, "Your parents are coming. They just turned into the driveway!"

With that, people started running in all directions. I didn't know if this was a joke, or if it was for real. Then, out of nowhere, the host (oldest brother) spotted me, ran over to where I stood, and said, "Terry, where's your car?"

"It's over there," I said, pointing in the direction of where I'd parked.

"I need your help. Let's take the keg and put it in your car," he said, motioning for me to follow him.

Between the two of us, we carried the heavy keg to my car and stuck it in the trunk. Meanwhile, cars were flowing in all directions. Some were using the fields to get to the highway, while others were getting back onto the driveway and fleeing.

"Terry, I want that keg back," the host said as I slid inside my car. Without answering, I pulled onto the driveway and took off for Fergus.

As I drove the twenty miles to town, I kept hearing rumbling noises coming from the trunk. *The keg's rolling around*, I thought. But, with no way of securing it, I kept driving.

It wasn't until I reached town that I heard another noise. As I was driving down Main Street, I began to hear a rhythmic hissing sound. Looking in the rearview mirror I saw a wet streak in the middle of the pavement—the keg was leaking beer onto the road.

Fearful of the police, I pulled over and parked against the curb. Getting out, I opened the trunk and, sure enough, the empty spare tire well was filled with foaming beer, which was leaking onto the road through a hole at the bottom of the well. In his haste to put the keg into my trunk, the host had failed to take the pump handle out and replace it with the plug that came with the keg.

Not having any options to speak of, I turned the keg around so the handle faced upward. Then, looking around to make sure there were no police in the vicinity, I got back in the car, and drove to the Kanton's. Once there, I told the gathering what had taken place, and everyone had a good laugh. After that, they proceeded to drink what was left of the beer.

A week or two later, I ran into the older brother at the pavilion and returned the empty keg. When I told him what had happened, he laughed and that ended the kegger party.

I didn't return home again until the start of football practice. On the first day back and before practice began, Dad and I had a short conversation, during which he made a point of telling me that he had missed my common sense and my work habits.

Unbeknownst to me, someone had been helping him around the farm while I was gone and he had become frustrated with the help. How much help he didn't say, and I didn't ask.

The common-sense part was rather interesting. According to my father, the person in question, was disking in the field one day when a rock got stuck between two disks. Instead of coming up with a solution, his helper brought the disk all the way back to the farmyard. As Dad put it, "If that would've happened to you, you would've found a way to solve the problem on the spot."

The work habit suggestion, on the other hand, struck me as wishful—it almost sounded as if he had thoughts of me taking over the farm someday.

On another note, while I was gone Dad had purchased an Allis Chalmers diesel tractor to replace the H and the 44. Both had aged, and neither had a built-in hydraulic system. The Allis Chalmers was powerful enough to pull our three-bottom plow, and the hydraulic system made it possible to lift the plow out of the ground mechanically, instead of manually.

My social life had also changed. I wasn't the church goer I had been in my youth, and even when I lived at home, I wasn't around most Friday or Saturday evenings. I loved dancing, so I would go to dances in Elbow Lake or to the American Legion pavilion in Fergus. I did have a few dates, but nothing that amounted to anything. That wouldn't happen until later in the fall of my senior year.

The biggest change that summer had to do with my size. I had finally grown. I now stood at five feet ten, and weighed one hundred and forty-five pounds. I still had skinny legs, but I had a thick and powerful chest. *Finally, a force to be reckoned with in football,* I thought.

CHAPTER 44
Homecoming

Senior Year

For some students, twelfth grade is anticlimactic. For me, the school year was filled with drama and highpoints, and even a few unsettling moments. It all started when the football coach announced on the first day of practice that we were switching from the T formation, to the San Francisco 49ers shotgun formation.

With the T formation, the quarterback stands directly behind the center and some ten feet directly behind him is a fullback; flanked by two running backs. With the shotgun formation, the quarterback; instead of taking the snap directly from the center, stands where the fullback used to stand; flanking by a fullback and one running back. The third, or missing running back, instead of standing in the backfield, is now a second receiver.

The 49ers first introduced this system in 1960 but instead of using it only on third downs, as many teams do today, they used it on every down. At first it worked, but opposing teams quickly adjusted and the 49ers dropped back down into the losing column.

Why Mr. Hoskins decided to use this formation and, worse yet, why he eliminated the position of quarterback is unknown, but he did. Instead, of the quarterback calling plays and taking the snap, the center would snap the ball directly to the fullback or to one of the two running backs and the fullback called the play in the huddle. Upon hearing this, I realized that my play calling and passing skills were no longer needed and my height and weight gain had been for naught.

An answer to what I could do to make the team came when I saw Butch Beckman watching from the sideline. Butch, a past member of the team and a Wendell boy, was not only a well-known football and basketball player, but at the time, he was the starting running back for St. John's University.

Walking over to where he stood, I said, "Hi Butch, what are you doing here?"

"We don't have practice until the end of the week, so I thought I'd drop by to see how things are shaping up."

"Can you give me some pointers?" I asked.

"I'll try," he said. "What do you need?"

"I've always been a quarterback, but because of this new system, I was thinking of switching to running back. What would I have to do to become a starter?"

"That's simple," he said, "if you're the best blocker on the team, the coach can't keep you out of the starting lineup."

With those words of wisdom and some pointers, I began to work on my blocking skills. I imagined I was the best blocker on the team, and then I went about proving it. When I ran interference, I did what Butch showed me. I used finesse. First and foremost, I made sure the opponent in front of me was a direct threat to the runner. Then I either took him down at the legs, or I moved him out of the running lane. Like Butch said, "If you're the best blocker, the coach can't keep you out of the starting lineup." And that's exactly what happened—when the season opened, Jimmy Melville and I were the starting running backs.

Nothing dramatic occurred during the first couple of games. As planned, most of the ball carrying revolved around Jimmy, with me or the fullback blocking. With one exception, I do not recall running with the ball; although I believe I did, and we seldom, if ever, passed the ball.

That one exception took place during homecoming game. It was an end run to my left. The center hiked the ball directly to me and I took off running. When I was about ten feet beyond where the tight end normally stood, I saw an opening to my right. I planted my left foot to make a cutback against the grain, but as I did, a defensive lineman came down on top of me, driving my leg into the ground. I immediately felt a searing pain and went down screaming. Several teammates helped me off the field, and I sat on the bench for the remainder of the game.

Despite the injury, I was back at practice the next week. The coach, upon seeing me limp onto the field, said, "Terry, why don't you go to the other end of the field and practice punting."

Looking around, he spotted a center and yelled, "Lonnie, go with Terry. He needs someone to hike the ball to him."

It only took one attempt at punting for me to realize that the injury was more serious than I'd thought. To punt, I had to plant my left foot into the ground and then follow through with my right foot. When I attempted this, the searing pain returned. I kept trying, but the pain persisted until I finally gave up.

Mom took me to the doctor the next day. He took an X-ray and the scan showed a fracture in my femur bone. He then told me my playing days were over, and when I saw the X-ray, I knew he was right. I was lucky it hadn't snapped in two.

"But, here's the good news," the doctor said. "After the crack heals, the bone will be even stronger."

"How can that be?" I asked.

"Well, the simple answer," he said, "is that when the fracture heals, the bone will be thicker."

The doctor, to his credit, was trying to make me feel better and in a way he did, but my high school football days were over.

CHAPTER 45

"A Death in the Family"

Senior Year Continued....

Of all the teachers I had in high school, Bruce Wilcox was my favorite. He had been my English teacher for three straight years and at the end of each year a "D" appeared on my report card." But, I have reason to believe that he knew the grade did not fit the student.

At the very beginning of my senior year, Mr. Wilcox encouraged me to start writing the year-end paper.

"I know you don't have a lot of time on your hands, Terry, but if you start writing your year-end paper now, you'll have it done by the end of the school year and then I won't have to give you a D."

Those were his very words and he said it with kindness. He also saw something else in me. At the end of October, Mr. Wilcox handed me the lead role in a one-act play titled, *For Titus Two*. I say "handed" because I didn't try out for the part, he just told me, "Terry, the part's yours if you want it," and to this day, some members of the class remember vividly the first words spoken on the day the play was put on.

The play itself was, by all accounts, unremarkable, but the idea of playing the lead was both challenging and uplifting. I took the script home and I had the dialog memorized before the first rehearsal.

I should state here that our class put on two one-act plays. The other play was the comedy *The Trysting Place*. The main character in that play was played by Ronald Duda. In some ways, Ronald was my stage rival. I doubt if anyone other than Ronald and Mr. Wilcox knew about the rivalry, because it was low key and not something we, or maybe I should say, I, discussed—it wasn't gossip. When I asked Mr. Wilcox why we were putting on two plays, he said, "I thought both you and Ronald deserved to have leading roles."

The schedule had us performing the play for the student body in the afternoon of November 22, 1963. On the day of the performance, we (the cast) attended class in the morning as we normally did. Changing into costumes and putting on makeup had been scheduled for the early afternoon, and that's when another, more worldly, event stepped into the picture.

Around 1:15 p.m., the superintendent's voice came over the intercom. "Boys and girls, staff, and teachers," he said, "I have some sad news to tell you. We've just been informed that our beloved president, Mr. John F. Kennedy, has been shot. As we understand it, the president is on the way to the hospital, so we don't know the seriousness of his injury. We'll keep you informed of what's going on as the day progresses. For those of you who are in the class play, things will go on as scheduled, unless you hear otherwise."

The announcement came as a shock to everyone. Mr. Wilcox didn't know what to say, and the students didn't know how to react to this tragic news. After a brief pause, Mr. Wilcox excused himself, stating, "Keep studying. I'll be back in a few minutes," and with that he left the classroom. I assumed, as I'm sure the other students did, that he left to learn if there was more to the announcement than the superintendent had let on.

The room was silent at first but after a while the whole classroom erupted into what I can only describe as chaos—restrained but chaos, nonetheless.

"OK, those of you in the play can leave to get your makeup on," Mr. Wilcox said, when he walked back into the classroom a few minutes later.

"Why can't we go home?" or "Why don't they cancel classes?" shouted some of the students.

Mr. Wilcox answered by saying something about "not getting the busses to the school before the end of the school day," which made perfect sense. Besides, from a student management standpoint, both the students and the teachers needed something to take their minds off what was going on in the outside world—and the play was the perfect solution, or so they thought.

It was around two o'clock when Mr. Wilcox told the cast to leave for the lunchroom. Getting ready didn't take long. My makeup took the longest because I played an elderly lawyer, but even that didn't take long. In truth, the makeup and my costume looked ridiculous. Instead of a conservative pinstriped suit, I wore my one and only sports coat, a pair of tight, dark pants, and white socks. In the seated position, a good foot of the socks where in plain view to the audience. I doubt if any lawyer in the entire country, or in any other country for that matter, would have been caught dead in that outfit.

To give me an elderly look, the makeup artist whitened my hair. When done, it looked like someone had squeezed an entire tube of toothpaste in my hair and forgot to brush it out. I didn't blame the makeup artist, because she was given limited instructions and resources, but I certainly didn't look the part of an elderly gentleman.

Throughout the makeup process, the room was somber. I can't say with any certainty that the shooting of Kennedy was on the minds of the other cast members, but I must admit that it was the furthest thing from my mind. I had my part down, but the anxiety that comes with performing in front of a live audience is all-consuming; at least that's how it was for me.

About a half hour before curtain call, Mr. Wilcox came into the lunchroom and told us to take our places on stage. Instead of going through the auditorium, which is what we normally would have done, we walked through the kitchen and entered the stage through the back door.

The set was nonexistent. It consisted of one rectangular table taken from the lunchroom and seven folding chairs; also taken from the lunchroom. The backdrop was the cream-colored curtain that had been hanging against the back wall of the stage for as long as I could remember.

Upon reaching the stage, I walked over and took my seat at the head of the table, while the other cast members sat in chairs to my right, facing the audience. Then, we sat in silence for what seemed like an eternity, listening to the student body talking and moving about in the gymnasium.

The curtain was scheduled to open at 3:00 p.m. but before it did, I, again, heard the crack of the intercom. "Please, listen up." The superintendent said. "I have some more sad news to tell you. We've just been informed that President Kennedy was pronounced dead upon arrival at the hospital." There was a short pause and then, continuing, he said, "I know this is upsetting, but we've decided to go ahead with the play," and with those words, I heard sobbing coming from the other side of the curtain and several of the girls in the cast also began to cry. Then, very slowly, the curtain began to part.

When it was fully open, I stood and looking down at the cast, I said, in a voice that could clearly be heard by everyone in the audience, "This is a very sad and solemn occasion for all of us. There's been a death in the family."

It's difficult to describe what took place after I spoke those words as almost everyone in the building burst into tears—cries of anguish were every-where and they were loud. The cast, especially the girls, forgot half their lines. I found myself constantly reminding them of where we were at in the play. According to one person, we skipped six pages, but no one seemed to care—it was time to go home.

This is one of those, "what were you doing when" moments in life—one that I will never forget. Almost everyone born before 1955 has a story of what they were doing on the day President John F. Kennedy was shot. Over the years I've heard some good ones, but I believe this story is right up there near the top.

As for the year-end paper, Mr. Wilcox asked me in the middle of the school year if I had started writing it and I told him no. Then, one week before the end of the year, he asked again. When I told him no again, he said, "Give me one paragraph and I'll give you a C for the year." I ended up with another D,

Mr. Wilcox would, over the years, keep track of my academic and professional career through my mother. Once he even told her, "I knew he had it in him." I wish I had told him how much I enjoyed the opportunities he gave me. Unfortunately, I had more pressing things on my mind at the time, and now it's too late. I'll thank him in the next life but, for now, this will have to do. Thank you, Mr. Wilcox.

The full cast of *For Titus Two*. Terry is sitting to the far right in the photo.

CHAPTER 46

Back to Wrestling

Senior Year Continued....

On the day after the start of the winter sports season, two unexpected things occurred. As I was leaving the lunchroom one day, Mr. Jacobson, the varsity basketball coach, stopped me. "Terry," he said, "I understand you didn't go out for wrestling. Would you give some thought to playing basketball?"

The first thought that ran through my mind was, *Wow, now there's a sport I suck at.* I had played some basketball against the varsity when I had been on the wrestling team, but I certainly wouldn't have impressed him with my skills unless, of course, he was looking for a goon.

Then he added, "By the way, what grade are you in now?"

What? Why was he asking me that? I had had him as a teacher and as a football coach...and he didn't know I was a senior?

"I'm a senior," I answered.

"Oh!" He paused and then he looked quizzically at me, and said, "Well, it's probably a little too late to start playing now," and with that, my interview for a role on the basketball team ended.

The unexpected didn't end with Mr. Jacobson. Within the hour, Coach Neilson appeared out of nowhere. "Terry," he said. "We miss you. Would you consider coming out for wrestling again?"

He had never gone out of his way to talk to me during the school day. I would occasionally see him in the lunchroom with some of the other teachers, but this was a complete departure from anything he had ever done in the past.

"No, I don't think so," I answered. I wanted to tell him about my conversation with the basketball coach, just to see what his reaction would be, but I let it pass.

Then he said the unexpected, "The team voted you in as captain, Terry. They would really like it if you would reconsider joining the team."

I was astonished—I didn't know what to say. I had never imagined that members of the wrestling team would vote me in as their as captain.

"They voted me in as the captain?" I finally asked, my ego beginning to grasp what this meant.

"Actually, you'll be a co-captain. Keith Olson is the other captain but, yes, you'll be a captain.

The ego is a strange thing. I should have realized right then and there that he was making this up as he went along. The team hadn't voted me in as anything. Over the years I had never voted for a captain in football, wrestling, or baseball. The coach called the shots, not the team. In fact, I don't believe our wrestling team ever had a captain, let alone co-captains. They certainly didn't wear a 'C' on their uniforms.

"I'm not going down in weight," I shouted as he walked

away, and with that, I returned to wrestling.

I opened the season by taking first place in a tri-meet. From there I went on to win seventeen in a row, including the Heart-O-Lakes Conference championship. According to the coach, no one scored against me during the streak—a statistic that I can't verify because scores weren't recorded, but I will say the matches were generally easy.

I did manage to get the coaches ire up and he made a point of letting me know that he wasn't happy about what I had done.

Due to poor audience attendance at wrestling matches, the superintendent arranged for one match to take place during school hours. I do not remember the opposing school, but I remember my match and the impact it had on everyone involved, including me.

Within seconds of the start of the match, I had my opponent on his back but, as I pushed for the pin. a student in the stands started shouting, "Don't pin him, Terry, don't pin him."

He was laughing as he shouted those words and shortly afterwards some of the other students sitting next to him joined in.

Upon hearing and seeing this, the coach, who was sitting on a chair with my teammates, stood and shouted, "pin him, pin him, Terry, we need the points."

I continued playing with him, or so it seemed. Then between the second and third period the coach grabbed my arm, "Terry," he said, angrily," stop playing around—pin him. The team needs the points." I knew what he meant, a pin meant five team points, a non-pin, regardless of the score, meant three.

When the match came to an end and the referee raised my arm in victory, I heard loud laughter and cheering erupted from the bleachers but only silence from the bench.

I have long remained silent on what really took place. When I first wrote this paper, I failed to put the whole truth into words. This is what really happened. It appeared as if I was playing with my opponent, but in reality, I couldn't pin him. He was double jointed. No matter how hard I pressed down, I could not get his entire back flattened onto the mat. I could get one arm and shoulder and the arm on the opposite side of his body flattened onto the mat, but not the opposite shoulder blade. I can do the same thing myself, but not to the extreme he was able to do it. The referee was down on his hands and knees with his hands raised in the air the entire match, but with the obvious gap, he couldn't bring himself to slap the mat and give me the pin and I understood why.

It was for that reason, not because I wanted to play with him, that I failed to pin him. The reason the crowd thought I was playing with him is because he was, overall, a weak wrestler. Getting him onto his back not only looked easy, it was easy. I won by a score of 21-0 and when he left the mat, I saw tears rolling down his cheeks—he had been crying.

The coach, of course, didn't see it that way. To him, I had failed the team so, on Monday of the following week, he took some unusual steps to demonstrate his displeasure.

Towards the end of practice, he shouted, "Dick, come over here. I want you and Terry to wrestle." The Dick he had summoned was Dick Enderly, our heavy weight,

"You want us to wrestle?" I asked, in astonishment.

"Yes, I want you and Dick out there on the mat."

"Are you talking about a real wrestling match?"

"Yes, a full, six-minute match."

"If I win, do I have to wrestle heavyweight on Friday?" I said, somewhat sarcastically.

"Let's see if you win first," he countered, and with that Dick and I shook hands and the other team members circled around the mat to watch.

Dick was a good six feet something and a solid two hundred and thirty-five pounds, while I stood at five feet ten and one hundred and forty-five pounds. That's almost a one-hundred-pound difference—and Dick was a good wrestler. He would not only go on to be a professional football player, but a wrestler at the University of Minnesota.

Going into the match, I knew I didn't stand a chance if I stayed in close. I had to play it loose to survive. The approach I took was simple: I stayed away from him. In the up position, I made repeated attempts to get behind him with my quickness, while he kept trying to go for the legs. To counter this, I would use his superior weight to push myself away from him—flying backwards at times and landing in the prone position. Because of his size and strength, he didn't bother to protect his legs. If I had gone for them all he would have had to have done is fall on top of me and it would have been over. Instead, he stood completely erect, a no, no position in most cases—but against me it was good strategy. To stay away from my attempts to use quickness to get behind him, he simply turned his entire body to the right or left to counter my move. It didn't require quickness. Getting behind him was like trying to run around a skyscraper; no matter what I did, I was always facing the front.

I found myself in the up position at the start of the second round and my strategy was again simple. I didn't hold onto him tightly. When he did a sit-out, instead of me trying to contain him, I let him do it, and then I followed. If he landed on his back, instead of trying to pin him, I tied up his legs. At all times, I made sure that my hands were touching him. Had I completely let him go, he would have gotten points. When he did a roll, I made sure he couldn't grab my arm. I would let him roll, and then follow, keeping my hands on him.

The score was tied at 0–0 when we went into the third round. This was the most dangerous round for me because Dick would be in the up position. This meant I would be in the prone position with his arm wrapped tightly around my waist. I had one chance to escape and, if it failed, all he would have had to do was use his superior weight to push me over and that would be the end of the match.

I considered my options. I knew I couldn't simply stand and attempt to force his hands apart—a move that is difficult even with wrestlers my own weight. I couldn't grab his arm and roll over; all he had to do was go with it and his weight would do the rest. The only option I had was a sit out, and even that was dangerous because I could easily end up with my back to the mat. I had to clear him completely, turn, and get up, or it would be over.

I chose the sit out and my quickness made the difference. Not only did I clear his arms—which was the only thing that could have worked—but I flew far enough away from him to allow me to turn and get to my feet.

The rest of the match went the same way as the first period with him going for my legs and me trying to get behind him. I won by a score of 1–0, but that didn't end Mr. Neilson's wrath.

The next day, with the coach oddly absent, Mr. Hoskins, the football coach, showed up. Walking up to me, he said, "Terry, let's wrestle."

"You want to wrestle me?" I asked, raising my eyebrows in disbelief.

"Yeah, I think I can show you a thing or two," and that was

it. He didn't say anything about the coach, but it was obvious to me that Mr. Neilson had asked him to do this and from what I could tell, Mr. Hoskins intended on giving me a good threshing.

He had the body of a wrestler and, from what I had been told, he had wrestled at the college level. He was well-built with large femoral muscles—this alone gave him the weight advantage. Not like Dick Enderly but an advantage, nonetheless. I had a large upper body but skinny legs. I was quick; whereas, he was fast

I pinned him in forty-eight seconds. Embarrassed, he got to his feet, and said, "I slipped. Let's try it again."

Again, I pinned him. This time it was in less than forty-eight seconds and when he got up he muttered, "All right, let's do this one more time—one out of three."

I could tell from the way he spoke that his confidence was gone and he might have been a little ticked at Mr. Neilson as well.

After pinning him in under thirty seconds, he walked off the mat grumbling something about, "What the heck did I get myself into," and with that he was gone.

Mr. Neilson didn't show for practice until the next day. I have no proof of his role in what had taken place, but I have every reason to believe that he was behind it.

Over the course of the season my weight went down naturally. By the end of the season, I was wrestling at one thirty-three and that's where I should have stayed, but, like a fool without a safety net, I went down to one twenty-seven for the District and it turned out to be my undoing. However, it wasn't until the first match in the Region that it affected me. I was exhausted but ahead of my opponent by one point with thirteen seconds left in the match when my knees collapsed—they simply gave out. If it hadn't been for the bell, he could have easily pinned me. He won by a point, went to the state, and I was done with wrestling.

As stated in the Prologue, I received scholarship offers from the four top wrestling programs in the country. I can still see myself standing in my bedroom tossing the offers into the wastebasket. I may not have liked wrestling, but it had served a basic need—it had given me self-esteem. By the time I graduated from high school, my ego knew with certainty that physically I could compete with my peers. In my youth, that was what I needed; the intellectual part would come later.

Co-captains Keith Olson and Terry Degner

CHAPTER 47

The Town Drunk

Senior Year Continued....

I missed the start of baseball due to a minor injury. During my last wrestling match, I had landed on the mat with my arm outstretched. Unbeknownst to me at the time, a small sliver of bone had chipped off my right elbow. I could feel the sliver moving around, but it wasn't painful. Not until I started throwing my curveball, that is. I told the coach about the pain I felt when I snapped the ball and he suggested that I squeeze a tennis ball to see if that would help. For a good two weeks, I took the ball everywhere with me, even to the classroom, and eventually the pain subsided to the point where it didn't bother me.

My first pitching assignment was against the small town of Donnelly. I wasn't the starting pitcher. I relieved our starter in the fourth inning and pitched a shutout. Then, I started the following week, and this continued for the greater part of the season as I was the only real pitcher on the team.

The first and second basemen also pitched but they were what the coach called throwers. When they threw the ball, the windup and motion they used was that of a catcher throwing the ball back to the pitcher. They would bring the ball behind their head and let it fly from close to their ear. They threw hard and straight, but they had nothing on the ball; no spin.

I do not recall the number of games or the team's win/loss record as the season began to wind down, but I will never forget one game. The game prior to this had been a disappointment. We were leading the Fergus Falls Otters by a score of 1–0 with two outs going into the seventh inning when our first baseman, teased by an opponent on third base, made the mistake of throwing the ball over the backstop. The opponent, and a player who had been on second base, scored and the Otters won by a score of 2–1.

On the following Friday, we again played the Otters and again it was in Fergus Falls. It was unusual to play two games in a row against the same opponent and even more unusual to play both games on their turf.

The cause for the incident, or maybe a better word is happening, came to my attention before the start of the gam.

As I was warming up on the sidelines, my buddy Byron Stock walked over and said, "I see you've got the town drunk for a referee."

I held up my arm to let Lourn Lysne, the catcher, know that I would be talking to Byron and then I turned to him and asked, "What do you mean, the town drunk?"

"Look," he said, pointing in the direction of home plate.

I turned my head and there, standing behind the home plate fence, stood a man dressed in the uniform of an umpire. But, it wasn't his uniform that caught my full attention, it was what he was doing. Right there, in front of my eyes, and in front of anyone else that might have been looking, he reached into his suit and pulled out what looked like a small glass flask, put it to his lips, tilted his head back, and took what I had to believe was a swig of something. What that something was, I didn't know, but it looked like a liquor bottle.

"He's the umpire?" I asked, in disbelief.

"Yup. He's the umpire and the town drunk and he pretty much lives at one of the bars downtown."

"Why do they let him umpire?"

"Ask the coach. I don't know but good luck," and with that, Byron left.

"What was that all about?" Lourn asked, now standing next to me.

"He told me the umpire is the town drunk and when I looked in his direction he was taking a swig from what looked like a liquor bottle."

"Wow, that's interesting," Lourn said, and with that, we went back to warming up.

I had gained a reputation as a reputation as a control pitcher. I would work the count with a sinker and screwball that moved in on right-handed batters. My strikeout pitch was a curve ball that dropped straight down. I seldom used a fastball. It tended to rise on me. Years later, when I pitched senior baseball, I used it against the heavy hitters who would pop the ball up, but in high school, I didn't know how to apply it to my advantage. Besides, my screwball worked great against the heavy hitters who would swing hard at the pitch as it came in on them and then stand at the pate admiring the ball as it sailed out of bounds.

Putting the "drunk umpire" warning out of my mind, I continued warming up. Then, just before heading to the mound, Lourn walked up to me and said, "Your pitches were coming right over the plate Terry. Let's give them hell," and with that, I walked to the mound.

The umpire called my first pitch a ball and the next and the next, until the bases were loaded and players started walking home. From the mound I could hear the slur in the umpire's voice as he roared, "BALL, BALL, BALL." Some of the the first batters took swings at my pitches and missed, but when the apposing players realized what was taking place they stopped swinging. Some even stood at the plate with the bat resting on their shoulders while the umpire kept yelling, "BALL."

I could hear laughter and shouting coming from the opponents' bench. I had played baseball with some of them when I had stayed at the Reesers and I had wrestled one of them.

"I don't know what to tell you, Terry," Lourn said, when he met me halfway between the mound and the plate. "The balls are coming right over the plate. I hate to say this, but I think your friend is right."

I had walked toward home plate, not to talk to Lourn, but to confront the umpire. I wanted to pull the flask out of his jacket and hold it up for everyone to see. I was not only throwing the ball right over the plate by this time, I was doing so with the intent of letting the batter hit the ball and still they stood there with the bat resting on their shoulders.

Finally, our coach had had enough. He walked out to were we were standing and held out his hand as a signal for me to give him the ball. I couldn't believe it; he was taking me out of the game without a word to the umpire.

"The umpire's drunk," I hissed.

"Give me the ball, Terry, and go sit on the bench," he said, in a commanding voice.

It wasn't what the coach said; it was how he said it that really hurt me. He was angry at me for challenging the authority of the umpire. By this time, everyone at the park knew the umpire was drunk and here he was kicking me out of the game.

I handed the ball to him and angrily walked over to the bench and threw my glove on the ground. I was steaming mad.

When the coach later returned to the bench, he said, "I'm afraid I'll have to ask you to go out and play in center field."

"I'm not going anywhere," I said, sternly.

"You have to, Terry. If you don't we'll have to forfeit the game."

I looked at him in disgust, picked up the mitt I had thrown on the ground, and ran out to center field. *If they hit the ball to me, I'll miss it intentionally,* I told myself, but fortunately it never happened

That game and my response to being thrown out essentially ended my pitching days for Elbow Lake. We didn't have substitutes, so I played second base the following week and the team lost. Then we moved into the playoffs and the coach again didn't start me. It wasn't until we were behind by six points in the first inning of the game that he called on me. This time it had nothing to do with the umpire; our opponents simply were having a field day at the plate.

I went on to pitch a no hitter for the rest of the game. We ended up losing 6–1. I was the only one to cross the plate. To the coach's credit, he did congratulate me, but it was too little and too late.

I've been an umpire myself, so I understand the need to call the game the way you see it without interference from the players or the coaches but "drunk" is another matter and he was most definitely drunk.

It was a sad ending in a sport that I enjoyed, but with the baseball season behind me, the school year came to an end. I was eighteen going on nineteen, and it was time for me to make some decisions about my immediate future. Would I take over the farm, go to college, or go into the military?

This photo, scanned from the 1964 Year Book, shows pitcher Terry Degner at the plate.

EPILOGUE

When Career Day arrived, the juniors and seniors were excused from class in the afternoon to visit the many exhibits in the gymnasium. I say many but in truth there were only a few. We had sixty students in our graduating class, not six hundred. How many colleges or companies would bother to send a recruiter to our small, country school? Most of the students going on to college had already made up their minds about where they were headed. As far as I know, there were no company recruiters present, but all the branches of the military were there. They loved country boys. We were tough and ready to see the world.

I walked the gymnasium, quickly brushing past the booths. I went by the Air Force, the Army, and the Navy recruiters without bothering to stop because I knew what I wanted—I wanted to be a Marine. The area assigned to them was the last stop in the U-shaped circle. To my surprise, it held the greatest number of interested students. Whereas the other recruiting stations were holding one-on-one discussions, the marines were giving a presentation to as many as five or six students who were all sitting at one end of the bleachers

"Wait here," a man in a Marine's uniform said, just as I was about to walk over to the bleachers. "The presentation will be over in a few minutes and then you can go and sit down."

"Is he going to give another presentation?" I asked.

"Yes, just wait here, he'll be done shortly," he said, and with that he walked over to stand by another Marine. Each one was smartly dressed in their red, white, and blue uniforms and each had ribbons tacked on their chest—one had more than the other. I didn't know what the ribbons stood for, but they looked impressive.

Suddenly, the one with the greater number of ribbons pointed across the gymnasium and said, "See that boy over there?"

I looked in the direction he was pointing and saw one of my classmates.

"That's the kind of guy we want in the Marines. We'll make a man out of him."

I couldn't believe my ears. The classmate he was pointing at was a butterball. I could've taken him in wrestling in a second.

Well, if that's the kind of guy they want in the Marines, I said to myself. *I'm joining the Navy to get an education,* and with that, I turned and walked over to the booth set up for the Navy.

Thank you, Mom! Your wisdom and perhaps my ego, to some extent, kept me from the horrors of Vietnam. As for my classmate, he also joined the Navy but, regrettably, they stationed him in Vietnam as a medic. Another classmate and a fellow wrestler who had seldom, if ever, made varsity did join the Marines. He made it through his tour in Vietnam, but committed suicide six months after returning.

After graduating Summa Cum "D" at the end of May, I

joined the Navy on June 14, 1964, bringing my personality with me—a personality some members of the Navy would come to know very well, but that's a story for Book III - Growing Skin.

About The Author

Terry Degner is a husband, father, grandfather, and great-grandfather. For over twenty-three years, he designed, wrote, directed, and edited hundreds of video, sound, and multimedia productions; including children's shows, documentaries, dramas, and training and promotional programs. For twelve of those years, he owned and managed his own production company, and his skill at script-writing is what brought in the repeat business. In addition to his media career, the author spent twelve years in sales and marketing, climbing the corporate ladder and winning many awards along the way. He got an education in electronics from the U.S. Navy, a degree from the University of Minnesota in speech (broadcast) journalism, and he is a certified webmaster. Terry was ideally suited to write, with captivating dialogue, this continuing true account of his life—a goal he set for himself at the age of twelve.